U.S. COAST GUARD WORLD WAR TWO NAVAL EXPLOITS

A MEMOIR
BOOK TWO

AND

MEN OF THE MENKAR

A MEMOIR
BOOK THREE

BY

CAPTAIN NIELS PETER THOMSEN, USCG (RET)

Captain Thomsen

VON BUCHHOLDT PRESS
1999

COVER PHOTOGRAPH:

UNITED STATES COAST GUARD-MANNED COMBAT TRANSPORT
U.S.S. HUNTER LIGGETT APA-14
FLAGSHIP OF COMMODORE LAURENCE FAIRFAX REIFSNIDER, USN
COMMANDER THIRD AMPHIBIOUS GROUP LEADING TWELVE ATTACK
TRANSPORTS AT EMPRESS AUGUSTA BAY AT THE INVASION OF
BOUGAINVILLE, SOLOMON ISLANDS ON "D" DAY
NOVEMBER FIRST, 1943

1 - VOYAGE OF THE FOREST DREAM
2 - U.S. COAST GUARD WORLD WAR TWO NAVAL EXPLOITS
3 - MEN OF THE MENKAR

A MEMOIR
BY
NIELS PETER THOMSEN

PUBLISHER
VON BUCHHOLDT PRESS
19222 OLYMPIC VIEW DRIVE
EDMONDS, WASHINGTON
98020

PRINTED IN USA
BY SNOHOMISH PUBLISHING COMPANY

In Memory
OF
The living and the dead
Who with lofty dreams
Were sent to places far away
Believing
That by their sacrifices
They were helping
To create
A better and more beautiful world
For those they loved
And
Who found
That on the field of Battle
There is no true glory
There is only food for tears.
To these
Courageous men and women
These memoirs are dedicated.

UNITED STATES COAST GUARD
WORLD WAR TWO NAVAL EXPLOITS

A MEMOIR

BY
CAPTAIN NIELS PETER THOMSEN, USCG (RET)

BOOK TWO

I
UNITED STATES LIGHTHOUSE SERVICE

II
UNITED STATES COAST GUARD

USS YP-251

USS HUNTER LIGGETT APA-14
ADDENDUM ONE
ADDENDUM TWO

12TH COAST GUARD DISTRICT
MORRO BAY, CALIFORNIA

YP-251

APA-14
USS HUNTER LIGGETT

AK-(123)
USS MENKAR

TABLE OF CONTENTS

PHOTOGRAPHS, MAPS AND DOCUMENTS
1937 to 1945

Chapter 1

THE SAILOR AND THE HEIRESS

 I was twenty-three years of age and serving as an Third Officer on the Standard Oil Company tanker S/S W.S. RHEEM. The vessel lay at the dock in Richmond on the east side of San Francisco Bay for a month of repairs. One day while seated at the bar of the St. Francis Hotel in San Francisco, I met a Mr. Kenneth Smith, the President and manager of the Yellow Cab Company. In our conversation it developed that at one time he had lived in Fresno. We exchanged telephone numbers and a week later he called, saying he would like me to be a dinner guest at his home in San Francisco so he could introduce me to his niece, a student at the University of California in Berkeley. Clarabelle Ashley was nineteen, unworldly, and shared an apartment with a girl friend from Fresno, where Clarabelle resided with her widowed mother.

We were attracted to one another and several days later had dinner and attended a movie together. We met several times, never getting beyond the handholding and kissing stage, when she suggested marriage. Being lonely and having no family, I thought it to be an interesting idea and we planned to marry before my ship departed for the East Coast two weeks hence. Clarabelle told her mother of our plans and pandemonium broke loose, as though a dam had burst or an earthquake had occurred. I learned that Clarabelle's grandfather who resided on a large estate in Hillsborough (a suburb of San Francisco) was a socially prominent multi-millionaire with vast timber and mining interests and Clarabelle's mother was his only child.

Two days later there was a gathering of the clan at Clarabelle's apartment. Those present were Clarabelle, her roommate, her uncle who had introduced this so-called fortune hunter to young and innocent Clarabelle, the mother, both grandparents, and yours truly. I recall sitting in the kitchen on a counter stool while a great deal of arguing was taking place in the living room. At intervals, the uncle who favored me would come to the kitchen and report on the latest developments. I do recall that my feelings were somewhat neutral concerning the outcome.

Finally after approximately two hours the verdict was announced. The granddaughter had won and we would be married in the Berkeley Methodist church the following Sunday, after which Clarabelle and I would spend a week at the grandparents estate in Hillsborough. So the marriage of the Sailor and the Heiress took place as planned and we both vowed to honor and cherish one another until death did us part.

The estate was magnificent, a mansion of twenty or so rooms staffed by a butler and numerous servants. We were royally treated, the grandparents particularly friendly to me, but I recall that I had some resentful feelings that I was being patronized. I also sensed that Clarabelle's mother who had led the opposition to the marriage was unhappy. But I kept my reservations to myself and the week went very well.

On our return to Clarabelle's apartment we attempted to have sexual relations, an act which turned out to be a complete disaster, as she was a virgin and I was too inexperienced to handle the situation. The next day we visited a clinic for advice where the doctor advised that Clarabelle required minor surgery, which he performed. Owing to the ship's imminent departure and my concern over her recent medical attention we decided to postpone sexual relations until my ship returned from the trip to the East Coast. The parting was very emotional and we promised to write each day. On the ten-day trip to Panama I wrote every day, the letters being mailed from Panama. A dozen letters were waiting for me on arrival at the Panama Canal, all filled with declarations of love and the happy future we would share. A week later on arrival at the Standard Oil dock in New Jersey, I received another dozen letters of love and unfulfilled romance. I mailed my dozen letters and after discharging cargo three days later we sailed on the return trip to Richmond.

When the W.S. RHEEM arrived at the Richmond dock in San Francisco Bay I was the first man ashore, with a small suitcase headed for Berkeley. I was filled with anticipation that home from a long sea voyage, for the first time in my life I had someone to come home to. The previous night I had been pouring over the many loving letters I had received from Clarabelle during the voyage.

I boarded the streetcar for Berkeley and arrived at the apartment to find the door locked and no response to my ringing of the doorbell. I then looked up the apartment manager who seemed to be expecting me. She told me she had instructions from Clarabelle to let me into the apartment where I would find a letter on the mantel. On the way to the apartment the landlady offered the information that Clarabelle had left with her mother three days earlier.

The letter was brief, as though from a stranger. Clarabelle said in her letter that her mother had arranged to have the marriage annulled and she was leaving the following day with her mother on a six-week tour of Europe, and she was sorry about what had happened to our plans. I was devastated, and I can recall after sixty-five years that on my way back to the ship in Richmond I stopped in at a restaurant for breakfast and that it was a Sunday, because my tears were falling on the pictures of Mutt and Jeff in the comic strip in the newspaper. I was sorely wounded and a week later sailed again for Marcus Hook, Pennsylvania on the East Coast, another thirty days at sea to console myself with books; the story of my life. It would be months before I ventured ashore again.

To keep occupied on these long voyages I enrolled with the La Salle Extension University for a four-year correspondence course leading to a Bachelor of Law Degree. Having so much time at my disposal, I completed the course in eighteen months and looked forward to further studies and ultimate admission to the Bar. After six months on the W.S. RHEEM I was promoted to Second Officer, sailing on several other Standard Oil tankers on the West Coast, plying between San Francisco, Oregon, and Washington ports. I rarely went ashore, other than to make an occasional trip to Fresno to visit Chris and Adelheid. Because I was years younger than most other ship's officers I had very little in common with them as far as shoreside activities were concerned, especially as most of them were married and others spent time in bars and casual relationships, neither of which held any special interest for me.

In May of 1931, I had the sea-time needed to sit for my unlimited Chief Mate's license. I requested and was granted thirty days leave of absence with full pay, to upgrade my license, with the assurance that when an opening occurred I would be sailing as Chief Officer. After brushing up for a week at Captain Taylor's Academy I reported to the Examiners and a week later on May 28,1931 I received my Chief Mate's license. I had no reason to stay in the Bay Area, for though I had been sailing out of San Francisco for two years I had few, if any, friends ashore.

So I boarded the Greyhound bus for Seattle, intending to spend the next two weeks of my leave looking up former shipmates from the HOLMES, or perhaps I would run into some old shipmate such as one-eyed Louie from the FOREST DREAM. There was also a chance that the HOLMES might still be in Seattle loading cargo for her annual trip to the Arctic and I would be able to visit with Captain Backland and Gus Carlson. I stopped at the Columbia Hotel out of habit and stayed for several days. The HOLMES had left for the Arctic and I found no former shipmates. I had a thousand dollars in the bank in San Francisco saved up for further law studies, so instead of taking the bus I decided I would return to San Francisco as a bonafide passenger on the EMMA ALEXANDER to report to the Standard Oil Company for assignment to my next ship.

Chapter 2

HOLLYWOOD

 The EMMA ALEXANDER departed from Seattle at Midnight on June 10, 1931, and her first stop after leaving Seattle would be Victoria, British Columbia where she would take on freight and passengers for California ports. In the next few days my life would be changed completely by an emotional experience over which I would have no control. I would never report to the Standard Oil Company offices, and all my well-laid plans for the future law career I had planned would be in shambles – for I met Laurena Dauncey.

Laurena was my age, twenty-four. She was born in Birmingham, England. Lithe of build, of medium height, rosy-cheeked, and with a vibrant outgoing personality. Her eyes were a deep blue and her coal-black hair, reaching to her shoulders, was naturally curly. She possessed a fine contralto singing voice and was an accomplished pianist. She had lived the greater part of her life in the small town of Courtney on the northern part of Vancouver Island, British Columbia. She had married at eighteen, and a year later, after the birth of her daughter, Gloria, had separated from her husband whom she had not seen for over four years. She was not divorced and lived with her child at her parents' home. She was an extremely unsophisticated young woman, the winner of a local beauty contest and on her way to Hollywood, California in search of a movie career.

Our meeting was the beginning of an implausible, romantic relationship with a tragically sad ending. She brought to flower in me the purest and most unselfish feelings of which a man is capable. After her career aspirations to which she was wholly dedicated, I would be by her own admission, the most important being in her life.

5

When she boarded the ship in Victoria I was standing on the ship's deck next to the gangway. She looked directly at me as she passed and I was hopelessly in love. I had the presence of mind to know that I must move quickly and so I stationed myself at the head of the dining room stairs hoping she would be coming to breakfast.

She soon appeared, the waiter seating her at a table for four. I do not know how I summoned the courage, but I walked over to her and asked permission to share her table. She graciously invited me to be seated.

For the next three days we found that we had much in common and became friends. I was due to report to the office of the Standard Oil Company in San Francisco for assignment to the W.S. RHEEM, shortly to depart for the East Coast; but by the time we reached San Francisco, I knew that I could not let Laurena go alone to face the jungle that was Hollywood. During the four hours that the ship was docked in San Francisco, I found time to withdraw my savings from the bank and arrange for passage on the ship to Los Angeles. We agreed to live together and that I would join her in seeking a career in motion pictures.

On arrival in San Pedro (then the port for Los Angeles) we took a bus to Hollywood, where we rented a room from a Mrs. Stephens, a widow. The room had two single beds and we shared the kitchen with Mrs. Stephens. On the second and third day we checked out several acting schools Laurena had corresponded with. While making these inquiries, we met and talked with other movie career aspirants who directed us to a photographer, where we had professional photos made for presentation to studios. We enrolled in a theatrical school, signing up for classes in acting, dancing and voice training. Our voice teacher was David Hutton, who had as one of his pupils the celebrated evangelist, Aimee Semple McPherson, whom he later married.

Aimee McPherson was the Billy Graham and Jimmy Swaggart of her era and presided over a large group of religious converts in a magnificent temple. David Hutton took an interest in us and on occasion we accompanied him to the temple and to private dinner parties at the home of Aimee McPherson, all of which we enjoyed.

Our studies were moving according to plan. Laurena was with an adagio dance group. With the help of Aimee McPherson I had the good fortune to get work at Warner Brothers studio as a stand-in for an actor named Conrad Nagel. In those days cameras were not as sophisticated as they are today and during filming, should an actor or actress need to absent themselves from the set for a cup of coffee, a cigarette, or to use the restroom, it was necessary that a person of the same height and coloring stand on the spot of the performer so the camera could be kept constantly focused and ready for the next scene. Being the same height and coloring as the star actor, I became his stand-in at ten dollars per day – a very happy arrangement.

The work was exciting, as were the acting school and voice lessons. It was an adventurous time, going from studio to studio for auditions, and in the process meeting and socializing with others who like Laurena and I were hopeful of success in a movie career. I even found that I had a talent for singing that David Hutton said

WARNER BROS. – HOLLYWOOD – 1931

6-A

LAURENA DAUNCEY – HOLLYWOOD – 1931

should be developed. All appeared to be going well. Mrs. Stephens treated us as though we were her children. We were both very interested in our work and Laurena and I were happy in each other's company, and there seemed to be no clouds on the horizon.

Laurena had been brought up in a home with high moral standards, and regarded it a sin for persons to indulge in intimate sexual behavior outside of marriage. I knew what her standards were and could respect them without a problem. We lived together and slept in the same room for over six months, romantically never sexually intimate; and in the long run this may have been a mistake. It was a relationship, which in retrospect now seems unbelievable. It was that I idolized her and she mirrored my most romantic ideals of Victorian womanhood.

Then one day, Laurena collapsed on the stage where she was working with her adagio dance group. Adagio dancing consists mainly of a dance group of three persons (a woman and two men) who toss the woman back and forth between them. A doctor was called in and after an examination diagnosed her as having a severe heart murmur. He said it would be dangerous for her to continue her stage work and imperative that she have a prolonged rest. Joe was in San Francisco at the time and when I phoned him he came to Hollywood to assist me in getting Laurena home to her parents. I needed an automobile, so I found a second hand Model A Ford on a parking lot priced at $300.00, made a down payment of fifty dollars and Joe and I drove Laurena home to Courtney. On the return trip coming over the mountains nearing Los Angeles, the car heated up and the engine block became bright red. After it cooled off we coasted into Los Angeles, long strips of vulcanizing rubber coming off the tires. After dark I returned the car to the lot where I had bought it. We then took the bus to San Francisco, checked in at a hotel on Mission Street and made our way to the Sailors' Union Hall, hoping to find a ship. It was during the 1931 Depression and Merchant Marine shipping was at an all-time low; the Union Hall filled with sailors looking for a berth.

Because of my abrupt departure from the Standard Oil Company, I was too embarrassed to contact them, so decided to ship out as an Able Seaman, joining Joe at the Union Hall. The scarcity in shipping had resulted in a new hiring rule that gave American citizens preference over alien seamen. This posed a real hardship for Joe, who was citizen of New Zealand. The Federal Maritime Law pertaining to Alien Seamen allowed for only a ninety day period ashore in the United States, after which time they were required to ship out on a foreign vessel or be deported. Joe's chances of getting a ship were nil. I gave Joe's problem a great deal of thought and came up with a plan that might work. I said to Joe, "If you could have the status of a United States Citizen, would you be willing to change your name?"

Joe promptly replied in the affirmative. That night weighing all the pros and cons, I laid out to Joe my plan on how to make him an instant United States Citizen.

Part one of the plan would necessitate finding someone approximately Joe,s age, height and coloring of eyes and hair. There were about sixty men in the hall and

I noted three people who would qualify as candidates. The first two I approached in a sociable manner turned out to be uncooperative when I became interested in their birthplace and date of birth, but the third man was more agreeable and after some lengthy, round-about conversation, revealed his age, and the County in which he was born, which happened to be Contra Costa County just across the Bay from San Francisco.

We then returned to our hotel room where I wrote a letter to the County Clerk of Contra Costa County, giving our benefactor's name and requesting a copy of his birth certificate, enclosing one dollar. The birth certificate arrived several days later and Joe became William Windrick, a Citizen of the United States. Joe lived under that name for sixteen years, until after World War II, when the Social Security System records revealed that there were two William Windricks with identical statistics and Joe was called in for questioning. Because he had been employed by the Gulf Oil Company on one of their tankers on especially hazardous duty in the Atlantic during World War II, the Company went to bat for him, and the government not only forgave him, but granted him immediate citizenship, and Joe resumed his original name of Joseph Bone.

We realized that shipping was not going to improve in San Francisco, and that for the time being it was not possible for Joe to use his new identity on the West Coast. I visited the Public Library where I studied newspapers from the Atlantic and Gulf Coasts to determine which ports had the most seagoing traffic. Port Arthur, Texas, a Gulf of Mexico port, appeared to have more arrivals and departures than East Coast ports and the bus fare cheaper, I suggested to Joe that we hitchhike, but Joe was never an adventurous person. However, it developed that Joe had one hundred dollars tucked away in mothballs. After our fare, our combined net worth was about twenty dollars.

Chapter 3

BEAUMONT, TEXAS

 We arrived in Beaumont, Texas the first week in November 1931, each carrying a small suitcase containing our worldly goods. What a wonderful carefree feeling. The rain was coming down in torrents, very depressing. It was some distance from Beaumont to Port Arthur, another four dollars each in bus fare. Port Arthur was small community of approximately eight square blocks on the edge of Sabine Canal, which was used by oil tankers enroute to Smith's Bluff, a major port of discharge. There were no buildings over two stories and with four or five small hotels and restaurants. It looked like the end of the world. Its only excuse for existing was to service fishing boats and oil tankers with food supplies. This was the prohibition era and there were a dozen homes selling homemade beer and corn whiskey, all doing a brisk business with crews of ships. A dismal looking place. It seemed as though half the Seamen in the United States Merchant Marine had converged here, all looking for a Seaman's billet.

We were desperately in need of two things, a place to sleep, and something to eat and with less than twenty dollars between us in a strange land, the prospects of sustained food and lodging until we found work were dim. The first small rooming house I approached was owned by a woman in her forties. I did all the talking and after going into some detail explaining our situation, we were given a small double room with two iron cots, all on credit. At least we had place to sleep and park our two suitcases.

I stopped at a third-rate restaurant and explained our circumstances to the owner, showing him my Chief Mate's license, with assurance that I would soon find employployment. He gave us each a month's roll of meal tickets on credit. The trust these Texans had in strangers was incredible. Never before or since have I run into such kindly people.

After three weeks I walked on board a small oil tanker of the Texas Company, the oil tanker S/S LOUISIANA and was hired as relief for the regular Second Mate who was going on vacation. The LOUISIANA was on a run between Port Arthur and New Orleans. The crew of the ship were all from the Cayman Islands and spoke with a strong West Indian accent. All were very friendly and I had a happy time on board. Joe and I were now able to take care of our bills at the hotel and restaurant with money to spare. Joe had not been able to ship out and was getting despondent. We had made friends with a Jewish family who operated a second-hand clothing store in Port Arthur. Their daughter Esther worked in the store, and Joe and I stopped in daily, socializing with the owner and his daughter, who had us at their home for dinner every Sunday. Now having funds, we took the bus to Beaumont each week and called on the various steamship companies. On the fourth trip, Joe was able to ship out on an oil tanker bound for New York. Three weeks later I shipped out as Second Mate on the Sun Oil Company tanker, S/S SUNBEAM, which was on a regular run between Beaumont and Marcus Hook, Pennsylvania.

Marcus Hook was the site of the Sun Oil Company refinery which processed Texas crude oil. It was on the Delaware River below the City of Chester, which in turn was down-river from the city of Philadelphia.

Laurena and I had been corresponding regularly since her return to her parents in Courtney, Vancouver Island. After being with the Sun Oil Company for about six months, which would have been in August of 1932, Laurena wrote that she wanted to come to me in Pennsylvania, that she had filed for a divorce, and could expect her final papers in several months. She wanted to bring her five-year-old daughter, Gloria, with her as well as her mother, who would assist her in getting located. Laurena said she had abandoned her movie career aspirations, but felt that she would like to have a try at becoming a night club singer. I was elated over the prospect of her coming and made the travel arrangements. At this time I was Second Officer on the tanker SUN-BEAM, sailing between Texas and Marcus Hook, making a round trip every three weeks, with three days in Marcus Hook discharging cargo.

When they arrived I met them in Philadelphia and we rented a flat in Chester. While the ship was in port I stayed at the flat, Laurena and I occupying one bedroom, and Gloria and her mother the other bedroom. As her divorce was not yet final, I respected her principles and made no demands for more intimate relationship than that we had enjoyed when we lived together in Hollywood the year earlier.
After several weeks Laurena began making the rounds of nightclubs in Philadelphia in search of employment and soon was singing and playing the piano nightly in a supper club. Neither her mother nor I were enthusiastic over this type of employment and the late hours, but I did not strenuously voice any objections. Now that Laurena was working it was necessary for Mrs. Dauncey to remain with us to take care of

Gloria, which pleased all of us.

When two months had passed, Laurena's mother much disturbed, told me that Laurena was being escorted home in the early morning hours by an older married man, the Chief of Detectives in Philadelphia, who, Laurena told her, would be able to further her career through his influence with night club operators. She felt the man was unprincipled and feared that a serious relationship might develop and that I should speak to Laurena. When I brought the subject up to Laurena she said that I had no right to interfere with her singing career, and if I was unhappy with the situation I could take my leave. I was crushed and Mrs. Dauncey stunned at this turn of events. I packed my belongings and returned to my ship. For the next five voyages I did not go ashore, either in Texas or Marcus Hook.

The main form of shipboard recreation was our nightly bridge game, the players being the Captain, Chief Engineer, the Chief Steward and myself. Murray, the Chief Steward, knowing of my unhappiness, had for several trips been urging me to come ashore with him in Smith's Bluff, Texas and have dinner with him and Mrs. Murray. On the fifth trip after parting from Laurena, Murray came to me, saying, "Niels, my wife has asked me to bring you home for dinner. We have a friend we would like to have you meet." I agreed to come with him, providing I could return to the ship early, as we were due to sail for Marcus Hook at noon the following day. On arriving at Murray's home I was introduced to my dinner partner, an attractive, slender young woman. Her name was Bernice Asbury, about nineteen years old, bright, vivacious, and one quarter Choctaw Indian. She had lovely, high cheekbones, was quick, intelligent and moved with an uncommon grace. After dinner she washed the dishes while I dried and I recall how impressed I was with her domestic capabilities. In retrospect it seems ridiculous that this trait affected me so deeply. We were playing the oldest game in the world.

Later we danced to some new records and she felt wonderful in my arms. We all had a few brandies and played a game of cards. Bernice and I found ourselves quite taken with each other and shared the spare bedroom. At breakfast she looked adorable, so we decided to be married when the City Clerk's office opened at ten o'clock. All went according to plan and at ten-thirty we were man and wife, to have and to hold, to love and to cherish, until death do us part. For the seven years we would be together and beyond, no harsh or unkind word or action would ever pass between us. I sailed with my ship at noon and Bernice went to her mother in Beaumont to make arrangements to move to Pennsylvania after the next voyage.

I had not seen or heard from Laurena for three months. After my initial period of grief, I had locked my memories of her in the chambers of my heart. I was on the bridge of the ship as we approached the dock in Marcus Hook, and there on the dock waving up at me was Laurena, as startlingly beautiful as when I first laid eyes on her in Victoria, almost two years earlier. It has been over sixty years and I still vividly remember that terrible moment walking down the gangway in a state of shock, my throat so dry I could scarcely speak. She ran to meet me with wide-open arms, saying,

11

"Niels, I love you." "I have my divorce and now we can be married."

I was speechless as she talked about the life we now would share. Never again would I endure the agony and heartbreak of the next half-hour. For so long a time I had idolized, dreamed of and desired this lovely woman. So many long night watches of pacing the bridge breathing poems to the stars in the sky, telling of my love for her, and now I had to explain to her that I had never expected to see her again. There was no future for us, as I now had a wife in Texas. It did not occur to me to abandon Bernice. I could not rationalize my impulsive marriage to her, other than it had to do with my Victorian attitude towards women, that sexual intimacy made marriage a prerequisite. Such feelings are still a part of my being, and to this day I have never been able to engage in a casual love affair.

After an hour we said our good-byes and twenty years would elapse before we would meet again. I sent Laurena money for the fares that would take them home to Vancouver Island, but later learned they went to New York instead of returning to Canada. Two years later I saw a write-up in Walter Winchell's column in the New York Times, describing Laurena as being a featured singer in an exclusive New York nightspot.

When I returned to Marcus Hook from Texas the next trip, Bernice was waiting for me. We rented an upstairs apartment in Boothwyn, a small village near Marcus Hook and I took a three-week leave of absence. The Prohibition Act had just been repealed and liquor was legally available. We bought a two-week supply of groceries, and several cases of alcohol drinks of different varieties, and without leaving our apartment for two weeks, celebrated a belated, glowing honeymoon. I made two round trips to Texas, and on my return from the second trip the Landlady in the apartment below us told me that whenever I was away she could hear Bernice crying in the night. I was puzzled and surprised, as she seemed totally happy when we were to-gether. That night I asked her what was troubling her, and she told me that she had a three-year old son in Beaumont being cared for by her mother and she sorely missed him. I told her that as soon as my ship sailed, she should take a bus to Texas and bring him home with her and that was how Jerry became part of the family.

Bernice made a quick trip to Texas, bringing Jerry home with her. I remained on the ATLANTIC SUN as regular Second Mate and relieving First Mate and acquired my First Class Pilot License for Delaware Bay and River to Philadelphia. Jerry was a lively little blonde youngster and we all got along fine as a family. In May of 1934, we decided to move to San Francisco, hoping that the West Coast might offer more opportunities for a berth on coastwise vessels, where I could be home more often. Also the winter had been severely cold and Bernice welcomed the prospect of a milder climate. I resigned from the Sun Oil Company and we took the bus to San Francisco, a carefree, happy trip across the country. On arrival in San Francisco, I registered at the Union Hall of the Masters, Mates and Pilots before going on to Fresno to visit with Chris and Adelheid, whom I had not seen for several years. They both took an instant liking to Bernice.

We moved to a small two-room house in the garden at the rear of Chris and Adelheid's house. We planned to live temporarily in Fresno, while I traveled to San Francisco by overnight freight train every two weeks to check in at the Master, Mates and Pilots Union Hall.

Approximately ten days after our arrival in San Francisco the Bloody Thursday West Coast Longshore and Maritime Strike was declared, and all maritime shipping came to a complete standstill. For the next six months I would be reporting each weekend to the Master, Mates and Pilots for duty in the picket line on the San Francisco waterfront.

The leader of the Longshoremen's Union was Harry Bridges, and a former shipmate of mine, Harry Lundberg, headed the Sailors' Union of the Pacific. The Madsen boys, Holger and Einar, worked for the Santa Fe Railroad in the Calwa freight yards and were instrumental in getting me a job sweeping out empty box cars, which paid fifty cents hourly. I would work Monday through Friday evening, then hop a freight train for the overnight ride to San Francisco, put in one day marching on the picket line, and hustle back to Fresno in time to get to work on Monday.

The Maritime strike continued through Christmas of 1934. I continued to ride the freight train regularly, sweep out box cars at the Santa Fe, my face wrapped in a towel to keep the dust out of my lungs. Life in Fresno went on without incident until February 1935 when the strike ended and shipping resumed. I found relief employment with the States Steamship Company that operated a fleet of freighters between West Coast ports and the Orient. When their ships arrived in San Francisco it was the policy to give several of the Mates leave of absence for the two week period the vessel loaded and discharged cargo in West Coast ports of San Francisco, Portland, and Seattle. I stayed with the company until August of 1935, serving on two of their vessels, SAN BERNADINO and SAN LUCAS. I then shipped out as Second Mate on a Tanker of the Associated Oil Company. In the meantime I sat for and received my Unlimited Master's License.

Bernice and I had initially moved to San Francisco, but as the Associated Oil tankers berthed in Martinez ten miles up the Sacramento River, we rented a house in that small community. My ship, the S/S Frank Drum, was on the intercoastal run to New Jersey via the Panama Canal, a round trip taking a little over two months, with a ten day layover in Martinez between trips. On my second trip to the East Coast I received a telegram when the ship arrived in Panama saying that Bernice was hospitalized and dangerously ill from an operation for a ruptured ectopic pregnancy. I telephoned the hospital and was told that she was out of danger. On my return I found Bernice extremely despondent over the aborted pregnancy and the hospital experience. Bernice was a generous, loving person, bright and caring. I do not think that we ever had a serious argument or difference in the years we were together. In the first years of our marriage we drank alcohol in a moderate fashion, but we discovered that Bernice because of her Indian heritage had a low tolerance for alcohol, so we had more or less restricted our drinking socially and at home.

13

We were both unhappy over the long periods apart, but shipping was so depressed I had no choice. I sailed on the S/S FRANK DRUM until the summer of 1937, when I was assigned to the S/S PAUL SHOUP as Chief Mate. The SHOUP was on the Trans-Pacific run to Chefoo, China, making round trips of three months duration. I was so involved in advancing in my profession that I could not foresee this assignment might destroy my marriage to Bernice.

In my thirteen years as a career seaman, I had seen more than half of the marriages of my shipmates, seamen and officers alike, eventually end in heartbreak and disaster because of long separations. Searching for a normal family life I decided to give up the Merchant Marine, and apply for employment with a Government Marine oriented agency, where I could practice my profession as a Deck Officer, Shipmaster and Pilot, and still have time home with my family. Prior to the sailing of the SHOUP to China, I had made application to the U.S. Government for a position as a Deck Officer and Pilot with three separate agencies, the Panama Canal Pilotage authority, the U.S. Army Corps of Engineers, and the U.S. Lighthouse Service.

In September on returning from China we arrived a day earlier than scheduled and instead of proceeding upriver to Martinez the ship docked at the Standard Oil Company dock at Richmond on San Francisco Bay. I was eager to get home to Martinez, so the Captain gave me permission to leave the ship at Richmond. I phoned Bernice in Martinez, and receiving no answer, I took the bus for the thirty-minute ride to Martinez. I arrived at the apartment about one in the afternoon to find no one at home, Jerry being at school and Bernice away. I spoke to a neighbor of ours who told me that he had seen Bernice in the company of a local bartender, and suggested she might be at his apartment, giving me his address. I learned later that this man had on a number of occasions made advances to Bernice, and been rejected, which could have accounted for his eagerness to enlighten me as to her possible whereabouts.
On the way to the address given me I was confused over what was transpiring. It was as though I were high up, looking down on a scenario in which I was a spectator and that it all really had nothing to do with me. I knew that our marriage was a happy one, except for the long periods of separation we had to endure.

I located the apartment and after knocking on the door several times, a pajama-clad man about twenty-five years old came to the door. I pushed past him and saw Bernice in the bedroom, unclothed. I have never really understood my behavior in this dramatic incident. It would have seemed that our culture would have required that I be enraged and furiously angry with Bernice, instead of detached and full of sadness for both of us. I said only a few words and all I can remember saying to Bernice was, "Is this the man you want?"

She replied, "Yes."

I turned and grabbed the man by the throat, shaking him and saying, "You Son of a Bitch, you take good care of her and Jerry or I will be coming after you." He gurgled and professed his intention to do just that, scared to death.

I said to Bernice, "I will continue to send you money for a few months, stay

away from the apartment until tomorrow, when I will be gone." I then walked out –
stunned. I returned to the apartment, packed my clothes and left a note asking her to
pack whatever things she thought I should have, and I would send for them when I
had found a place to stay.

The next morning I returned to my ship which had docked in Martinez. In the
mail was a letter from the United States Lighthouse Service in San Francisco, offering me an appointment as Second Officer of the Lighthouse Tender SEQUOIA. The
following day I reported to the office of the Lighthouse Service in San Francisco,
accepted the appointment and resigned from the Associated Oil Company. I rented a
small, furnished apartment in San Francisco and a friend in Martinez collected and
delivered to me the items given to him by Bernice. Thankfully my new duties as an
Officer on the SEQUOIA, a large ocean-going ship which served the lighthouses and
sea buoys on the California Coast kept me occupied, with little time to dwell on the
wreckage of what had been insofar as I knew, a five-year, happy and trouble-free
marriage.

Chapter 4

U.S. LIGHTHOUSE SERVICE

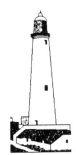The SEQUOIA was stationed at the Lighthouse maintenance dock and base on YERBA BUENA ISLAND in San Francisco Bay. It was one of several tenders in the San Francisco District, being responsible for the maintenance of aids to navigation on the California Coast that included shore lights and sea buoys. It was equipped with a workboat for landing supplies at light stations and for surf landings, a very heavy boat rowed by four sailors, with the Second Mate at the rudder in charge of the boat. It was a change for me, very interesting, and an assignment that required much skill and physical dexterity. I also had to acquire skill in acetylene welding and cutting of anchor chain.

The rest of the ship's officers had been together on the ship for many years. Captain Bode for thirty years, First Mate and Chief Engineer for over twenty-five years, and the First and Second Engineers over twenty years. It was a month before I felt secure enough to ask to have the salt passed. The Officers and crew were a dedicated group of men, performing a very special and unique service to the maritime industry, and it was a good feeling to be part of such a service.

A month after I had moved to San Francisco I was at my apartment and in the act of hanging curtains when there was a knock on the door. I opened the door and there stood Bernice. After we exchanged greetings she asked if I would take her back and without any conditions, or discussion, I agreed to her request and we moved to a larger apartment in Oakland and tried to put our lives together again.

We both wanted it to work and tried hard, but though we cared for each other it was not the same as before. It was as though a golden thread had been broken and would not mend. I treated her with consideration, never mentioning what had transpired in Martinez, but I was miserable. One day we sat down like two friends and talked about our situation and as a result I proposed she determine what she could do to become self-sufficient. She thought she would like to become a beauty operator. We both felt that it would be a good career for her, as she was quick and energetic. We then agreed that she would take a six-month course at a local beauty school and when her course was completed and she was employed we would live separately.

During this period of my life I was emotionally confused, nursing my hurt, and with no desire for any further emotional entanglements. I remained wholly wrapped up in my work, probably a defensive reaction that would last for a long time. Bernice completed her schooling and was retained by the beauty school as an instructor. She had her own apartment, and with me carrying the expense of Jerry's boarding school in San Mateo, was able to support herself.

Bernice was an honest, loving, generous person, remarkably alert, capable and sensitive. Her only failing was her addiction to alcohol to which in her lonesomeness during my three months absence from home had helped to bring about, and which my immaturity prevented me from recognizing and forgiving her completely. Because of her Cherokee Indian heritage she was especially vulnerable genetically to alcohol, a disease which would eventually destroy her chances for an orderly, happy, productive life. In our years together, I cannot recall our ever having exchanged an unkind word. I saw little of Bernice during the turmoil that existed during the transfer of the Lighthouse Service to the Coast Guard. We talked over the phone and exchanged birthday and Christmas cards with affectionate greetings, a practice that would continue for fifteen or twenty years.

When Bernice moved to her own apartment I rented a room with a delightful French family in Oakland. It was a large, old-fashioned turn-of-the-century home wherein I occupied a spacious room with a working fireplace. They accepted me as part of the family.

Mr. and Mrs. de Paulliac, the French family in whose home I lived, introduced me to a young Englishman visiting from the West Indies. He belonged to an English Plantocracy family, and had been brought up on a sugar plantation owned by his family for generations. Of my own age, he had traveled extensively in India, and was an ardent Theosophist. We were attracted to one another, and over a period of several weeks, spent many hours discussing religious philosophy. This association left an indelible mark on my spiritual views, causing me to question the validity of my Christian beliefs. At this period in my life I was without the maturity to carry to conclusion my exploration into the possibility of an existence beyond this lifetime. How I have wished to again meet and know this man whose name I have long ago lost in memory.

I had a used Ford automobile and sometimes on a weekend I would drive South along the East shore of San Francisco Bay to an isolated wooded area. Here flowed a small, sparkling stream which reminded me of Fancher Creek several miles from

Fresno, where as an eleven year old boy I spent many summer weekends, alone with my books and a blanket. I would catch crayfish to cook and eat, and with romantic dreams would comb the shallow creek bottom for freshwater clams in a search for fresh water pearls. This creek was such a place. So a thirty-three year-old boy would take with him a six-foot long broomstick handle, a bit of string and raw liver as bait, as he had done as a child twenty years earlier. I have since marveled and wondered at the healing contentment of this experience.

I usually shared my catch of crayfish with the de Paulliacs, so one Sunday on my way home to Oakland I saw a small wooden sailboat (a 38 foot Tahiti Ketch) pulled up on the beach, with a man close to my age scraping the bottom of the boat.
I was filled with nostalgia at the sight, thinking of the Schooner C.S. HOLMES and the Barkentine FOREST DREAM, so I walked to the boat and introduced myself. His name was Carl Tilden, a machinist originally from Salt Lake City, Utah. He and his wife Cina had a dream of homesteading on some farming land in Brazil. They had come to San Francisco, and with their savings had bought a small sailboat, Tahiti Ketch, which they planned to sail to Rio de Janeiro in Brazil. They both worked, he as a machinist and she as a waitress, with all of their money going into the repair and outfitting of their boat.

Carl appreciated my knowledge and experience with sailboats and was grateful for my interest and advice. I drove him home, met Cina, and we ate crayfish for dinner. As the weeks went by I spent each available weekend working on the boat with Carl, and we became friends. Several months later I was transferred from the SEQUOIA to the COLUMBINE as First Officer, and my visits to Carl and Cina became less frequent.

One weekend I noticed that Carl seemed very depressed. After some urging he told me that Cina was two months pregnant, and were struggling to come to a decision. They were both Mormons, and having an abortion was a major sin. To have a child at this time meant that they would have to forego their cherished dream to sail to Brazil, or so they thought.

The following day I drove into a second hand auto dealer's lot in Oakland and sold my Ford for $650.00 that I gave to Carl. I could get along without an automobile. I continued to visit them whenever I could, and in due time Cina gave birth to a baby girl whom they named Noel. A year later they set sail for Brazil. Then came 1940 and the changeover of the Lighthouse Service to the Coast Guard, and my subsequent transfer to Alaska. I was serving in the Coast Guard in Ketchikan, Alaska when I received a wooden box from Rio de Janeiro. It contained a letter with photos of Carl and Cina and two children, together with a picture of their ranch. The box also contained souvenirs, one a large tray made of mahogany and ornamented with butterfly wings and many small items, all of which I still have. All was well with them.

Then came World War II, and it was not until the end of the war that I wrote to their address in Brazil, only to have my letters returned as undeliverable. I never heard from the Tildens again. I will always remember them with a warm, pleasurable feeling, thinking that perhaps this rare, spontaneous action of mine might offset one of the many thoughtless sins of omission I have unwittingly committed in my lifetime.

Memories of this portion of my life have faded with the years, but I can recall with great clarity a number of incidents that transpired, one particularly humorous. Bernice and I had for some years been friends with a couple fifteen years older than we were, Owen and Mary Burns, with one daughter the age of Bernice. They were all from Atlanta, Georgia, Owen being the scion of a wealthy family and very much an alcoholic, who having dissipated his patrimony was employed as a used car salesman. He was tall and imposing and the most cultured and charming person I have ever met. His wife, Mary, was a busty, volatile, imaginative woman. They were a devoted couple and Mary had spent most of her married life trying to keep him away from alcohol. Owen and I were very companionable, and occasionally I would spend an evening with them. Fond of Chinese food, we would tour San Francisco's Chinatown. One day I visited Owen at his workplace and on the way to his apartment we stopped at a number of Owen's favorite bars. I did not know that he had been drinking for a week. We were in a joyful mood and as we approached his home, we noticed that the sidewalk trees in front of his third floor apartment, which in winter were barren of leaves, appeared to be in full bloom. On closer examination we saw long streamers of multicolored silk hanging from the branches. Mary in her frustration over his week of drinking, had cut all of his shirts and pajamas into strips and thrown them out of the window and five minutes after we entered the apartment, the three of us were laughing hilariously over the incident.

In the spring of 1937 while on a weekend visit to Chris and Adelheid in Fresno, Adelheid took me to one side and said, "I have received a letter from my sister in Denmark saying she has discovered the address of your father and mother, Hans Christian and Jenny. Your father is still an Officer in the Army, living in Krusaa, and for many years has been the Commander of the border between Denmark and Germany. She also said your brother Jens died of tuberculosis thirteen years ago when he was 19 years old. I am giving you their address, so you can write to them."

I had to think it over for several weeks before I could bring myself to write to parents that I had never known. I discovered I had harbored a deep resentment towards my mother for having abandoned me, and could not write to her at this time. I very much wanted to know my father, towards whom I attached no blame for the circumstances of my birth. So I wrote to my father, who was fluent in several languages, including English. After exchanging several letters, I included Jenny in the heading. He suggested that I come to Denmark and spend Christmas with him and Jenny, and I agreed to do so.

In the first week of October, I received a letter from Jenny, that my father had died instantly of a cerebral hemorrhage on September 23, 1937 at the age of 54. I continued to correspond with Jenny four or five times yearly. Ten years were to elapse before I would meet her.

I enjoyed my work as Second Mate on the SEQUOIA, performing varied and challenging tasks that required a high degree of seamanship. Annually we serviced lights located on the highest points on the isolated, desolate San Clemente Islands off the Southern California coast. In charge of a dozen seamen carrying 100-pound acetylene cylinders on their backs, I would clamber up what seemed to us to be mountains. At other times we had to take a twenty foot heavy wooden boat loaded with a ton of coal and provisions through a pounding surf at isolated coastal light stations. Six men would be at the oars, with me in the stern steering the boat and ready to drop a sea anchor to keep the boat from broaching and to enable us to pull off the beach on the return to the ship. Sometimes the boat would capsize in the breakers, casting all of us into the sea along with the cargo. Together with the First Mate, I had to be on the foredeck when working buoys, some weighing as much as nine tons and thirty or more feet in length. We had to scurry about the deck securing heavy buoy anchor chain, so we could burn out sections of chain and add new chain. The work was hard and dangerous, and I enjoyed it.

Ten years later, as Captain of a buoy tender I would invent and patent a device called a mechanical chain stopper and safety lead that would be used by buoy tenders throughout the world and save scores of lives and reduce serious injuries to almost nil. During the summer months some of our trips would take us away from our home port of San Francisco for as long as three weeks. In the winter months, adverse weather conditions kept us moored at the base, or tending aids to navigation in San Francisco Bay.

The U.S. Lighthouse Service was a civilian service operating under the jurisdiction of the Department of Commerce. Their mission was to maintain and operate the Aids to Navigational System of the United States, which consisted of hundreds of coastal and inland light stations, as well as thousands of sea buoys, river buoys, and channel markers. It was an extremely dedicated service. Many persons manning the lighthouses and life saving stations had fathers and grandfathers who had held the same positions. The ship's officers were all professional former Merchant Marine officers licensed by the Marine Inspection Office, many having been employed for over twenty or more years. The duties of a vessel handling large sea buoys weighing many tons and the servicing of coastal lighthouses was dangerous and challenging, requiring a high level of sea-going knowledge and skill. It can be said that the Lighthouse Service had an intimate knowledge of every foot of the coastline of the United States. In 1939 the Lighthouse Service had under its command a total of 108 vessels and 39 lightships manned by seagoing personnel.

Chapter 5

US COAST GUARD

FROM ALASKA TO THE SOUTH PACIFIC

 The United States Coast Guard was a paramilitary service, which by law became part of the United States Navy in time of war. President Franklin Delano Roosevelt, certain that the United States would eventually be drawn into a world war and recognizing the value of the role the ships and personnel of the Lighthouse Service could play in the coastal defense, decided to have the Lighthouse Service absorbed into the United States Coast Guard and placed under the Secretary of the Treasury.

The details of this Coast Guard takeover was left to Coast Guard Headquarters staff and the senior Lighthouse Service Administrative Staff members located in Washington, D.C. A committee consisting of high-ranking Coast Guard officers and Superintendents of Lighthouse Districts convened in Washington D.C. to arrange for the consolidation of the two Services. While the Coast Guard was very eager to triple the size of the Coast Guard, they were determined not to dilute their Commissioned Officer complement of Coast Guard Academy Officers with former Merchant Marine Officers, or shoreside personnel, who were not college graduates. The Coast Guard Academy Officers were a relatively small, closely knit, fraternal group, whose guiding principle was to protect one another's careers by covering up all negative actions and characteristics of their fellow officers, half of whom were productive, and the other half enjoying a protected, pleasurable, and carefree existence.

The Lighthouse officer personnel, with their Merchant Marine background were far more experienced in seamanship than the Academy officers, whose background consisted of four years of academics along with two or three short training cruises at sea. The committee was entirely dominated by the Coast Guard, who placated the Lighthouse Service Administrative Members, all engineering college graduates, by granting them the 37 officer commissions doled out to the Lighthouse Service. There was no one to speak for the interests of the sea-going personnel of the Lighthouse Service vessels.

To accomplish their purpose the committee arbitrarily decided that the military ranks and ratings to be offered to U.S. Lighthouse Service employees would be predicated by equating the pay scales of the two services, irrespective of the positions held, or the responsibilities inherent in the position. By this ruling they justified their planned allocation of military ranks and ratings to be granted U.S. Lighthouse personnel.

An examining board, composed of Coast Guard officers was convened at Coast Guard Headquarters in Washington, D.C. and eventually word filtered down to the Lighthouse Service in San Francisco that Masters of major Lighthouse vessels were to be offered the rank of Chief Warrant Boatswain. Masters of smaller vessels, such as 125-foot tenders that serviced rivers and bays, would be offered the rank of Warrant Boatswain, providing their pay scale was equal to the pay scale of that rank. To the Deck Officers of Lighthouse tenders this was disconcerting. They were for the most part in command of ships of equal or greater size than Coast Guard vessels commanded by Coast Guard commissioned officers. Furthermore, they had far greater responsibilities performing hazardous duties that no Coast Guard officer was qualified or prepared to undertake without extensive training. These men were proud professional seamen, many with twenty or thirty years of government service as Shipmasters. Humiliated, many chose to retire or resign.

In the summer of 1939 while the Coast Guard Examining Board in Washington was deciding the fate of Lighthouse personnel, I was Chief Officer of the vessel "COLUMBINE," a 125 foot vessel with a crew of (4) officers and (20) deck and engine room personnel. The Captain was Eric Hesse, a twenty-year employee who had elected to retire rather than enter the Coast Guard, and I had been selected to be his relief. The COLUMBINE operated on San Francisco Bay and tributaries, including the Sacramento River. It was an interesting assignment with our home base on Yerba Buena Island in San Francisco Bay. One week we would tend lights and buoys in the Bay, and the next week we would do the Sacramento River. We worked hard all day and in the evenings we would tie up in one of the small towns (villages), go to a movie and stop in our favorite bar on our way back to the ship.

In March of 1939, thinking a change of scenery might help me recover from the loss of Bernice, I had requested a transfer to a vessel in Honolulu, Hawaii. In December of 1939 all Lighthouse personnel received a letter from the examining board in Washington which set forth the number of Commissioned Officers, Chief Warrant,

San Francisco, California
November 13, 1939

From: Niels P. Thomsen
      First Officer, Tender Colombine
      U.S. Lighthouse Service
      San Francisco District.

To: Assistant Secretary of the Treasury
      Washington, D.C.

Via: 1. Commander, U.S. Coast Guard District
         San Francisco, California
      2. Commandant, U.S. Coast Guard
         Washington, D.C.

Subject: Inadequacy of proposed Coast Guard rank and ratings
         for Tender Officers.

Reference: Recent Headquarters release showing present
           grades of Lighthouse personnel, and proposed
           Coast Guard ranks and ratings to be offered
           to U.S.LIghthouse shipboard personnel.

The Coast Guard is primarily a Maritime Organization of vessels
composed of Seamen and Nautical Specialists, and in the same
category is found the large and efficient fleet of Vessels
and personnel of the Lighthouse Service. These ships and men
are responsible, not only for the safe efficient
maintenance, and economical operation of this fleet of
splendid ships, but for the maintenance and accuracy of the
thousands of floating aids to navigation, as well as the
construction and repairs to thousands of fixed aids on
submarine sites. It appears that neither our ability, nor
the importance or reponsibility of our duties is fully
appreciated.

It is understood that approximately forty of the former
Lighthouse District Headquarters Staff of Engineers, etc.,
are to be commissioned with ranks from Ensign to Captain.
Why cannot like consideration be given to ships Officers.
A number of the more experienced in nautical affairs among
those commissioned, are former Officers of Lighthouse
Service vessels. The former District Commanders of the
Life-saving section of the Lighthouse Service have been
commissioned as lieutenant Commanders and Commanders. We
ships' Officers, have the same educational background, with
possibily more nautical experience in equally hazardous,
and exacting duties on the high seas. Why cannot we, who
speak the language of the Mariner for whom the aids to
navigation are maintained, be accorded similar recognition.

If we cannot be given rank commensurate with our responsibilities, then could we not remain as we are as present, with the same opportunity for advancement and promotion on Tenders, rather than be inducted into the Military organization. The clerks and depot personnel are permitted to retain their civilian status, and we would prefer that to the humiliation incident to inadequate Military rank. Under the proposed ratings some of the present Officers on Tenders would be compelled to go from the wardroom, where they have been for years, to the forecastle as Blue-jackets.

Insofar as economy is concerned, it is not clear how this can be affected, consistent with a continued maintenance of past efficiency, inasmuch as the Lighthouse Service has carried that to an extent that borders on penurious.
A double standard cannot be successfully and harmoniously maintained for vessels of the service, one for the vessels of the former Revenue Cutter Service and another for the vessels of the Former Lighthouse Service. Compensation, complements of vessels and hours of duty, the times a vessels must be in and out of port and at sea, must eventually conform to a single standard, and that will mean a material augmentation in vessels, personnel, and all expenses incident thereto. The average American believes in Justice, and it will be difficult to explain so that he can understand the line of reasoning whereby, for instance, the PANDORA and the NEMISIS, two Coast Guard vessels half the size and tonnage of the Lighthouse tender IVY, should have over twice the personnel, be commanded by a Lieutenant Commander, and spending a substantial time alongside a dock, while the IVY commanded by a Warrant or Chief Warrant Officer, with half the personnel, has only ten days a quarter in port for cleaning boilers, painting buoys, plus ship repair and maintenance.

The lighthouse Service has always been engaged 365 days a year in safeguarding life and property from the perils of the sea, and in addition thereto, when disaster overtakes a vessel, then the lighthouse tenders also render effective salvage service. Heretofore, during a National Emergency they have taken their proper place as a military Maritime organization, and have rendered conspicuous service. In the performance of their daily duties which at times are extremely hazardous, especially when relieving a buoy with appendages weighs fifteen tons, is about forty feet long and nine feet in diameter at its largest part, with the vessel rolling in a seaway Men have lost their lives, or been seriously crippled, but the work must be done, and the vast commerce of the United States must move, and the Lighthouse Service has always done it's part to keep it so.

Under the circumstances, it is respectfully requested that
further consideration be given to the subject of this
letter, with a view to more equitable rank for Lighthouse
tender Officers under consideration for induction into the
military organization, or that the seagoing personnel of
the Lighthouse Service be continued in a civilian status
with all the privileges and benefits we have heretofore
enjoyed.

Niels P. Thomsen
First Officer
USLHS Tender COLUMBINE

NOTE: After forty years I now know that I should have addressed
this letter to the Coast Guard Commandant, with a copy
direct to the Secretary of the Treasury. I do not believe
that it ever went further than the Coast Guard Commandant,
and may not have gone further than San Francisco.

3 February, 1940

From: Niels P. Thomsen
             First Officer, Tender COLUMBINE
             San Francisco, California

To: Commandant,
             United States Coast Guard,
             Washinngton, D.C.

Via: Official Channels

Subject: Induction into the United States Coast Guard.

Reference: Consideration of proposed Coast Guard status.

    1. I understand, through the examing board, that my present
pay and allowances are $10.00 per month short of the amount which
would permit the board to recommend me for an appointment as
Warrant Boatswain.

    2. For twelve years I have served as a Senior Deck Officer
in the American Merchant Marine in both sail and steam vessels. I
hold an unlimited Masters License, together with First Class
pilotage for both Atlantic and Pacific Coast ports. My official
record will show that I am fully qualified to hold any position
as a master Mariner in the Lighthouse Unit of the Coast Guard. On
two occasions in the past year I have been recommended by the
Superintendent of the Lighthouse Service for promotion to a grade
that would have qualified me for a Warrant Officers appointment.
These positions subsequently were filled by Coast Guard Warrant
Officers.

    3. Having held a Commission in the United States Naval
Reserve as an Ensign for six years, and having had active
training duty together with numerous corresondence courses, I am
in every way aware of the duties and responsibilities of a
Warrant Officer.

    4.   Paragraph 7, of the Commandant´s letter of November 25,
1939 states; "The rank or rate and pay of Officers and men in the
Coast Guard are based on many factors, not the least of which is
the potential ability of the person concerned to perform assigned
duty". With this thought in mind I trust that my application for
appointment will deserve the attention and consideration of the
Commandant.

                                          Niels P. Thomsen

Forwarded: E Hesse, Master

NIELS PETER THOMSEN - AGE THIRTY

24-E

MF/THOMSEN, Niels P,
Ensign, D-M, USNR, #68769,
(3173-63-Rys)

TWELFTH NAVAL DISTRICT
FEDERAL OFFICE BUILDING CIVIC CENTER
SAN FRANCISCO · CALIFORNIA

27 March, 1940

FIRST ENDORSEMENT.

From: Commandant, Twelfth Naval District and Naval
           Operating Base.
To: -   Ensign Niels P. Thomsen, D-M, USNR.,
           Room 425, Custom House,
           San Francisco, California.

Subject: Resignation.

1.   Forwarded, for compliance in accordance with paragraph 3.

2.   The Commandant also regrets that you find it necessary to resign from the U.S. Naval Reserve.

A.J.HEPBURN.

WARRANT OFFICER'S APPOINTMENT

UNITED STATES COAST GUARD.

In accordance with the provisions of the Regulations for the Government of the

Coast Guard, NIELS P. THOMSEN is hereby appointed

a BOATSWAIN in the Coast Guard of the United States

from (24 April, 1940), 19___. He is therefore carefully and diligently to discharge

DATE OF OATH

all the duties of a BOATSWAIN , and is to obey the orders and directions

which he shall receive from his superior officers, according to the rules and discipline

of the Coast Guard; and all Petty Officers, Seamen, Surfmen, and others under his

direction are strictly charged and required to be obedient to his orders.

This appointment to continue in force only during the pleasure of the Secretary

of the Treasury.

Washington, D. C. 9 APRIL, 1940

Secretary.

2-7871

GOVERNMENT PRINTING OFFICE

24-G

DECEMBER,1939 REPORT OF U.S. COAST GUARD EXAMINING BOARD

COMMISSIONED OFFICERS

	- 1939 - COAST GUARD	- ALLOCATED - USLHS	- 1940 - TOTAL
Rear Admirals	3	0	3
Captains	23	2	25
Commanders	41	12	53
Lt. Commanders	94	6	100
Lieutenants	200	0	200
Lieutenant JG	333	15	348
Ensign	346	2	348
	1,040	37	1,077

WARRANT OFFICERS

Chief Boatswain	144	64	208
Boatswain	203	150	353
	347	214	561

The remaining Lighthouse Personnel were offered enlisted ratings ranging from Seaman to Chief Petty Officer. Many Employees refused the ratings offered, and resigned.

Warrant Officers and Enlisted Men to be inducted into the Coast Guard. A short while later each employee received a letter stating the rank or rating for which the Board had recommended that he be offered.

In the first week in January I received my letter from the Coast Guard Examining Board. It stated that I had been selected for the enlisted rating of a Chief Boatswains' Mate. The letter furthermore advised me that my present pay and allowances were $15.00 a month short of the amount that would permit the Board to recommend me for an appointment as a Warrant Officer. I was shocked. I had many things to consider and did not send in my reply until February 3rd.

I had served in the Merchant Marine for seventeen years, twelve years of which had been as an Officer. I had an unlimited Masters' License to command ships of any tonnage on any ocean, as well as East and West Coast Pilot licenses. I had been a Naval Reserve Officer for five years, having taken in each of those years the required two weeks training cruise on the battleship USS NEVADA. I had completed many Navy correspondence courses in naval procedure and technical subjects, always acquiring top grades. I had no intention of accepting, or being locked into an Enlisted rating. I had the option of returning to the Merchant Marine at twice the salary of a Warrant Officer, and I could look forward to a command in one or two year's time. I no longer had a family, so there was no reason for not returning to a career that required protracted periods of sea duty.

The disciplined life of a Naval Officer held some appeal for me, and I had first-hand knowledge of the high regard accorded to Navy Warrant Officers, a rare appointment only attainable by the elite of Enlisted Chief Petty Officers. Inasmuch as a Warrant Officer appointment carried with it the option of resigning on request, except in time of war, I wrote to the Commandant of the Coast Guard that I could not accept any appointment below the rank of Warrant Boatswain. Several months later I received an appointment as Warrant Boatswain to rank from April 24, 1940. On receipt of the appointment, I requested to be transferred to a Coast Guard Patrol Cutter, to more rapidly become familiar with Coast Guard military customs and procedure. Had I known of the roadblocks that lay ahead for a "Mustang" (a non-Academy Officer) of my ambition, temperament and self-esteem, I might have chosen an easier route to the top.

On May 11, 1940, I received orders to report to the U.S. Coast Guard Cutter ARIADNE for duty. The ARIADNE and her sister ship the DAPHNE, were two 135 foot patrol vessels based in San Francisco as search and rescue vessels covering the Pacific Coast between Point Arguello to the South, and Point Arena to the North. They were manned by two Commissioned Officers, two Warrant Boatswains, a Chief Warrant Machinist and twenty-four Enlisted ratings. Lieutenant John Stewart, USCG was Commanding Officer, and Lieutenant Charles Ashley, USCG the Executive Officer and were Coast Guard Academy classmates. I found them both to be considerate, fair-minded and capable men. They were accustomed to a somewhat privileged lifestyle, free of career concerns other than the date of their inevitable advancement

REPORT ON THE FITNESS OF OFFICERS

CON

OCT 11 1940

FILE

The following six questions are to be answered by the officer reported on:

Period covered by this report, from _____ 11 May _____, 19 40 to _____ 30 September _____

_____ THOMSEN, Niels Peter _____; Grade _____ Boatswain _____;
(Surname first—other names in full)

1. Regular station and duties _____ Gunnery and Commissary Officer, ARIADNE; Watch Of _____

2. Additional duties performed _____ Clothing Officer, ARIADNE. _____

3. Permanent home address _____ 201 Orange Street, Oakland, California. _____

4. Next of kin _____ Wife _____ Bernice Eula Thomsen, 201 Orange St., Oaklar
(Relationship) _____ (Name) _____ (Address)

5. (a) For what class of duty have you a prefer-   (b) For what station have you a p
ence?
   (1) Present (2) Maritime ✓ _____   _____ Gulf Coast ✓
   (If more than one, state order of preference)   (If more than one, state order of pref

6. Proficiency in foreign languages, stating which ones, and ability therein, giving mark:

   (a) As interpreter _____ Danish - 4.0 _____

   (b) As translator _____ Danish - 4.0 _____

   Signature _____ Niels P. Thomsen _____ Rank _ Boatswain

Following to be made out by reporting officer:

7. Reporting officer: Name _____ John R. Stewart _____, Rank _____ Lieutenant _____,

8. Reporting officer's official status relative to officer reported on _____ Commanding Offi

9. Assign marks on scale of 0–4 in appropriate subdivisions given below, and any other quali
which observation has been sufficient to justify marking—a mark of 2.5 or less will be r
the officer reported upon.

   Present assignment _ 3.3 _ Ability to command _ 3.2 _ As executive or division officer

   As deck watch officer _ 3.4 _ In administration _ 3.4 _

10. Has the work of this officer been reported on either in a commendatory way or adversely c

    period of this report? _ No _. If so, state the substance of the report.

11. In case any unfavorable entries have been made by you on this report, were the deficiencies
    hereon brought to the attention of the officer concerned while under your command and

    the rendition of this report? _ None _ If yes, what improvement, if any, was noted? __

12. Considering the possible requirements of the service in peace or war, indicate your attitu

    having this officer under your command. Would you (1) Especially desire to have him ✓

    (2) Be satisfied to have him? _____ (3) Prefer not to have him? _____ (If (3
    officer for statement.)

13. Has he any weakness—mental, moral, physical, etc.—which adversely affect his efficier
    "Yes," give details.)

    _____ None _____

5. Consider cooperativeness; ability to work for and with others; readiness to give new i and methods a fair trial; desire to observe and conform with the policies of his superi

(___) (✓) (___) (___) (___)
Superior in this respect   Very cooperative   Cooperative   Difficult to handle   Obstructive

6. Consider initiative; resourcefulness; success in doing things in new and better ways in adapting improved methods to his own work; constructive thinking.

(___) (✓) (___) (___) (___)
Superior in this respect   Very resourceful   Progressive   Rarely suggests   Needs detailed instr

7. Consider adaptability for Service; personal habits, neatness, punctuality, conversati temperament, and personality.

(___) (✓) (___) (___) (___)
Greatest possible   Very adaptable   Adaptable   Doubtful Adaptability   Not adaptable
adaptability

8. Considering the emergent nature of Coast Guard duty in all of its phases in time of pea and war, answer affirmatively one of the three following:

(a) Do you particularly desire to have this officer with you?   *Yes*
(b) Would you be satisfied to have this officer with you?   _____
(c) Would you prefer not to have him?   _____

9. REMARKS.   (State anything that you may desire regarding your opinion of this office:

This officer entered the service last April. At first certain radical elements caused by his past environment were noted. However in the process of his induction these traits have disappeared. He will be an outstanding and a very adaptable warrant officer

I certify that the answers to the above questions have been carefully determined a are made without prejudice or partiality, and represent my true and honest opinion.

C. St. Lley
(Signature)

This officer entered the service last April. At first certain radical elements caused by his past enviroment were noted. However, in the process of his induction these traits have disappeared. He will be an outstanding and very adaptable warrant officer.

in rank and pay. For some unexplainable reason I had no difficulty in relating to them both.

I was assigned as Deck Officer, with collateral duties as Gunnery and Commissary Officer. The other Warrant Boatswain was Mr. Leonard White, a man fifty-two years old, with over twenty years of Coast Guard Service. Here I must add a note concerning the Warrant Officer Corps of the Coast Guard. Practically all Warrant Officers in the Coast Guard were over fifty years of age, having been appointed with the onset of prohibition when the Coast Guard built and had in commission scores of small patrol craft to combat rum running. These officers were for the most part from the Enlisted ranks of the Coast Guard, generally men of limited education.

In 1933 the prohibition law was repealed and these Warrant Officers were assigned as Junior Deck Officers of Cutters and as officers in charge of small craft. Because of the practically non-existent opportunities for advancement in rank most of these Warrant Officers lost all incentive and ambition. Being former Enlisted men their standards of military discipline were unbelievably low. The lack of military conduct and discipline on the ARIADNE, which had been tolerated by Mr. White and the Warrant Officer who had preceded me, disturbed me and I felt it my duty to bring the crew up to Navy military standards. I discussed my views with the Captain and Executive Officer, who gave me their support.

The assignment was not an easy one, yet I made progress despite resistance from the crew and Mr. White. I refer to the comments contained in my fitness report as made out by Captain Stewart. It was a week on duty, and a week alongside the dock in Alameda, alternating with our sister ship, the Cutter DAPHNE. During the week we were on duty we spent 80 percent of our sea time at anchor in San Francisco Bay near the Yacht Club, with a launch going ashore daily to pick up ship's mail. Captain Stewart was a pleasant, carefree person whose primary ambition was to have a photograph of him and his wife attending a fashionable San Francisco night club appear in the Examiner social column. Mr. Ashley was a high strung officer of approximately my age. He was of very slight build, always with a worried look. For some reason, probably medical, he had been placed out of line of promotion, and would never rise above Lieutenant. He was quiet, thoughtful, and a thorough gentleman. We both felt the crew was not up to proper naval discipline, and he appreciated my views on this subject. We got along well together.

After eight months I tired of the routine aboard the ARIADNE and felt I was ready for a more active assignment. I spoke to Mr. Ashley about my feelings, and he convinced the Captain to arrange a transfer for me to the Alaskan District Headquarters in Ketchikan, Alaska, which I had visited while in the Merchant Marine fifteen years earlier. On the first of February 1941, I received orders to report for duty to the Coast Guard District in Ketchikan, Alaska. When I told Bernice of my impending transfer, she asked if she and Jerry could accompany me. So the three of us headed by train to Seattle and on to Alaska by an Alaska Steamship Company passenger vessel. On March 12, 1941, we arrived in Ketchikan as passengers on the Alaska Steamship

BARANOFF. We rented a furnished apartment on Millar Street and Bernice set about arranging for Jerry's schooling and several days later I reported to the Commander of the 17th Coast Guard District, Commander F.A. Zeusler, USCG. The 17th Coast Guard District included all Alaskan waters, including the Aleutian Islands and the Bering Sea, as well as annual patrols as far North as Point Barrow in the Arctic Ocean. In addition to being the location of the 17th Coast Guard Headquarters, Ketchikan had been the headquarters of the former Lighthouse Service, which maintained a large ship and buoy repair base with many artisan shops, all manned by Civil Service employees. Though the base was now part of the Coast Guard, the former U.S. Lighthouse Civil Service employees had retained their civilian status. However, Coast Guard military personnel had been placed in all supervisory positions, an act that was causing considerable conflict.

The three seagoing buoy tenders stationed here were the CEDAR, HEMLOCK and ALDER. The Coast Guard vessels in the District were the Arctic Patrol Cutter HAIDA, the 165-foot Cutter CYANE, a sister ship to the ARIADNE, and two slightly smaller 125 foot Patrol Cutters the BONHAM and the NEMAHA. Although the BONHAM and the NEMAHA were sister ships and their duties identical, the NEMAHA was commanded by a Coast Guard Academy full Lieutenant and the BONHAM by a Warrant Boatswain from the former Lighthouse Service, an example of the Coast Guard's inequitable policy in the award of military ranks to Lighthouse Service officers.

I do not wish it to appear that I was still harboring any resentment towards the treatment of Lighthouse Service officers. I refer to it only because I was brought face to face with a gross example of this act of injustice on my first duty assignment when I reported to the District.

The Master of the tender CEDAR, the largest Lighthouse tender afloat, was Captain John W. Leadbetter, a former Merchant Marine Shipmaster from the State of Maine. He was 65 years old and had been Master of the CEDAR for thirty-seven years. Without question, the duties performed annually by his vessel were the most difficult and perilous in the Lighthouse Service or Coast Guard. It serviced all the aids to navigation from Ketchikan to the Arctic Ocean and when it departed on its annual Bering Sea voyage it would be six months or longer away from its base at Ketchikan, where the crew's families, including the Captain's wife and six children made their home. The CEDAR and her Captain were a thirty-seven year old legend throughout all of Alaska. He was an imperious, six-foot, strong, goateed, and genteel person, a "State of Mainer," stern and straight as a ramrod in all his dealings with his ship and his fellow men. When the Coast Guard took over the Lighthouse Service, he was assigned the rank of Chief Warrant Boatswain, an overwhelming insult to this proud man of legendary stature. But his ship was his life, and he could not bring himself to resign. He continued to carry out his assignment with his civilian crew in the same tried, true and efficient way he had done for thirty-seven years. He was unfamiliar with military procedures and would never fit the Coast Guard mold.

Chapter 6

KETCHIKAN, ALASKA

 Ketchikan was a small insular town, where all inhabitants were acquainted with one another and the entire town had first or second-hand knowledge of everyone's intimate life, similar to "Peyton Place." By the same token, no one was openly criticized for their moral lapses, not that they were an amoral group, but there was always in the back of their minds that they one day might covet their neighbor's wife or husband, and thus be found wanting. Everyone knew who was likely to become pregnant and by whom. The townspeople fitted into various social levels. At the top level were the creme de la creme, the firmly entrenched, longtime Ketchikan resident families, who belonged to the Holy Order of Masons. Of this group, the less desirable, along with successful local businessmen, favored the Elks club. On the next lower level, were the Scandinavian fishermen and their families, who were referred to as "squareheads." They were regarded as not very bright, but were grudgingly accepted by the creme de la creme, as the existence of the town depended entirely on their fishing efforts. They preferred the ethnic comfort of the Sons of Norway Hall, except for the most affluent boat owners, who favored the Elks Club. Coast Guard personnel were considered to be transients, and were not favorably regarded, having taken over the Lighthouse Service and disturbed the status quo of the many former Lighthouse Service employees. They did however, represent to some of the towns bored and restless young women, the opportunity to marry and leave the "rainforest" of Ketchikan behind them for the bright lights of Stateside. Except for an enlightened few, the classes of inhabitants mentioned above, had not as yet made up their minds whether or not the local Native-Americans were a part of the Human Race.

For appearance sake, as in all small communities, the local prostitutes occupied **a** place on the lower rung of the social ladder. Even the clergymen of the many churches in Ketchikan had to acknowledge the important role this profession played in a town where men outnumbered women ten to one. Their establishments were located on Creek Street, which bordered on a spawning salmon stream of the same name, which flowed through the center of the town, past the Post Office and the Federal Building which housed the Headquarters of the Coast Guard. Many of them were long-time residents, and were accorded a certain degree of respect by the townspeople. They were restricted to Creek Street after dark, and in the afternoons could be seen strolling down Main Street walking their poodles. Their place in the community was secure, with most of them on a nodding acquaintance with the more liberal minded of the creme de la creme, men and women alike.

I thought the pioneer atmosphere of Ketchikan to be honest, refreshing, and for the most part non-hypocritical. A town with values I had no trouble relating to. I would have liked to have lived my entire life in this Alaskan town. While I served in the Coast Guard, it was always number one on my requests for assignment to the next duty station.

The District Commander was Commander Frederick A. Zeusler, USCG who would shortly be promoted to Captain, and later to Rear Admiral. He was a Coast Guard Academy graduate of the class of 1908, the year after I was born. He had held the rank of commander since 1929. During World War II he had served as an officer in the U.S. Navy, and was an outstanding example of what one would visualize a senior Naval Officer to be, in administrative ability, character, intelligence and fairness. He and Mrs. Zeusler were both religiously inclined. His Alaskan assignment was the most difficult in the Coast Guard, chiefly because of the vast area for which he was responsible. His assignment was further complicated by a long-standing Coast Guard policy to treat Alaskan duty as a form of punishment for officers and men who were chronic alcoholics, or those with negative characteristics which might embarrass the Coast Guard. Coast Guard service in Alaska could be compared to the Russian use of Siberian duty assignments. With the possibility of war in the Pacific, this policy was beginning to do an about face.

Prior to World War II, the Coast Guard was a relatively small Military Service, and promotion in the officer ranks unbelievably slow. As an example, Commander Zeusler graduated from the Coast Guard Academy as a Cadet in 1908, became an Ensign in 1911, a Lieutenant (jg) in 1915, a full Lieutenant in 1923, and Lieutenant Commander in 1924, a Commander in 1929, and a Captain in December of 1941. Thirty-three years from graduation as cadet to the rank of Captain, a long haul. Promotion in rank for military services was determined by an Order of Precedence list which establishes by number each officer's standing in the line of promotion. As an example, an officer graduating in the class of 1940 will be given a number corresponding to his grade standing in the class of 1940. This class is then entered in the Order of Precedence list behind the class of the previous year. Deviations from this

CAPTAIN FREDERICK ZEUSLER, USCG / JACK DEMPSEY WORLD CHAMPION BOXER

order were uncommon, but could occur in two instances. An Officer found to be outstanding in personal characteristics and professional competence could be selected by a board of senior officers for promotion ahead of officers who outranked him on the Order of Precedence list. Conversely, if an officer's fitness reports are consistently unfavorable to the point where it seriously threatened his ability to perform the duties of a higher rank, he could be placed out of the line of promotion, and would remain in his present rank until early retirement. This latter action could also occur should an officer be found unqualified for medical reasons. A confidential, detailed officer's fitness report was prepared by his commanding officer on each of the following occasions; routinely every six months, on his detachment from an assignment, or on detachment of the commanding officer from his command. This system had a tendency to reduce Academy Officers to a group of "yes men," fearful of incurring the displeasure of their reporting officer, should they challenge his opinions. It affected their performance by stifling their imagination and initiative. This type of behavior would be highly dangerous in time of war under combat conditions.

Several days after reporting to the District Office, the District Commander informed me that I would be temporarily assigned to the former Lighthouse tender CEDAR for a two-week period. He said to me,

"We have a problem with the CEDAR. Headquarters insists that the ship be militarized, and that the Master of the vessel, who for thirty-seven years has commanded the CEDAR, has refused to accept retirement. He must be replaced to make way for an officer who will carry out the military indoctrination program set forth in the Commandant's directive. This is a very sensitive assignment and you will encounter considerable resentment on board the vessel. You are to observe Captain Leadbetter, and come up with a recommendation as to what duty he should be assigned in the District Office."

I reported to Captain Leadbetter on the CEDAR. I have described him in some detail on a previous page, so will dispense with my impressions of him, except to say that he was old enough to be my father. I had tremendous respect for him as a person and a renowned Shipmaster. I felt like a small boy in his presence. It was not a duty assignment I was comfortable with, knowing the injustices having been inflicted on him by the Coast Guard in the takeover of the Lighthouse Service.

When the CEDAR returned to port two weeks later, I recommended to District Commander Zeusler that he be assigned to the District Office as Port Captain, an independent position of considerable prestige, and for which he was uniquely qualified because of his reputation and vast knowledge. As Port Captain he would report directly to the District Commander, bypassing all other District officers.

Following my CEDAR assignment, I was assigned to the District Office. This was a period when the District Commander was swamped with a great many directives from Washington. Commander Zeusler felt he needed someone to assist him with the voluminous correspondence this entailed, and appointed me his unofficial Aide. He gave me a desk in a corner of his office and I took on the duties of a Secretary. This assignment did not sit well with the Chief of Staff, Lieutenant Commander Tomkiel, who had personal problems. He had been involved in an automobile accident several years earlier in which a man lost his life. Not having liability coverage, he was ordered to pay a substantial amount of his monthly salary to the victim's family. He was also in poor health, and was retired several years later. I accurately regarded him as a future adversary.

Just being in the District Commander's office was an education in itself. I noted that the higher the rank of an officer when appearing before the Commander, the greater his nervousness, and the more apprehensive he seemed. I concluded that perhaps it was because he had more to lose. I also took note that in the weekly District Staff conferences, no one ever challenged the Commander's plans or suggestions. I had no intention of making the Coast Guard my career, so I had nothing to lose by challenging my senior officer's ideas or suggestions, and I became the "Devil's Advocate" at the meetings, which did nothing to increase my popularity with other District Officers. In retrospect, I now view my behavior among this group of senior officers as having been interpreted as being pretentious and unseemly, given my youth and lowly warrant rank.

A directive was received at the District to immediately establish a U.S. Coast Guard Auxiliary and Reserve, and the Commander assigned me to this project. It involved persuading the several hundred local fishing boats to enroll in the Auxiliary by offering their boats and crews to the Government for patrol services. I spent some time setting up the organization, and then began contacting the fishing fleet. Practically all of the boats were owned and manned by Scandinavians, by nature very suspicious of any military entanglement.
On my first day visiting the boats I met with a dozen fishermen on board one of the larger vessels. I did not reveal to them that I was fluent in all three Scandinavian languages.

While I was elaborating on the importance of establishing a Coast Guard Auxiliary and Reserve Unit in Ketchikan, explaining why they should join, and appealing to their patriotism, the fishermen in their native language were openly discussing me among themselves. Their remarks were personal and quite crude, referring to me as an upstart in a fancy uniform, still wet behind the ears, and believing them so foolish as to pledge themselves and their boats to some Coast Guard Unit. I concluded my sales pitch, and as I left I shook hands with each of them, and in Danish, Swedish and Norwegian said, "I thank you all very much for listening to me, you have all been so kind." They were all taken aback and visibly embarrassed.

The following day I signed up twelve boats and their crews, and within a month the Auxiliary was formally established with over fifty boats and crews. Commander Zeusler in a military ceremony, officially blessed the Coast Guard Auxiliary and election of officers was held. Commander Zeusler commended me for completing my assignment and I returned to my desk in his office, much to the discomfort of the Academy Officers in the District Office, particularly the Chief of Staff, Lieutenant

Commander Tomkiel.

Pearl Harbor was six months away, and Ketchikan was still a small community with very little entertainment. Like any small town, most social activities were cliquish and limited to established local residents, and Senior Coast Guard Officers. The single movie house and Saturday night dances were the only form of entertainment except for the numerous bars, saloons and honky-tonks scattered about the town. I was totally wrapped up in my Coast Guard duties, while Bernice, an energetic person, was finding Ketchikan very boring.

I cannot remember what our life together was like during this period, other than we never quarreled or were unkind to one another. What now seems strange, is that our relations were harmonious and our friendship never threatened. It may have been that I recognized and appreciated how she was successfully handling her dependence on alcohol. I continued to carry on my duties in the District Commander's Office. Commander Zeusler received a promotion in rank to Captain. One day he said to me, "Thomsen, the Coast Guard is going to appoint a number of Chief Warrant and Warrant Boatswains to the rank of Ensign and Lieutenant (jg) in the Coast Guard Reserve, and I have recommended you for promotion to Lieutenant (jg). If your promotion is approved, you will be assigned to sea duty. I am convinced that you will make a good Commissioned Coast Guard Officer, and be a credit to the service."

Chapter 7

USCG CUTTER CYANE

Several weeks later, word was received at the District that I had been promoted to the rank of Lieutenant (jg) in the Coast Guard Reserve. Out of five hundred and sixty Chief Warrant and Warrant Officers only five had been selected for promotion to Lieutenant (jg). I had leapfrogged over five hundred Warrant Officers who were senior to me in the Order of Precedence for promotion, and was now number three, and holding the temporary rank of Lieutenant (jg) in the Coast Guard Reserve.

Seven days later I was transferred to the U.S. Coast Guard Cutter CYANE. The CYANE was a sister ship to the ARIADNE, stationed in Ketchikan, and commanded by Lieutenant Frank K. Johnson, USCG, a 1928 Coast Guard Academy graduate, who had been promoted to Lieutenant Commander, and was about to be transferred.

On June 20, 1941, I walked on board the CYANE reporting to the Executive Officer, Lt. (jg) Julius R. Richey, USCG a graduate of the Academy Class of 1932, who had been assigned to the CYANE a year earlier. I was taken to the Commanding Officer and assigned to duty as a Deck Watch Officer, and Treasurer of the Mess. The CYANE was a happy ship, made so by the Captain and Executive Officer and I felt comfortable with my assignment, CYANE being on patrol, performing rescue work and servicing isolated Light Stations in Southeastern Alaska. Captain Johnson recognized my capabilities, giving me a full measure of trust and responsibility.

In August the CYANE received orders to proceed to Seattle for annual dry-docking. Bernice expressed a desire to return to San Francisco, and Captain Johnson gave me permission to take Bernice and Jerry south to Seattle on the CYANE, Bernice in my room, and Jerry berthing with Mr. Richey. Bernice and Jerry enjoyed the trip to Seattle, and for some reason Bernice and I never felt closer, and when I took her to the train station, we were both saddened at the thought of parting. We never ceased to retain this mutual affection for one another, and exchanged birthday and Christmas cards of remembrance for years to come, until we lost track of one another years later after World War II. I provided for her financially until she found employment, and became self-supporting.

In September of 1941, Captain Johnson was promoted to Lieutenant Commander, and having completed his two years of Alaskan duty, was transferred to a new duty station in the United States. Lieutenant Richey assumed command of the CYANE, pending the arrival of the new Commanding Officer, Lieutenant Commander Leslie Tollaksen, USCG. Commander Tollaksen had completed a three-year tour of duty in Honolulu, as communications Officer of the Cutter TANEY, one of the newest and largest Coast Guard vessels. He was known to several officers on the District Staff, who viewed his arrival with some apprehension. He had served for six years as an Aide to the Commandant of the Coast Guard in Washington, D.C. and was said to have a habit of bypassing his District office superiors by contacting friends in Washington, a trait which had led to his transfer to Alaskan sea duty on the CYANE, which normally was a Lieutenant's command, a considerable comedown in his career.

Lieutenant Commander Tollaksen reported to the District and the CYANE on September 20, 1941, and from that day forward, peace and tranquility disappeared from the CYANE. Lieutenant Richey was an amiable person. His Coast Guard Academy training had conditioned him to accept a superior officer's tyrannical peculiarities without protest. Also, he knew that he was shortly due for promotion to full Lieutenant and an accompanying transfer from Alaska. A month later he received his promotion and was transferred to the District Office, and I became the Executive Officer of the CYANE, and my troubles began.

Except for the short summer months the weather in Southeastern Alaska was cold and inclement. During the two years Captain Johnson commanded the CYANE, the crew had been permitted to wear non-regulation, casual, warm jackets. At his first inspection of the ship and crew, Commander Tollaksen announced that henceforth the crew would wear only regulation uniform, and non-regulation jackets could no longer be worn. Under the circumstances, this was an unreasonable edict, and was received by the enlisted crew with resistance, creating an animosity towards Mr. Richey and myself by our efforts to force compliance with the order.

In the month of October the CYANE performed an unusual and memorable rescue operation. A light airplane belonging to Ketchikan Air Service was being flown from Seattle to Ketchikan by two local Pilots. A radio distress message was picked up stating they were caught in a severe snowstorm and were making an emergency crash landing in a small inlet in Canadian British Columbia two hundred miles south of Ketchikan. Receiving an approximate location, the CYANE left immediately, arriving in the vicinity the following day.

On the second day of our search, while exploring an isolated inlet, we sighted the wreckage of an airplane that had mowed a fifty-foot wide path for several hundred feet through a stand of trees. When we stepped on the beach we saw the plane about one hundred yards from the beach. Both wings had been ripped away from the fuselage, which was still intact. In the Pilot and Co-pilot seats were two dead men, their heads smashed by contact with the glass windshield. In the back of the plane were two injured men, both of whom I recognized as the two Ketchikan pilots. One of them suffered from a broken shoulder blade, the other a broken arm. Both men were badly bruised about the face and head. They had this story to tell. "When our plane struck the water in the middle of the inlet we managed to get clear before it sank about two hundred and fifty feet from the shoreline. Lucky for us, one of the floats had separated from the plane and we were able to keep afloat by clinging to it, each of us having only one good arm. The water was very cold and it was snowing, but we managed to paddle to the beach. When we stood up on reaching the beach we could see a stretch of freshly broken trees with an airplane at the far end, a hundred feet distant. The wings were broken off, but the fuselage appeared to be intact. By holding on to one another we were able to reach the plane. Inside were two dead men. The man in the co-pilot seat had a map in one hand and a pair of dividers in the other. They must not have been dead very long as their bodies were not stiffened or frozen. In the plane were two down sleeping bags and a supply of food, among which were several cartons of eggs, which remarkably had not broken. Were it not for the shelter and food in the plane, we would never have survived."

When we returned to the CYANE, a message had been received saying a plane bound from Anchorage to Seattle was missing with two men on board. We had found both planes. Two men had died so two others might live, an unbelievable coincidence. The CYANE alternated with the Cutter McLANE, one week on patrol and one week in port. When in port I kept a room at the Ingersoll hotel. One Saturday evening, depressed, and drowning my sorrows at the bar in the hotel's cocktail lounge where a dance was in progress, I caught the eye of an attractive, dark-haired woman on the dance floor. By asking the bartender, I learned that her name was Ethel Bevan, the daughter of Captain Leadbetter of the legendary Lighthouse Tender CEDAR, whom I had encountered on my first assignment on reporting to the Coast Guard for duty in Alaska. Captain Leadbetter and his family, partly because it was erroneously believed I was responsible for his removal from his beloved CEDAR, had every reason to put me at the head of the list of persona-non-grata in his home.

Ethel was my age (35) and a widow with a five-year-old daughter, Carol Ann. She taught school in one of the lower grades in Ketchikan. I asked her for a dance, and we were attracted to one another. We arranged to meet the following day. She told me she had been keeping company with a local person for over a year and expected to marry him. They had quarreled a week earlier, which was why she was celebrating the evening with friends at the hotel. Her boyfriend, Nathan Warner, was a member in good standing at the local Masonic Hall, the Holy Temple and meeting place of the creme de la creme and of which Captain Leadbetter was the Grand Potentate. Warner was therefore welcomed as a potential member of the family, who found Ethel's interest in an itinerant Junior Coast Guard Officer, and a "squarehead" as well, to be highly disturbing, to say the least. For several weeks the only way Ethel and I were able to meet, was at a restaurant, movie theater, or on the street corner. During the months of November and December of 1941, three newly appointed Coast Guard Reserve Ensigns reported to the CYANE for training duty. The CYANE was kept busy servicing outlying lighthouse stations in Southeastern Alaska. On December 3rd, the CYANE departed from Ketchikan for Cape Decision Light Station on the West Coast. Cape Decision could only be serviced at extreme high tide, which on this occasion was in the morning shortly after 0600. We anchored in a small cove near Cape Decision in the late evening. At midnight a light feathery snow began to fall. There was no wind, and we were surrounded by a soft quietness. After anchoring, the Captain gave me verbal orders to call him at 0555, heave up the anchor at 0600 and then have him called. (TURN TO ADDENDUM ONE FOR A COMPLETE ACCOUNT OF THIS INCIDENT)

Captain Tollaksen instructed the Chief Boatswains' Mate and the Reserve Ensigns that I was incommunicado. At first the entire incident appeared to me to be humorous, if not outright ridiculous. The Steward served my breakfast in my room. In reviewing the events, and having completed a course in Naval Regulations while a Naval Reserve Officer, I came to the conclusion that Tollaksen had acted illegally. I then sent the Steward for a copy of Naval Regulations and sure enough Tollaksen could be in trouble. When the CYANE returned to Ketchikan the following evening, word had reached the District Office that I was confined to the ship. Later in the evening a Yeoman from the District Office came on board with a message from the District Office instructing Captain Tollaksen to have me report ashore to the District Commander, Captain Zeusler. It was apparent that Tollaksen had good reason to be nervous.

I distinctly recall my meeting that evening with the District Commander, Captain Zeusler and the Chief of Staff, Commander Tomkiel. In the three months Lieutenant Commander Tollaksen had been attached to the District as Captain of the CYANE, history had been repeating itself. He had been a thorn in the side of the District Commander by constantly going over the heads of the District by writing and telephoning his friends at Headquarters in Washington, not only on matters regarding the CYANE, but on District policies that were not his concern. Captain Zeusler and Commander Tomkiel wanted him out of the District, and they viewed his action in illegally suspending me from duty a way of discrediting him. After hearing my recitation of the suspension incident they suggested that I file a formal complaint against Tollaksen. For some unexplainable reason, I could not bring myself to accede to their wishes. It may be that I sensed that Tollaksen was mentally disturbed, or that my training and principles would not permit me to waver in my loyalty to my Commanding Officer, though I knew he was my mortal enemy where my career was concerned, and there would never be a lasting peace between us. I have always felt good about my decision that evening, and as my fitness report reveals, Captain Zeusler could appreciate my conduct. This was the point in my life where I began to develop a philosophy of wiping the slate clean of any animosity towards any human being before closing my eyes at the end of each day.

On my return to the CYANE that evening, I gave the Captain an account of my meeting with the District Commander and the Chief of Staff, Commander Tomkiel. He thanked me profusely, seemingly grateful and much relieved. I considered the incident closed. Two days later the United States was at war with Japan. The ship's portholes were painted black, and we were scheduled to be sent out to patrol the entrance to Dixon Entrance, the gateway to the Inside Passage of Southeast Alaska. Dixon Entrance was about forty miles in width, and separated United States and Canadian waters. There was much confusion in the town of Ketchikan. Many of the inhabitants were scurrying about constructing shelters in the nearby woods and stocking them with provisions in   preparations of an enemy attack. The local bank declared that all Japanese-owned bank accounts were frozen. The local laundry was owned and operated by the Tatsuda family who had lived in Ketchikan for more than thirty years. The Tatsuda family were well liked and highly thought of in the community and the townspeople were indignant at the hardship being inflicted on them. The ship's laundry had been handled by the Tatsudas for years, but the Captain instructed me not to pay our laundry bill, which amounted to four hundred dollars. Each day for the next seven days some of Tatsuda's employees would stop by the ship to tell me that they had not been able to receive any of the salaries owed them. I agonized over their plight for several days, and after some deliberation, fully realizing Captain Tollaksen would be furious, I paid the accounts and so informed the Captain. From that day forward, he was determined to ruin me and I had no quarrel with his reaction. I had committed an outright act of disobeying a lawful order.

Whenever I am totally surprised, shocked, or rendered speechless, I have an uncontrollable urge to come out with an expletive that can be interpreted as having several meanings, but usually and properly conveys my response to a silly, asinine suggestion or remark. It has happened to me on three memorable occasions. The first time it occurred was on the CYANE, when I was the Deck Officer in charge of the bridge.

Captain Tollaksen came on the bridge while I was at the chart table, and said, "Thomsen I think that instead of cruising back and forth across Dixon Strait, we should pay out the anchor with thirty fathoms of chain on both anchors, and just let the current drag the anchors along the bottom."

I looked at him in amazement, and before I could collect my thoughts, I gave a long, drawn-out "JESUS CHRIST." He looked at me intently, and without a word went below to his cabin. The next day after we docked at the base in Ketchikan, he went post haste to the District Office and when he returned to the ship, called me to his cabin and said I was to report to the District Office for further assignment to duty.

He then shook my hand and wished me well.

The reason for my outburst was that the area we were patrolling varied in depths from twenty fathoms (120 feet) to one hundred fathoms (600 feet), with steep drop-offs. Had we followed his plan we would have dragged the anchors and chain along the twenty-fathom bottom to the brink of a one hundred fathoms deep, and the tons of falling anchor and chain would have ripped the anchor windlass from the vessel.

Chapter 8

THE GENERAL AND THE PROSTITUTES

 On my arrival at the District Office I was again assigned to my former desk in the District Commander's Office, which was heaped high with directives, not only from Coast Guard Headquarters, but from General Simon Bolivar Buckner, U.S. Army, based in Anchorage, and overall Commander of the Alaskan Area. Of special interest to me was a letter from Coast Guard Headquarters, changing my rank as a Lieutenant (jg) in the Coast Guard Reserve to Lieutenant (jg) (Temporary) in the regular Coast Guard. Neither Captain Zeusler, nor any other District Officer made mention of my problems on the CYANE.

On leaving the CYANE in January 1942 for the District Office, I moved into the Bachelor Officer Quarters (BOQ) at the Coast Guard Base. I was given a small desk just inside Captain Zeusler's Office, which was heaped with correspondence from a dozen Coast Guard, Army and Navy Agencies. On top of the pile, lay a directive from U.S. Army General Simon Buckner stationed in Anchorage, and the overall Commander of the Alaskan Area. It was marked urgent and instructed Captain Zeusler to round up all the local prostitutes for deportation to the United States on the next weekly southbound passenger ship. Captain Zeusler told me to take care of the matter by writing a letter over his signature to each of the ladies, advising them of their impending deportation.

Inasmuch as these ladies all lived on Creek Street, a stone's throw from the District Office, I regarded the assignment as a relatively simple and assured Captain Zeusler I would complete the matter in a day or two at the most. The names and Creek Street addresses of the ladies filled two pages of the Ketchikan telephone book, but there was a problem in that only their first names were listed, such as Delores, Joan,

Ramona, Gloria, Phyllis, and Gwendolyn - just to mention a few I still remember. To make the notices legal I needed to know their surnames. To assist in my research I called on a Warrant Officer, Mr. Cash Slaghuis, newly married and attached to the Operations office. I told him that on the following day he was to call at all the Creek Street addresses listed in the telephone book, and obtain the surnames of the occupants.

Mr. Slaghuis was waiting for me in front of my office the following morning. He said his wife had been in tears all night and he had not slept. She was upset over the assignment I had given him and wanted him to refuse. I told him I would handle it myself. So dressed in full uniform, the telephone book in one hand and copies of the General's directive in the other I set out for Creek Street and began knocking on doors at ten in the morning. When the door opened at the first house, a lady in her nightgown, half-asleep, appeared before me. I introduced myself, and as I handed her the General's Order, asked for her surname. She read the order carefully, told me to what part of my anatomy I could shove it and slammed the door shut. The second call produced the same results, except that in this instance the lady was clad only in the lower part of her pajamas. I visited ten addresses, all with similar results, before I gave up and returned to my desk to review my battle plan, and prepare for my next assault. To quote Revolutionary Naval Captain John Paul Jones, I was not about to give up the ship, "I had just begun to fight."

At noon, when I walked down Main Street to a restaurant every person I met stopped to ask me if I was nuts, and what in the hell was I trying to do to my fisherman friends and the poor, defenseless, respectable ladies of Creek Street. I returned to my desk to ponder the wisdom of complying with the General's edict. If I continued to carry out Captain Zeusler's instructions, I would alienate all the fishermen whose membership in the Coast Guard Reserve I had worked so diligently to bring about. If I did not carry out his order, I would jeopardize my standing as the "IDEA BOY" who had managed to convince his Commander that he could solve every problem. I needed a way of carrying out the Captain's Orders and at the same time keep myself out of harms' way.

The next morning after weighing one idea against another, I hit upon a brilliant plan, which I felt was worthy of my blossoming reputation. I would write each Lady a letter over the Captain's signature, addressed "Dear Madam" followed by their given name. I then prepared thirty-some letters and had them signed by Captain Zeusler. I returned to my desk to prepare and seal the envelopes when I had a horrible thought. If the ladies left for Seattle with letters signed by a Senior Coast Guard Officer, certifying that they held the rank of "Madam," they would undoubtedly demand a higher fee for their work in whatever establishment they contacted, and if some zealous newspaper reporter got wind of the letters, it might very well cast a cloud over the image and prestige of the Coast Guard in general, and Captain Zeusler in particular. So I put the letters in my desk drawer, having decided to sleep on the problem.

As soon as the Captain arrived at his office the following morning, he sent for me. He appeared extremely agitated, and said, "Thomsen, forget the letter. When Mrs. Zeusler and I were walking down main street yesterday afternoon, fishermen in the company of prostitutes accosted us on four occasions. The fishermen loudly castigated us, calling Mrs. Zeusler and myself cruel and unfeeling for driving these poor, unfortunate, working women out of town. It was highly embarrassing to us both."

He was not the only one who breathed a sigh of relief when I told him the letters were still in my desk. None of the ladies were ever deported, and peace was restored between the Fishermen, the Ladies of Creek Street and the Coast Guard.

Captain Zeusler received a directive from the Alaska Army Command to devise and place in effect the camouflaging from the air of major defense-related facilities in Ketchikan, such as the waterfront area, cold storages, fuel storage areas, shipyards, and the Coast Guard Base. I was assigned the project. I rented a small seaplane (Grumman Goose) and took aerial color photos of the entire town, constructed a camouflage color map, and painted the roofs to conform to the plan. This project was completed in one month, to the Captain's amazement.

A request was received from the Alaskan Air Command stating there was an urgent need for Army Crash Rescue boats to be stationed in Bristol Bay, and they were of the opinion that rather than attempt to use Navy or Coast Guard personnel to man these boats, they would prefer to have the Coast Guard train an elite group of Airmen as boat operators, and could the Coast Guard in a three month period train fifty airmen for this purpose.

Lieutenant Richey, former Executive Officer of the CYANE and under whom I had served, was assigned the project and asked to have me as his assistant. We commandeered a small salmon cannery building, hastily converting it into barracks and a classroom. In less than a week fifty airmen arrived from an airfield in Texas. A fine group of men. We had ten-hour daily classes, with Lieutenant Richey teaching engineering and me seamanship. We both taught navigation, he in the classroom, and me on a sixty foot fishing boat cruising the inside channels. It was a very rewarding experience.

Several years later I had the satisfaction of reading accounts of outstanding service performed by these men and their small boats in aircraft rescue missions in Bristol Bay and the Bering Sea.

On March 28, 1942 Ethel Leadbetter and I decided to be married and rented a house on Millar Street, adjacent to the Leadbetter home, settling in to a very happy existence together.

Chapter 9

USS YP-251

 The largest fishing vessel enrolled in the Coast Guard Reserve was the 40 year-old halibut schooner FOREMOST. She was about ninety feet in length, deep in the water, and with a thirty year old, noisy, heavy-duty diesel engine. The CYANE, which was on patrol duty in Dixon Entrance, was to be transferred to Western Alaska and it was decided to activate the FOREMOST as a Navy Patrol Vessel to operate in conjunction with the Coast Guard Cutter McLANE in Dixon Entrance. She was to be turned over to the United States Navy and be named the YP-251. I was put in Command, with orders to proceed to Seattle for outfitting as a Navy Patrol vessel. The hundred and twenty five foot Coast Guard Cutter McLANE was under the command of Ensign Ralph Burns, a former Lighthouse Service Officer. As I have previously mentioned, I was not a favorite of the Chief of Staff, Commander Tomkiel, who from my first meeting with him on reporting to the District a year before as a Warrant Officer had resented the special relationship I had enjoyed with the District Commander, Captain Zeusler. He must have gloated over shipping me off to Seattle on the FOREMOST, a prototype, so to speak, of Humphrey Bogart's AFRICAN QUEEN. He would regret this action. My crew consisted of a Chief boatswain's Mate named Issacs, a twenty-year Coast Guard veteran, one cook, and sixteen seamen, all nineteen years of age. None of the seamen had any sea experience. We arrived in Seattle six days after leaving Ketchikan, encountering thick fog most of the way. We were rushed in and out of the shipyard. The hull was scraped and painted and armament was installed on board, consisting of a three inch gun on the forward deck, two fifty caliber machine guns on top of the pilot house and two depth charge racks on the stern of the vessel. Truckload after

truckload of equipment came on board, some having to be loaded on the open deck. A month later we arrived back in Ketchikan, where we unloaded over half of the supplies and equipment taken on in Seattle. Three days later we were out patrolling Dixon Entrance, alternating with the Cutter McLANE.

The YP-251 was the ex-FOREMOST, a former local halibut fishing boat that I had recruited into the Coast Guard Auxilliary. She looked like a fishing boat, rolled like a fishing boat, and no matter how often we scrubbed the holds and the decks, she still smelled like a fishing boat. When we first returned to Ketchikan from Seattle she was the butt of a dozen jokes, not only in the Coast Guard, but also by the townspeople, and Commander Tomkiel was much amused. My pride was suffering. I had recently been promoted to full Lieutenant, and Burns to Lieutenant (Junior Grade). In all fairness and according to custom, I should have had command of the Cutter McLANE, being Burns' senior by 214 numbers. Because of Commander Tomkiel, Burns commanded a 125-foot sleek Coast Guard cutter, with state of the art electronic equipment and armament while I commanded a lumbering forty-year old halibut fishing schooner that had seen better days. Not only was she Navy instead of Coast Guard, she didn't even have a name. To work out my frustration, I put my teenage crew of Nebraska farmhands practicing seamanship and anti-submarine procedure fifteen hours a day. The maximum speed of the YP-251 was ten knots.

On the morning of July 8, 1942, the YP-251 was docked at the Coast Guard base. I was having a cup of coffee in the galley when I received a telephone call from the District Office. It was from the operations officer who said, "We have just had a message from a Canadian patrol plane that he has spotted an enemy submarine on the ocean side of Prince of Wales Island, and that he dropped a bomb next to it as it was submerging. You will get underway immediately and join the cutter McLANE in Dixon Entrance in the event the submarine might attempt to enter inland waters."

As we raced at a breakneck speed of ten knots toward Dixon Entrance, I was mulling over in my mind how this joint McLANE and YP-251 operation was going to be handled. The situation was unprecedented, given the great disparity between the caliber of the two vessels, and with the Senior Officer Afloat being on a fish boat. Characteristically, I resolved that on my arrival at Dixon Entrance I would leave no doubt in the mind of anyone who was SOPA, (Senior Officer Present Afloat.) On the way to Dixon Entrance I went over all the anti-submarine manuals that had come on board the ship before we departed from Seattle. Of particular interest was a basic search plan that I brought to the pilothouse. There was a great deal of excitement among the crew, everyone pumped up at the thought of going into action. A radio blackout had been ordered, so our only communication would have to be by visual signals with lights or flags. It was still daylight when we arrived at Dixon Entrance and I was surprised to see a large Canadian frigate patrolling with the McLANE. I later learned that her commanding Officer was a navy three stripe Commander.

As I approached both ships I had Issacs run up the signal flags SOPA, actually intended only for the McLANE. The Canadian Frigate, not knowing my rank, acknowledged by running up their signal flags. I now had a fleet of three ships instead of two - I felt a little bit like NELSON must have felt at Trafalgar, or Admiral Beatty at the Battle of Copenhagen. Being SOPA on the bridge of the flagship was fun. I was coming along fast.

The basic submarine search plan recommended in the Navy Manual was simple. It consisted of the participating ships cruising along side by side about one-half mile apart creating ever-widening squares, each time increasing in size by one-half mile. I lined up my three vessels with the YP-251 on the inside. She had no sonar equipment, and with her noisy engine and propeller, would serve to drive a submarine out and away from her where she would be picked up by the McLANE and the frigate, the two outside vessels.

It was the month of July with long daylight hours. We continued with our search pattern until darkness fell, when the frigate requested permission to return to her base at Prince Rupert. I granted permission, and the McLANE and I continued through the night with our search pattern. When daylight came at about four in the morning, I spread out the small-scale ocean chart of the area where the submarine had been reported sighted and bombed. On close examination I noted that while the waters averaged from one hundred to two hundred fathoms in depth along the Coast, there appeared to be a small, fifty fathom shoal about six miles offshore in the area where the submarine was seen. I then reasoned that if I was a submarine commander, and under attack, I would look for a spot where I could lie on the bottom of the ocean. I then brought out a newer larger scale coastal chart of the same area, and what intrigued me was that the shallow fifty-fathom spot did not appear on the large-scale chart. I had another thought, and ordered Burns and the McLANE to follow me up the coast to the charted position of the shoal indicated on the chart.

We reached our position about 0700 and resumed our previous search pattern, the YP-251 on the inner leg with her noisy engine and propeller, and the McLANE on the outside leg, a quarter of a mile distant. We increased the size of the square one-quarter of a mile on the completion of each square. At about 0800 on July ninth, the McLANE made a contact. She dropped a depth charge that failed to explode, but picked up a contact an hour later and followed it. The contact was intermittent and zigzagged, indicating the submarine was running only at short intervals; then contact was lost. At 1540 the McLANE made another contact; putting about, she followed it for thirteen minutes, then dropped four depth charges. Numerous bubbles rose in the vicinity. The sea was oily smooth with little or no breeze, almost like a lazy tropical sea. Towards late afternoon, a light offshore breeze sprang up. At 1935, just completing a search pattern, heading southeast and parallel to the Coast, I decided to have a word with Burns, so I stopped my vessel, went to the after deck and motioned to Burns to bring the bow of the McLANE close to the stern of the YP-251. The breeze had increased so that ripplets were drawing a line in the water and we lay in a small trough, not enough to rock the vessel. I walked to the edge of the stern and began talking to Burns, who stood on the foredeck of the McLANE, bending over towards me. The ships were approximately fifty feet apart. While we were talking, an air driven torpedo came from upwind, passing just under the bow of the McLANE.

It looked to me like a column of fifty-cent pieces four feet high, or like a vertical row of bubbles coursing through the water. All Burns and I could do was to stare and follow the zooming path of the torpedo with pointing fingers. I dashed to the pilot-house, noting particularly the exact direction of the wind - hard on the port beam. I grabbed the wheel from the helmsman, swung it hard Left, and held it there until the wind was directly on the opposite beam (Starboard) which put me on the path down which had come the torpedo. The crew was at their battle stations. I then put the wheel hard right, swung ninety degrees and headed directly into the wind. After a run of perhaps a hundred yards or more a periscope barely broke the surface of the water several points on the port bow. It immediately disappeared as I headed directly for it. When we struck, it was not a hard contact, but more like striking a net or wire cable, and at that instant I pulled the whistle cord, signaling to the cook, Havelka, to release the two depth charges at our stern. They were set to a depth of one hundred and fifty feet, and when they exploded our boat leaped up in the water and the shock scattered items about, stunning us momentarily.

We stood by as the McLANE crisscrossed the area, dropping five or six depth charges, until the water was covered with oil and what appeared to be some form of rock wool came to the surface. We both remained at the scene until morning, when after ordering Burns to proceed to Ketchikan to report the encounter, I returned to Dixon Entrance to resume our patrol.

The crew was so keyed up there was no thought of sleep. As we neared Dixon Entrance, a small-unmarked floatplane approached the ship at a height of about five or six hundred feet. There was not a breath of wind and the sea was flat. The plane was flashing a light towards us and Issacs my Boatswain's Mate and a former signal-man relayed to me that the plane was repeating the words, "follow me." Issacs acknowledged the signal, after which the plane headed out to sea and we set out in the same direction. It was obvious that for some reason, at that moment, no one on the YP-251 was thinking clearly, least of all the erstwhile Senior Officer Present Afloat. I had no reason to think that the plane was not an American or Canadian plane so we headed out into the Pacific in the direction in which the plane had disappeared. I assumed we were being directed to a ship of some sort, perhaps an enemy ship. The crew was busily engaged in bringing up ropes of machine gun ammunition for our two fifty caliber guns and the three-inch gun on the fore deck.

During the next hour the plane returned twice, repeating the same signal, and again disappearing. After two hours elapsed and the coastline began to grow dim, I began to have some sobering thoughts. Meeting up with a surfacing submarine was the last thing I was looking for with my three-inch gun and two fifty-caliber popguns. We could be blown out of the water in less than thirty seconds. As soon as the possibility of this happening sunk in, I turned the ship about and headed for Dixon Entrance, looking apprehensively over my shoulder every five minutes. The plane did not reappear. [1,2]

Later I received a message to return to the Ketchikan Coast Guard Base, where each Member of the ship's crew was questioned individually as to what he had seen and heard in connection with the submarine encounter. I spent some time with Captain Zeusler, giving him all the particulars. Tomkiel did not appear too happy with the turn of events. All crew members of the McLANE and the YP-251 were instructed not to discuss the submarine incident, but of course there were rumors flying about. Later, we learned the Canadian frigate was monitoring the area where the incident occurred. All of us forgot entirely about the YP-251 and McLANE experience with the RO-32, and it was not until sixteen months later, when I returned from the South Pacific, that I would be ordered to the Alameda Training Station to be officially awarded a decoration.

On August 10, 1942, I received orders to report to San Francisco on September fifth for transfer to Auckland, New Zealand for eventual assignment as Assistant Navigator of the combat troop transport APA-14, the USS HUNTER LIGGETT, presently enroute from the Solomons to Auckland, New Zealand. Ethel and I packed our belongings, and with Carol Ann, boarded the passenger steamer to Seattle, and on to Fresno, California, where Ethel rented a house. I selected Fresno because Chris and Adelheid lived there and I felt they would assist her in any way possible. I since realized that sending them there was probably the last thing I should have done. I had forgotten how uneducated and narrow Chris and Adelheid were.

---

[1] THE RO-32 AND THE FIFTY FATHOM BANK. There can never be a positive solution to this enigma. The answer was destroyed along with the RO-32 on the afternoon of the ninth of July. It would be logical to assume that the submarine Commander's out-of-date small-scale coastal chart may have played a major part in the destruction of the submarine. At Dixon Entrance on the morning of the eighth of July, 1942, after a night of fruitless search for the submarine, I was in my pilot house studying two charts of the area where the RO-32 had been bombed. One of the charts was a ten-year-old small-scale coastal chart covering a considerable of the coast of Southeast Alaska. This chart showed a depth of several hundred fathoms extending offshore for several miles, and approximately six miles offshore a small fifty-fathom bank two miles in diameter.

On the more recent large-scale chart of the area, the fifty fathom bank was non-existent, a startling discovery. This difference in the two charts generated the thought that if I were the commander of a crippled submarine, I would seek the nearest area where I could lie on the ocean floor, and escape detection. I then ordered the McLANE to accompany the YP-251 to the bombing location to the North. It is my firm belief that the RO-32 was searching for the fifty-fathom bank, and which action led to his undoing. This theory was not my brainstorm - it was all contained in the submarine detection manual provided the YP-251, which I just finished reading that morning of July ninth.

[2] THE FLOATPLANE ENIGMA. At the close of World War II, Japanese records confirmed the sinking of the Japanese submarine RO-32 off the coast of Southeast Alaska. It also brought to light that during the month of June, 1942, two Japanese submarines were operating along the Northwest Pacific coastline between Oregon and Southeast Alaska, coinciding with the date the Lighthouse at Estanvan Point, British Columbia came under fire by one of these two submarines. The larger of the two subma-

rines was capable of carrying, and had on board, a small floatplane for observation purposes. A thorough investigation by American and Canadian authorities at the time of the submarine incident on July eighth and ninth revealed that no American or Canadian float plane was known to have been aloft in the Dixon Entrance area within that time frame. It can easily be surmised that the plane was Japanese, launched directly from the submarine, or from a location in one of the hundreds of hidden inlets in the Dixon Entrance area.

It is my personal belief that in response to distress signals transmitted by the RO-32 after the initial bombing by Canadian aircraft, the deployment of the float plane was an effort to lure the YP-251 away from the area, not knowing the submarine had been destroyed. The action taken by the YP-251 in following the floatplane was considered to be reckless, ill conceived and extremely fraught with danger, and the Commander of the YP-251 narrowly escaped being reprimanded by Captain Zeusler, the District Commander.

IMPERIVM NEPTVNI REGIS

WHEREVER YE MAY BE and to all Mermaid
Eels, Skates, Suckers, Crabs, Lobsters and all other Living
out on this **29TH** day of **SEPTEMBER** *1942* in Latitude *00000* and *2* ng to
cared within Our Royal Domain the **U.S.S. MOUNT VERNON** bound **SOUTH** for the
THE SOUTH PACIFIC OCEAN

BE IT REMEMBERED

said Vessel and Officers and Crew thereof have been inspected and passed on by Ourself and Our Roya
be It Known: By all ye Sailors, Marines, Sand Subbers and others who may be honored by his presence

Lieut. NIELS P. THOMSEN, U.S.C.G.

been found worthy to be numbered as one of our Trusty Shellbacks he has been duly initiated into
SOLEMN MYSTERIES OF THE ANCIENT ORDER OF THE DEEP

Be It Further Understood That by virtue of the power invested in me I do hereby command
all my subjects to show due honor and respect to him wherever he may be
Disobey this order under penalty of Our Royal Displeasure
Given under our hand and seal this **30TH DAY OF SEPTEMBER** *1942*

Davey Jones
His Majesty's Scribe

Neptunus Rex
Ruler of the Raging Main
By His Servant
Commanding

Chapter 10

USS HUNTER LIGGETT APA-14

On September 20, 1942, I boarded the USS MOUNT VERNON, a converted passenger ship fully loaded with Army and Marine Corps troops for New Zealand, for transportation to the Solomon Islands. I had been looking forward to seeing the Antipodes and the South Pacific Islands. In my early twenties I had contemplated taking part in a shark-fishing venture in the Solomons, operating out of Cookstown in Queensland, Northern Australia, so was familiar with the area. I knew that I had now to put my personal life aside for at least two years and perhaps even more, as well as give some thought to the possibility of leaving my bones in the South Pacific, so I resolved to devote all of my thoughts and efforts to my military commitments.

When the S/S MOUNT VERNON crossed the Equator, the traditional KING NEPTUNE ceremony was held, and in exchange for being dunked in a canvas pool, grease rubbed in our hair, and duly shaved, we received an elaborate document certifying that we were trusty shellbacks, who had been initiated into the Solemn Mysteries of the Ancient Order of the Deep, duly signed by His Majesty's Scribe, Davy Jones, and Neptunus Rex, Ruler of the Raging Main.

On arrival in Auckland a group of about sixty officers, urgently-needed replacements for the Guadalcanal invasion, of which I was one, were that same day of arrival bundled on board a small converted coastwise passenger ship for Guadalcanal. It was a five-day voyage. Strangely enough only one event stands out in memory.

The ship's dining room was too small to accommodate all the officers so a temporary dining room was erected on the enclosed promenade deck. A long table had been set up with a plywood wall parallel to the table, behind which a kitchen with two large ranges had been installed. I sat at the end of the table, where I could see into the kitchen. All of the waiters and kitchen staff were black. The first evening I took my place at the table, two Army officers seated on the side of the table, with their backs to the plywood wall, complained to their waiter that the steaks were underdone, and sent them back to the kitchen. I saw the waiter reach out both plates to the cook, who stuck his fork into the steaks, lifted them off the plates, spit on them, turned them over, and handed them back to the waiter. The waiter placed both plates before the officers, who thanked him profusely. For the next five days I ate what was put before me.

The HUNTER LIGGETT was a former Moore McCormack luxury passenger liner taken from the South American trade. As was the custom, all the woodwork throughout the ship had been removed for protection against wood splinters from bombing attacks and gunfire. She was moored near the shore off Lunga Beach at Guadalcanal, busy loading wounded Marines for a return trip to Wellington, New Zealand, where she would take on a capacity load of Marines for return to Guadalcanal. I was assigned a large single stateroom with a tiled bath, and a bed instead of a bunk.

After settling in my cabin, I reported to the Executive Officer, Commander Edward Hahn, USCG ten years older than I, who had joined the HUNTER LIGGETT two weeks earlier. He was a slightly built, very energetic person, who had served with the U.S. Navy in World War I as an enlisted man. After the war he served as an officer in the Merchant Marine for several years, and in 1926 when the Coast Guard needed to man scores of small rum-running cutters, had joined the Coast Guard and subsequently received a commission as an Ensign. We were to become good friends. He escorted me to the Captain's cabin, introduced me, and left me with Captain Louis Waite Perkins, U.S. Coast Guard, who said to me, "Our navigator, Lieutenant Commander Holtzman has been on board for eighteen months, and is scheduled for transfer back to the States. I made a special request to Headquarters for an outstanding navigator, and had expected to be assigned a regular Coast Guard Academy graduate of Lieutenant Commander Rank. The navigator of this ship in these waters carries a tremendous responsibility. Whenever the LIGGETT takes part in an amphibious landing, this ship becomes the Flagship of Commodore Laurence F. Reifsnider, U.S. Navy, Commander of the Third Amphibious Group of twelve combat transports. He and his staff of eighteen officers are expected to join us next trip while enroute North from Wellington, New Zealand."

Pausing briefly, he continued, "We are Coast Guard manned, and being a subordinate service, our relationship under the circumstances is highly sensitive. We must treat them with much tact, which may at times call for much forbearance from the navigational department. For the time being, you will take on the duties of the LIGGETT Assistant Navigator."

Captain Louis Waite Perkins was another "Captain Zeusler," with all his admirable qualities, a traditional officer and a gentleman, with the true heart and mind of a sailor. He was calm, and soft-spoken. I never met a person who did not hold him in great esteem, and I enjoyed every day I spent under his command. As a leader he possessed a quality of greatness I was never able to attain, in that he could inspire his men to heights of accomplishment by gentle persuasion and suggestion, and be well-liked while so doing. Since the age of twenty I have been a driver of men, making their lives miserable, forcing my will upon them, demanding they meet my standards of excellence and production. To achieve my ambitions, I have had to quell the compassionate side of my nature and often wear a mask of indifference to the feelings of others. The personal tragedy was that the mask became frozen, so I could not remove it whenever I came home to my family - and so lost them. I have always envied men like Captain Louis Waite Perkins.

The HUNTER LIGGETT was manned by thirty-six Coast Guard officers, one Army Major, three doctors, two dentists, and one chaplain, all Navy. The six hundred enlisted men were all Coast Guard. The Coast Guard Officers were a mixture of Coast Guard Academy Graduates, former Coast Guard Warrant Officers temporarily promoted to Commissioned officers, Coast Guard Warrant Officers, and Coast Guard Reserve Officers, who for the most part were graduates of Ivy League colleges. Except for Captain Perkins, the only other Coast Guard Academy graduates on board were Lieutenant Commander George Holtzman (navigator), Lieutenant Otis Estes (Assistant Engineer), Lieutenant (jg) Albert Frost (Deck W.O.), Lieutenant (jg) Bernhard Henry (Deck W.O.), and Ensign James McGary (Asst. First Lieutenant). Commander Hahn, Executive Officer and Commander Searcy Lowery, Gunnery Officer were appointed from the enlisted and Warrant ranks during the Prohibition period.

The wheels of the ship, under the overall control of the Captain and Executive Officer, were kept turning by the professional, knowledgeable eyes and hands of the former Chief Warrant, Warrant Officers and Chief Petty Officers of the regular Coast Guard, recently elevated in rank to temporary commissioned officer status. The Senior Officers of this group headed up departments such as Executive Officer, Gunnery Officer, First Lieutenant, Engineering Officer, Navigator, and Supply Officer. As Navigator, I spent most of my waking hours on the bridge. Each Deck Watch Officer had his division to maintain, and to which he had to devote most of his time when not on bridge watch. I never became close to any of the officers except the department heads, such as Lowery, Armstrong, Croteau, Jones and Commander Hahn. On the LIGGETT were a number of extra curricular duties, normally filled by junior officer volunteers, or assigned by the Executive Officer. The Officers Mess Treasurer and the Mail Officer required some supervision and effort and had no volunteers. I told Hahn I would take both assignments. I had the time, and each position carried with it a certain degree of status and education along with it.

Two days after reporting to the LIGGETT at Guadalcanal, we left for New Zealand with several hundred wounded Marines to be hospitalized in Wellington. Ten days later we were again on our way to Guadalcanal with a new contingent of Marine and

ROBIN

I WISH THAT I COULD WRITE A POEM
ABOUT THAT LITTLE SON OF OURS,
SO I HAVE WRACKED MY WEARY BRAIN
EACH DAY FOR HOURS AND HOURS.

IT SHOULD BE EASY FOR A MEN
WHO HAS AN ONLY SON,
TO WRITE A MILLION POEMS
YET I CANNOT THINK OF ONE.

COULD IT BE 'CAUSE HE'S SO PRECIOUS
TO THAT HUNGRY HEART OF MINE,
THAT I'M SO MUTELY TONGUE-TIED
THAT I CANNOT WRITE A LINE.

WHEN I HEARD YOU'D NAMED HIM "ROBIN"
I WAS HAPPY AS COULD BE,
FOR I KNEW THAT YOU WERE THINKING
OF THAT REDBREAST IN OUR TREE.

I'M SO GLAD TO HEAR HE'S CUNNING
AND THAT HE LOOKS LIKE ME,
LET'S PRAY HE'LL NEVER HAVE TO FIGHT
ON FOREIGN LAND OR SEA.

IS IT TRUE THAT HE CAN CRAWL
AND THAT HE'S LOSING ALL HIS HAIR,
THAT HIS EYES ARE HEAVEN BLUE
AND HIS SKIN SO VERY FAIR.

YOU SAY HE'S GETTING ROUNDER
THAT HE HAS THE SWEETEST SMILE,
HOW I'D LIKE TO BE THERE SWEETHEART
JUST TO HOLD HIM FOR AWHILE.

IT MAY BE MONTHS AND PERHAPS YEARS
BEFORE I'LL SEE THAT BOY,
BUT WITH YOU FOR A MOTHER
HE'LL BE SURE TO BE A JOY.

ONE THING WE KNOW FOR CERTAIN
THAT SHOULD HELP MAKE HIM A MAN,
IS THAT HE HAS A SISTER
WHOSE NAME IS CAROL-ANN.

I DID SO WANT TO SHOW HIM
ALL THE CREATURES IN THE PARK,
BUT MOST OF ALL TO TEACH HIM.
THAT HE SHOULD NOT FEAR THE DARK.

HE PROBABLY WILL NEVER KNOW
OF ALL THE DREAMS I'VE HAD,
IN WHICH HE WAS THE HERO
AND I WAS JUST HIS DAD.

AND IF IT SHOULD SO HAPPEN
THAT I NEVER SEE HIS FACE,
YOU'LL HAVE TO BE A FATHER TOO
AND TAKE HIS DADDYS PLACE.

> Niels Thomsen
> Guadalcanal 1942
> (On learning of the birth of my son.)

Army troops. On arriving in Wellington, I had received a letter from Ethel saying that a son had been born to us on September 29, 1942, and that his name was Robin Christian Thomsen. Ethel asked me to write a poem to him, and surprisingly I found this an easy assignment, sending it off from Wellington. Returning to the Solomons, we were bombed a number of times as we approached Guadalcanal, but arrived unscathed, unloaded troops and loaded wounded for transportation to Brisbane, Australia. For the next several months we shuttled reinforcements between New Caledonia, Brisbane, Australia, the Hebrides and Guadalcanal. Two months after I joined the ship, Lt. Commander Holtzman received his orders for transfer to the United States, and Captain Perkins appointed me Navigator of the HUNTER LIGGETT.

During the first week in November, the Commander of the Third Amphibious Group, Commodore Laurence Reifsnider, U.S. Navy, selected the HUNTER LIGGETT to be his Flagship and he and his staff of eighteen Navy Officers moved on board the LIGGETT. This could only mean that we would be seeing more close-up action. The Commodore and his Staff were held in much awe by the career Coast Guard officers on board the LIGGETT, primarily because of the formality they carried with them. It also imposed a multitude of additional burdens on the shoulders of Captain Perkins.

As ship,s Navigator, I had more contact with the Commodore than any of the other Coast Guard Officers, including Captain Perkins. There were two Navy Commanders acting as Navigators on the Navy Staff. I was appalled at their incompetence. As the weeks went by, the Commodore, who spent a great deal of time on the bridge and in the chartroom, chose to consult me on many occasions connected with navigation matters and ship-handling. His staff officers and the ships' Coast Guard officers, concerned about their careers, never voiced any of their own opinions. I was not planning a military career, and it made no difference to me what the Commodore, or for that matter, any of my senior officers, thought about my propensity to freely voice my opinions. The Commodore never minded. I think he was weary of having everyone always agreeing with everything he said. Being responsible for twelve ships in wartime, Commodore Reifsnider could not socialize, or be on close terms with his staff of Navy officers. His chief of Staff, Captain Thornhill, U.S. Navy, a man in his fifties, was a delightful individual for whom I had a great deal of admiration. He needed to get away from the Commodore and the Staff Officers, so he would come to my quarters in the afternoon for a game of cribbage, a card game he loved. I socialized very little with the Junior Coast Guard Officers after the Staff joined the ship, so I had to endure remarks about being the Staff pet, but Captain Perkins told me not to let anything bother me - just keep the Commodore happy with the Navigation department. After a period of several weeks, Commodore Reifsnider asked Captain Perkins to have me appointed additional duties as his Staff Navigator. Commander Hahn, the Executive Officer, was having some problems with the operation of the Ship's Service Store. I felt that I could find time to take on another collateral duty, and I agreed to take it on. I now was Officer's Mess Treasurer, Mail Officer and Ships Service Store Officer.

January and February of 1943 were stressful months. The United States Navy was suffering heavy losses in ships and men, as the Japanese Navy attempted desperately to retake Guadalcanal. All this while, the LIGGETT flitted back and forth ferrying in fresh troops and wounded out, luckily and routinely dodging torpedoes and bombs. Most of the time I was too occupied to feel fear. I can only think of two occasions when I felt a bit too personally involved. We were departing Guadalcanal, the LIGGETT at the head of a column of three ships, a freighter behind us, followed by an oil tanker. It was late in the afternoon. High in the sky, dueling above us, just tiny specks, were thirty or forty fighters. They were scarcely visible, except when one of them trailing smoke, spiraled into the sea about us. I was standing on the outside wing of the bridge deck with Farleigh S. Dickinson, Jr., a reserve Lieutenant whose family owned Dickinson College in Carlisle, PA, when from the port side a formation of eight or ten torpedo bombers, flying fifty feet above the water, headed directly towards us. Suddenly, seeing the nests of anti-aircraft armament on the LIGGETT, they swerved and headed for the oil tanker, which as we watched, took three torpedoes. We were loaded with wounded, so we scurried away at full speed, as did the freighter.

The other occasion occurred one day while we lay off Lunga Beach near the airfield at Guadalcanal. It was too dangerous to anchor, as high up in the hills a mobile piece of Japanese field artillery was shelling us every nine minutes all day long. Being on wheels the gun had to be adjusted after every firing. The Commodore and his staff were on the top bridge from where I handled the ship's controls. We would see a puff of smoke on the hill where the gun was positioned; next a screaming shell would land near the ship. I would then move the ship to the right or left, ahead or astern, to the spot where the salvo landed, knowing that the range or deflection was being changed. This was a distracting situation that lasted all day. I had to admire the Commodore's behavior throughout the afternoon. One would have thought he was attending a baseball game. He was a tall, heavily built man well over six feet tall, with a multiple-veined red nose and ruddy features. Reifsnider was a calm, quiet individual. He gave off an aura of self-confidence and inspiration which in some manner enveloped all his subordinantes. He was a real warrior, a forceful man who could lead in battle and I felt proud being on his team. I admired his courage and was his twenty-four hour a day navigator for over nine months.

About this time I began having severe stomach pains and passing black stools. I was sent ashore to the field hospital on Guadalcanal one afternoon and was told that I was suffering from bleeding stomach ulcers. The doctor recommended that I request to be transferred to the hospital in Wellington, or the United States. When I stated my preference for remaining on the LIGGETT, I was given medicine to take and placed on a diet.

In July the scope of ComTransGroupThirdPhib was enlarged, and Commodore Reifsnider left the LIGGETT to join Admiral Halsey's Staff. Captain H.E. Thornhill, U.S. Navy, his Executive Officer, temporarily appointed Commodore took over com-

One evening while anchored off Lunga Point at Guadalcanal,
I was standing the eight to twelve gangway watch, when a
small launch came alongside with a Navy Lieutenant Commander
from a destroyer taking on fuel from a nearby oil tanker.
He was the Commanding Officer of the Destroyer LOWELL. He
said," We will be finished fueling in two hours, I have not
had a bath for two weeks. Would it be possible for me to
have a shower on board." I said, " of course ", and had the
Quartermaster take him to my room. As he was leaving the
ship thirty or forty minutes later, I suggested he send over
any of his Officers who would like a shower, and so two of
his Officers came on board. When my duty watch ended at
midnight, and as I went to bed, I felt a lump under my pillow,
and Lo and behold, the Officers had left a quart of whiskey
under my pillow, worth a pouch of diamonds in that area.
At breakfast I was informed that the LOWELL had been engaged
by an Enemy Cruiser at Four o'clock that morning, and had sunk
with all on board. At the gangway I was handed a message sent
me by signal light from the Commanding Officer of the LOWELL
shortly after midnight. It is attached below - I never knew
the name of the Commander.

NAVSHIPS (250)
NCS 387

U.S. NAVAL COMMUNICATION SERVICE

SRS 77

(X523 r KOBC)

☆ GPO 16—16896-1

BT To Commander Thomsen X Certainly
appreciate favor you have done for
us X We are sailing soon X Hope
to see you X Best wishes from
captain and officers X The
Lowell BT K

For) a71 1215
FL) R.f

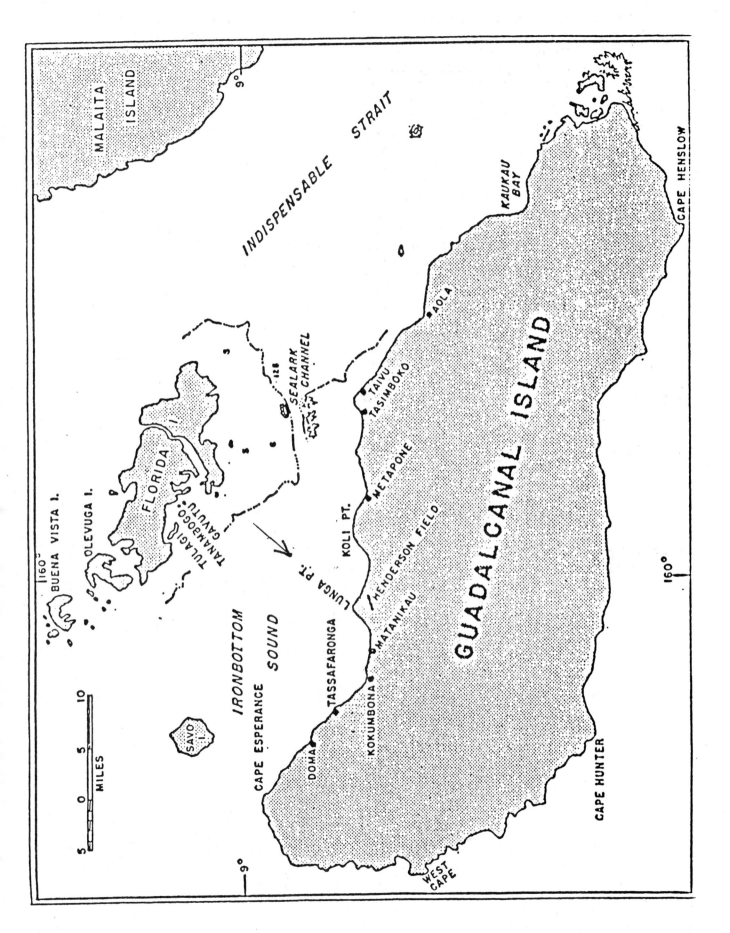

SAGA OF THE SOLOMONS

TO THE LEFT OF US LIES KOLI,
TO THE RIGHT STANDS HIGH SAVO,
STRAIGHT AHEAD THE BEACH OF LUNGA,
UP ABOVE THE CLOUDS HANG LOW.

DOWN THE VOICE-TUBE COMES A MESSAGE,
"THERE'S A SIGNAL IN THE AIR".
CAN THE O.D. GUESS THE ANSWER,
WITHOUT TEARING OUT HIS HAIR.

"UNDERSTOOD!" THE J.O. SHOUTED,
CLAWING WILDLY FOR THE BOOK,
NOW ALL HANDS ARE GATHERED ROUND HIM,
STRAINING NECKS TO HAVE A LOOK.

"WHAT'S THE COURSE, AND WHAT'S THE BEARING",
COMES DOWN FROM THE COMMODORE.
WHAT WILL TAKE HER THROUGH IN SAFETY,
BRING HER CLOSER TO THE SHORE.

ALL THE WHILE THE NAVIGATOR,
TEMPLES FASTLY TURNING GRAY,
FLITS FROM COMPASS TO THE CHARTROOM,
MUMBLING BEARINGS ON THE WAY.

NOW THE TIME IS FAST APPROACHING,
TO START CALLING NIPPON'S BETS,
BOATS ARE LOWERED ON THE RUN,
OVERSIDE ARE FLUNG THE NETS.

KNOWING THAT THE HOURS ARE GOLDEN,
ALL MEN STRIVE WITH MIGHT AND MAIN,
TROOPS ARE QUICKLY FERRIED SHOREWARD,
BOATS HAVE FORMED A CARGO TRAIN.

THEN APPEARS A PUFF OF SMOKE,
FROM ATOP A NEARBY RIDGE,
NEXT THE WHINE AND BURST OF SHRAPNEL,
SCREAMING PAST THE FLYING BRIDGE.

BUT THERE IS NO TURNING SEAWARD,
THERE CAN BE NO THOUGHT OF FLIGHT,
THIS IS WHY WE LEFT OUR HOMELAND,
WHY WE CREPT HERE THROUGH THE NIGHT.

ONCE AGAIN AND OFT' THEREAFTER,
DOES THIS METAL MONGREL BARK,
THERE'S A BREEZE, BUT NO DEFLECTION,
IT'S AS SAFE AS CENTRAL PARK.

BUT THE COMINCH* DOES NOT LIKE IT,
AND OUR BOMBERS TAKE THE SKY,
SOON TO RAIN ON SONS OF HEAVEN,
LITTLE GIFTS FROM YOU AND I.

WHERE IN ALL THIS VAST CONFUSION,
IS THE CAPTAIN**, LORD OF ALL,
IS HE SCREAMING AND EXCITED,
FULL OF ORDERS YET TO BAWL.

NO, HE STANDS IN SILENT STUDY,
HEAVING NOW AND THEN A SIGH,
PATIENCE IS HIS CROWNING VIRTUE,
GOD BE THANKED, BREATHE YOU AND I . . .

• Cominch (Commander in Chief)
** Captain Louis Perkins

Niels P. Thomsen, Navigator
Combat Transport HUNTER LIGGETT
Guadalcanal, Solomon Islands, 1942

55-D

SONG OF THE SOLOMONS

(A word to the wise)

AT BEAT TO QUARTERS OR ABANDON SHIP,
    ALTHOUGH IT IS A DRILL,
DON'T STOP FOR CLOCKS OR DIRTY SOCKS,
    BUT GET ON WITH A WILL.

IT'S OFT BEEN SAID, YOU MAKE YOUR BED,
    AND IN IT YOU MUST LIE,
BUT ALL WE KNOW IT'S JACK OR JOE,
    WHO WILL IT IF WE DIE.

WE'D GO TO HELL FOR THE LIBERTY BELL,
    IN THIS FIGHT FOR UNCLE SAM,
BUT MORE OF US WILL LIVE TO CUSS,
    IF WE MAKE IT ON THE LAM.

THERE'S MANY A LAD, BOTH GOOD AND BAD,
    WHO, HAD HE GOT THERE FIRST,
MIGHT STILL STROKE THE CURLS OF PRETTY GIRLS,
    AND READ OLD RANDOLPH HEARST.

IT'S PLENTY PUNK TO LEAVE THAT BUNK,
    EACH TIME YOU HEAR THE BELL,
BUT IT CAN'T LAST, SO MAKE IT FAST,
    LET'S SEND THOSE JAPS TO HELL.

LOOK HERE, BLOKE, THIS AIN'T NO JOKE,
    CAUSE IT'S NORTH BY WEST AND STEADY,
BUT WE'LL NOT FEEL THEIR RED HOT STEEL,
    IF WE ARE MANNED AND READY.

I KNOW A LOT OF THIS SOUNDS STALE,
    AND THAT ENOUGH'S ENOUGH,
BUT THINK OF HOME AND MOTHER, BOYS,
    GET UP! GET ROUGH! GET TOUGH!

Niels Thomsen
Guadalcanal – 1943

GUADALCANAL

DEATH IN THE MORNING
IS NOT SO BAD –
THINKING OF LIFE
AND THE FUN YOU'VE HAD.

DEATH IN THE AFTERNOON
FITS IN QUITE WELL –
WHEN YOU'RE HEARTSICK AND WEARY
OF MAN-MADE HELL.

DEATH IN THE NIGHT IS NOT FOR ME
FOR NO MATTER HOW I TRY –
I CAN'T HELP WISHING FOR ONE MORE GLIMPSE
OF THE SUN IN THE EASTERN SKY.

Niels Thomsen – 1942

CAPTAIN PATCH

LT. THOMSEN

mand of Division Ten, under ComTransGroupThirdPhib, a post still held by Commodore L.F. Reifsnider. In April 1943, Captain Perkins, much to the regret of all of the LIGGETT's crew, was transferred to the United States for shore duty, having been Captain of the LIGGETT for two years. The new commanding Officer was Captain Roderick Patch, U.S.C.G., in his late fifties. He was a grandfatherly type, more at home in an office than on board ship. He was a fair, kindly person, very low-keyed and unassertive. Anyone, no matter how competent, would have had difficulty in filling the shoes of the charismatic Captain Perkins. Captain Patch seemed somewhat awed by the Commodore and his Navy Staff. Captain Thornhill and I carried on with our daily cribbage game, except we now played in the Commodore's suite, with tea served by the Coast Guard Steward. This routine placed me in an awkward position, as Captain Patch acquired the habit of asking me how Captain Thornhill felt about various issues. The heads of the Departments, Commander Hahn, the Executive Officer; Searcy Lowery, the Gunnery Officer; and Croteau, the First Lieutenant, understood the situation, but the Junior Officers were not above referring to me as the Commodore's pet. The fact was that the Commodore and I never discussed matters having to do with the ship, or that it even existed. He talked about his life in the Navy and about his son who was a Naval Officer on a destroyer and he liked to hear my stories of sailing ship experiences.

We continued to shuttle Army and Marine Corps Troops between Guadalcanal and New Zealand for the next six months. In October, with the Solomons secured, there were rumors that we would soon be taking part in another full-scale invasion further to the North. On October tenth, Commodore Reifsnider rejoined the LIGGETT with his staff of eighteen officers and again he requested of Captain Patch that I be assigned to him as Staff Navigator, which was done. We learned that the LIGGETT would be the flagship for the invasion of Bougainville, with Commodore Reifsnider as Commander of the Third Amphibious Group of twelve troop transports carrying an invasion force of twelve thousand men.

On October 22, 1943, we arrived at Espiritu Santo, and made preparations for loading Army and Marine Corps troops. On October 24, 1943, Fleet Admiral William H. Halsey, USN came on board along with several Admirals to confer with Commodore Reifsnider. After several hours all officers departed except Admiral Halsey, who spent the night in the staff quarters. After Halsey's departure early the next morning, Commodore Reifsnider sent for me to come to his quarters. He motioned me to a table where he and his Chief of Staff, Captain Henry Thornhill, USN, stood beside a stack of dozens of aerial photographs.

The Commodore said, "Thomsen, we are going to Bougainville. The Dutch charts are obsolete, unreliable, and as much as ten miles out. I have here a stack of aerial photographs taken a few days ago.[3] I want you to construct a navigational chart that

---

[3] The Saturday Evening Post, April 19, 1947, Page 17, "Fleet Admiral Wm. F. Halsey, USN tells his story."

The TOROKINA OPERATION was christened CHERRY BLOSSOM, and November First

56

will take twelve transports and us to a landing beach off Torokina Point. Take these photographs and get going. If you require any assistance, use any of the Staff. I am counting on you. Our entire operation depends on this project."

For the next five days I spent eighteen hours daily bent over my chart table, with the Commodore looking over my shoulder a dozen times a day. I did not ask for help, it would have delayed me. On October 28, 1943, Commodore Reifsnider's Flagship, the HUNTER LIGGETT, leading a column of twelve Combat Transports loaded with Army and Marine Corps Invasion Forces, departed Espiritu Santos for Empress Augusta Bay on the Island of Bougainville. I turned my chart and pilotage work over to Commodore Reifsnider, detailing the problems I had with the aerial photos. While they clearly outlined reefs they did not provide contours and heights, I could not vouch as to the exactness of the bearings used to fix the position marking the 90 degree left turn into the transport unloading zone, and I felt I should be at his side during the approach to Puruata Island.

It was then agreed that the Commodore would be on the (port) left side of the helmsman directing him, and I would be on the (starboard) right hand side of the helm. Two staff Officers were assigned to the wing compasses to relay to the Commodore the bearings of the two points of reference; the North end of Puruata Island to bear 030 degrees, and the South end of Cape Torokina to bear 090 degrees. I gave the Commodore a piece of paper with the two bearings marking the course change 900 yards from Puruata Island. The new course would be 340 degrees to the anchoring and unloading zone parallel to the shoreline. I was very concerned as to the correctness of the charts I had constructed from the aerial charts.

---

was set as L day. On October twenty-fourth I flew up to Espiritu and spent the night on the Flagship of the Commander of the Transport Group, Commodore Laurence F. Reifsnider, USN. I have said that all of our charts of the Northern Solomons were sketchy and far from reliable; Hundreds of square miles of the interior were dismissed with "Unexplored." But my worries were nothing to those of Reifsnider, on whose pinpoint navigation the success of the landing depended.

Long stretches around Torokina were dotted, indicating mere guesses at the contour; Southern Bougainville was marked "Abnormal magnetic variation reported here;" and an aerial survey showed the whole island to be eight or ten miles northeast of the charted position.

Moreover, a last minute reconnaissance by the submarine GUARDFISH discovered two unmarked shoals of less than four fathoms close to Reif's run-in point, and he was afraid that other shoals even shallower might exist, and they did too. Reif is usually cool, but he admitted that his aplomb was being gnawed by the prospect of taking an invasion force through such waters, in total darkness towards a beach that might be ten miles off base.

I laughed and told him, "You won't have any trouble, Reif. You're too good of a sailorman. Besides, it's a simple job."

NOTICE TO ALL PERSONNEL

31 OCTOBER, 1943

PRIOR TO SOUNDING OF ALARM FOR GENERAL QUARTERS TOMORROW MORNING, 1 NOVEMBER, 1943, ALL PERSONNEL, OFFICERS, TROOPS AND CREW WILL TAKE A THOROUGH SOAP AND WATER SHOWER AND PUT ON ALL CLEAN, FRESHLY LAUNDERED CLOTHING FROM THE SKIN OUT. THIS TENDS TO MINIMIZE THE CHANCE OF INFECTION IN CASE OF WOUNDS OR ACCIDENTS.

IN CASE OF CAPTURE BY THE ENEMY ALL PERSONNEL ARE ADVISED THAT THE ONLY INFORMATION THEY ARE REQUIRED TO FURNISH IS AS FOLLOWS:

NAME
RANK
SERIAL NUMBER

DO NOT MENTION THE NAME OF ANY VESSEL, THE PLACE IT HAS BEEN, OR GIVE ANY INFORMATION RELATIVE TO TROOPS, SHIPS, OR ANY OTHER INFORMATION OF A MILITARY NATURE THAT MAY BE OF VALUE TO THE ENEMY.

E.E. HAHN,Jr
EXECUTIVE OFFICER
HUNTER LIGGETT

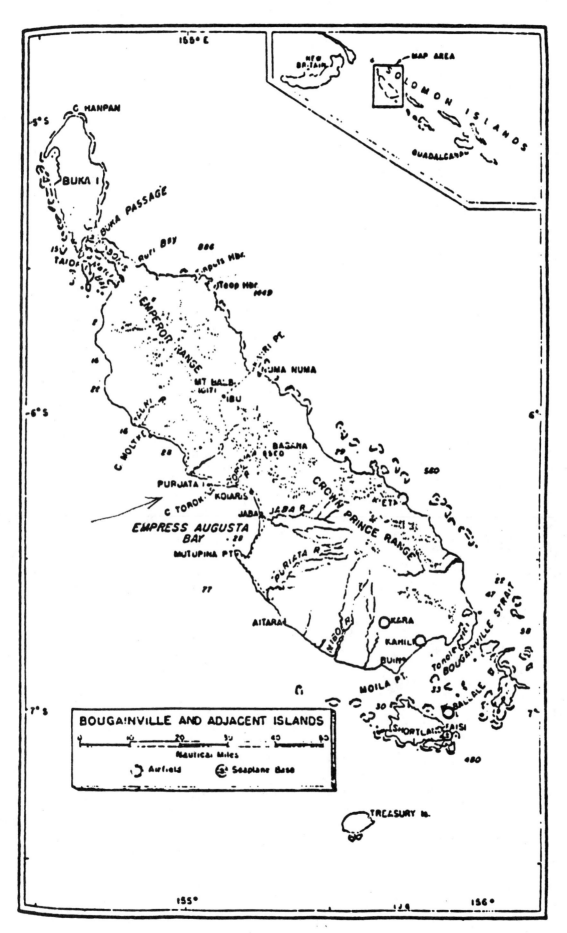

BOUGAINVILLE AND ADJACENT ISLANDS

Nautical Miles

Airfield   Seaplane Base

58-B

authority on Tibet and therefore, presumably, indispensable to the South Pacific campaign. He was so wrapped in his cloak-and-dagger role that he whispered even in my office, and I had great difficulty learning why he was there. I finally gathered that he was promoting a one-man collapsible rubber submarine. When I asked him to describe it, he breathed, "I'd rather not. It's highly confidential."

I assured him that he could trust my discretion, and finally he admitted, "The fact is, we haven't got one yet, but I'll tell Washington to develop it."

I told him, "Get out of here!"

Another hour was shot to hell.

(I don't mean to discredit the OSS. It did a splendid job in Europe and elsewhere, but there was simply no place for it in our part of the world.)

From New Georgia, we jumped to Vella Lavella, and from Vella we took a good look at Bougainville, the last major obstacle on the road to Rabaul. Bougainville is the largest of the Solomon Islands—150 miles long, fiddle-shaped, and split down the back by the Crown Prince Range, which features two active volcanoes. In the twenty-one months that the Japs had occupied it, they had made it a formidable fortress. They had built a seaplane base and four airfields; a fifth was on a small island a few miles southward; a sixth was under construction. The 35,000 troops in their ground forces included the infamous 6th Division which had raped Nanking in 1937.

Our invasion plan required us to establish a beachhead where opposition would be weak and difficult of reinforcement, and to carve out our own airfield. To discover a suitable place, our submarines, seaplanes and PT boats put combat reconnaissance teams ashore at several likely points. These teams reported that Cape Torokina, in Empress Augusta Bay, offered the best possibilities. Strategically, it would bring all the Bougainville airfields within a radius of sixty-five miles and Rabaul itself within 215 miles—a

flatly, "It's Torokina. Now get on your horses!"

The operation was christened CHERRYBLOSSOM, and November first was set as L Day. On October twenty-fourth I flew up to Espiritu and spent the night on the flagship of the Commander of the Transport Group, Commo. Lawrence F. Reifsnider. I have said that our charts of the Northern Solomons were sketchy and far from reliable; hundreds of square miles of the interior were dismissed with "Unexplored." But my worries were nothing to those of Reif, on whose pinpoint navigation the success of the landing depended. Long stretches of coastline around Torokina were dotted, indicating mere guesses at the contour; Southern Bougainville was marked "Abnormal magnetic variation reported here"; and an aerial survey showed the whole island to be eight to ten miles northeast of its charted position. Moreover, a last-minute reconnaissance by the submarine Guardfish discovered two uncharted shoals of less than four fathoms close to Reif's run-in point, and he was afraid that other shoals even shallower might exist—they did too.

Reif is usually cool, but he admitted that his aplomb was being gnawed by the prospect of taking an invasion force through such waters, in total darkness, toward a beach that might be ten miles off base.

I laughed and told him, "You won't have any trouble, Reif. You're too good a sailorman. Besides, it's a simple job!"

He didn't believe a word I said, and I didn't either. Fortunately, we were able to supply him with better air maps just before he sailed.

The break of L Day found us hitting the enemy on five fronts, some of them 200 miles apart. A New Zealand brigade landed on Treasury Island to protect our flank; a marine parachute battalion made a diversionary landing on Choiseul Island to suck reinforcements across from Bougainville; a cruiser-destroyer force commanded by

Princeton
churned
left.

Rear A
man, con
group, st
L Day a
before we
100 mile
position v
from air
forward
into the l
This pre
Three day
our scout
enemy fo
Rabaul fr
two light
Presumal
down to
and sink
our preca
most des
fronted
COMSOI

Even
and destr
and fresh
night bat
two bon
would no
ping such
BLOSSO
success of
upon its l

Captain
The CC
flown up
to be close
SOM. W
there whe
Doug Mc
operation
possible
task grou
northwar
wrote a d
assigning
first, dest
Chief of
miral's (
proval.

For the past fifty years I have been much too occupied with living to give thought to what occurred on the bridge of the Flagship USS HUNTER LIGGETT as she lead twelve troop-laden transports towards Puruata Island, Empress Augusta Bay, Bougainville, just before sunrise on November 1, 1943.

Six months ago I ran across the Memoirs of Fleet Admiral Wm. H. Halsey, USN published in the "Saturday Evening Post." I was appalled at the gamble taken by Admiral Halsey and his staff with respect to the navigational aspects of the operation, and my role therein. My feelings are mixed; on the one hand, I feel honored to have been the recipient of such total trust tendered me by Admiral Reifsnider, for whom I had great admiration. But, should such overwhelming responsibility have been laid solely on the shoulders of a Coast Guard Warrant Officer. The success of the entire operation was one that hinged on pin-point navigation, and no less than a senior Navy commander or Captain should have been given this assignment. However, when it came to the final approach at Puruata Island, it was not navigational expertise that saved the day. The bearings were meaningless. The only factor I felt I could trust was the aerial photos which showed the distance from the reefs to Puruata Island to be 2,000 yards. It was the art of judging distances acquired during coast Guard duty in Southeastern Alaskan inland waters by a permanent Coast Guard warrant officer with a propensity for challenging authority, a major character deficiency regularly noted in his officer fitness reports by the Coast Guard.

Admiral Reifsnider did keep the promise he made on the USS GEORGE CLYMER the afternoon of the invasion. He made certain that his Chief of Staff, Commodore Thornhill, USN, issued the letter of commendation, and eight months later when I wearied of my shore assignment and wrote him personally requesting a command in the forward area, he recommended the USS MENKAR (AK-123) on her secret Loran installation in the forward area, a rewarding and eventful challenge.

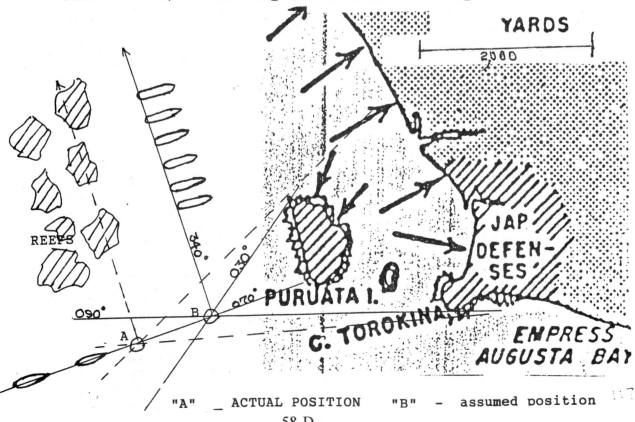

"A" _ ACTUAL POSITION   "B" - assumed position

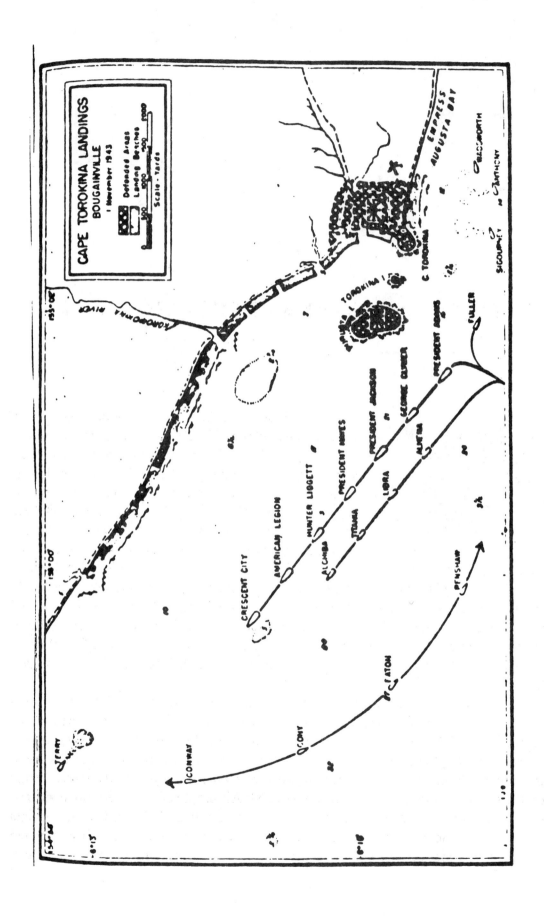

Chapter 11

CAPE TOROKINA, BOUGAINVILLE

At daybreak on November First, Cape Torokina was sighted. When Puruata Island bore 070 degrees, the approach course, we headed directly for it. Commodore Reifsnider was on the top navigating bridge standing to the left (port) of the Helmsman. I stood to the right (Starboard) of the helm. Also on the bridge were Captain Patch, two Junior Coast Guard Deck Officers and several signalmen standing by their hoisting stations. Each of the two bridge-wing compasses was manned by a Navy Staff Officer taking and relaying bearings to the Commodore. Flying high above us were planes diving and wheeling in combat, and now and then one would spiral into the sea, streaming smoke. As we neared Puruata Island, we commenced receiving heavy gunfire from the island and shore directly ahead. We were grateful for the forest of cargo masts and booms on the foredeck that screamingly deflected artillery and 40 millimeter shells that whistled past the bridge. Luckily, no one was hit.

Groups of fighters flew back and forth, strafing the beach and shore batteries. I was too occupied to feel fear, but I was perspiring with nervousness as we neared the turning point. The bearings were being called out by the two Staff Officers, and the Commodore kept checking the bearing note I had provided him with. I was unsure of the turn position, which was to be 900 yards from Puruata, now directly ahead. While on the CYANE piloting in inland waters in SE Alaska, I had acquired much experience in judging distances. I could see that we were at least 2000 yards from Puruata Point, and by the bearings we were almost on the turn position. When it was called out, the Commodore gave the Helmsman the order to come hard left with the wheel.

On sudden impulse I grabbed the wheel and held it fast with both hands.

The Commodore, with the note in one hand, and a confused look on his face, grasped the wheel at the other side of the Quartermaster. Meanwhile, I was holding fast to the wheel and shouting, "No! No! No!" for about two minutes until I was certain we were within 900 yards from Puruata Island, at which time I let go of the wheel and motioned to the Helmsman to put the wheel hard left and steady the ship on the new course of 340 degrees to our anchorage.

I was perspiring profusely. All ships anchored without incident, Commander Hahn, the Executive Officer anchoring the LIGGETT. The incident at the turning point was not referred to by the Commodore, or Captain Patch. Immediately the anchor left the hawsepipe, the nets were dropped down the ship's sides, the landing craft all set to drop into the water, and marines clambering into boats preparing to circle about near the ship, before heading in towards the beach in company with the landing craft of all twelve transports.

An hour later after the Marines were ashore, I went to Captain Patch's cabin and explained the incident that had taken place at the turning point off Puruata Island. He responded in a positive, understanding manner, saying that he hoped the incident would be forgotten, referring to a prior episode involving myself and the Commodore in the chartroom several days earlier, to which he had been a witness, and from which there had been no repercussions.[4]

Early in the afternoon, Commodore Reifsnider and his Staff moved the Flag from the HUNTER LIGGETT to the transport USS GEORGE CLYMER anchored nearby. Later in the afternoon, after the beaches had been secured, the LIGGETT received a signal from the GEORGE CLYMER that Lieutenant Thomsen was to report to Commodore Reifsnider on board the GEORGE CLYMER. I did not know

---

[4] As Flagship, the LIGGETT had on board Commodore Laurence Reifsnider, U.S. Navy, leading his Third Amphibious fleet of twelve combat transports enroute from Auckland, New Zealand. As Staff navigator, I was responsible to the Commodore for the route of the fleet. One afternoon, while I was on duty in the chartroom, Commodore Reifsnider walked in with an Army and Marine Corps General, and the Commander of the LIGGETT, Captain Roderick Patch, U.S. Coast Guard. The Commodore asked me to describe the route we were taking to pass through a group of islands in the Solomons. As I was laying out the route, he pointed with a ruler to a spot between two islands, saying, "Thomsen, why do we not take this passage, it appears more direct."

I came out with "JESUS CHRIST!!!" the same answer I had given Tollaksen on the CYANE, and one could have heard a pin drop. The Generals and Captain Patch looked at me in horror, but not a word or gesture from the Commodore.

Later I showed the Commodore a small notation at the bottom of the chart that called attention to the fact that the passage had not been wire-dragged and there was a possibility of hidden reefs undetected by aerial surveys. That evening at the Coast Guard Officer's table, there were a few remarks to the effect that the Commodore's pet was finally in trouble. I was in a somewhat uncomfortable position on the HUNTER LIGGETT, in that while Coast Guard manned, it also was the Navy Flagship, carrying on board the Navy Amphibious Commander and his eighteen man staff. I practically lived on the bridge twenty hours a day, which pleased both Commodore Reifsnider and Captain Patch.

COMMANDER TRANSPORT DIVISION TEN
U.S.S. HUNTER LIGGETT, Flagship,   Bd
%Fleet Post Office,
San Francisco, California.

24 November 1943

From: The Commander Transport Division TEN, Third
          Amphibious Force.
To :   The Commanding Officer, U.S.S. HUNTER LIGGETT.

Subject: Lieutenant Niels P. THOMSEN, U.S.C.G. - per-
          formance of duty, commendation for.

1.   During the last nine months the writer has
had occasion to use lieutenant THOMSEN, U.S.C.G., the
navigating officer of the U.S.S. HUNTER LIGGETT, for considerable staff work in connection with the operation of
task units throughout the South Pacific Area. Much of
this operating has been in advanced combat areas where
charts were either unavailable or at best unreliable.
Throughout the period mentioned above lieutenant THOMSEN's
work has been outstanding for its reliability and its excellence.

2.   It has been the observation of the undersigned that lieutenant THOMSEN performs his duty with far
greater skill than the average or the good officer. He is
industrious, conscientious and reliable to a high degree.
He seeks, and is considered capable of assuming, greater
responsibility. He is an excellent ship handler and is tem-
peramentally well fitted for such work.

3.   Lieutenant THOMSEN is considered well qualified for promotion, and well fitted for independent duty of
an important nature.

4.   It is directed that a copy of this letter be
attached to lieutenant THOMSEN's fitness report.

                                H. E. THORNHILL.

Copy to:
  U.S.C.G. Headquarters
  ComTransGroupThirdPhib
  Lieut. N. P. THOMSEN, USCG.

File in Officers File
copy for fitness report
RPP

FROM: COMMANDER TRANSPORT GROUP SOPAC.

TO: AMERICAN LEGION ; HUNTER LIGGETT.

INFO: COMMANDER TRANSPORT DIVISION 10.

YOU HAVE GREATLY CONTRIBUTED TO THE SUCCESS OF OUR
OPERATIONS X I WISH YOU A SAFE VOYAGE HOME A GOOD
OVERHAUL A WELL MERITED REST AND A SPEEDY RETURN
TO THE FORWARD AREA.

TOR: 2338/17 NOV/VIS.   172220

'Lucky Liggett' Has Not Lost Single Soldier

SAN FRANCISCO, March 28. (U.P.)-"Lucky Liggett" a navy transport ship, has carried thousands of soldiers, sailors and marines into battle theaters during nearly two years of war without losing a man, the 12th naval district has revealed.

Her coast guard crew dubbed the vessel "Lucky Liggett" after she escaped damage in the initial invasion of Guadalcanal when Jap bombs fell so close that "another coat of paint would mean a hit," naval headquarters said.

During the Bougainville invasion "Lucky Liggett" was the flagship of the transports in the amphibious force. Jap Zeros strafed the ship in Empress Augusta Bay while she sent landing boats ashore.

An enemy bomb tore a 10-inch hole in the ship and splinters pierced the uniform and flesh of Lt. William J. P. Parker, Glen Rock, N. J. Someone said something about a Purple Hart but Lt. Parker said he was more interested in red mercurochrome.

Capt. Roderick S. Patch, USCG, Alameda, Cal., commands the "Lucky Liggett."

BAGGERS OF JAP SUB OFF ALASKA COAST REWARDED

KETCHIKAN, Alaska, Dec. 8.— The Legion of Merit has been awarded Lieut. Ralph Burns, Ketchikan Coast Guardsman, and Lieut. Nils P. Thomsen, now in the South Pacific, by Secretary of Navy Frank Knox, for their role in bagging a Jap submarine off the Alaskan coast over a year ago, Coast Guard Headquarters here announces.

Lieut. Burns, 46, in old lighthouse service 10 years before entering the Coast Guard, commanded one patrol vessel, and Lieut. Thomsen commanded the old converted halibut schooner Foremost which lost part of her keel in ramming the sub and escaping a torpedo hit by only a few feet.

DAUGHTER OF P.M. OF NEW ZEALAND – LIEUT THOMSEN, USCG

what to expect, but feared the worst. A boat took me to the CLYMER, where I was escorted by a Marine Corporal to the door of the wardroom. Through the door I could see Commodore Reifsnider, two Marine Generals, and three Navy Captains sitting at a large table. They were all in a joyous mood, congratulating one another on the success of the landings, and toasting Reifsnider, who had just received official word of promotion to Rear Admiral.

The Marine escort instructed me to wait at the door while he walked to the table and spoke to the now Admiral Reifsnider, who arose from the table, walked over to me and holding out his hand, saying, "Thomsen, you will be happy to know that this morning one of our small craft surveyed the reef area off Puruata Island. We would all have piled up on the reef had we made our ninety-degree turn as originally planned. None of my Staff Officers would have had the guts to take the wheel away from me. You should have a medal. I am instructing Commodore Thornhill, who has just received a promotion and is now the new Commander of Division Ten, and is my relief as flag of the LIGGETT, to write a letter to your Commanding Officer, commending you for your services to me and my Staff over the past nine months. I have been relieved of duty in this area and am being transferred to Navy Headquarters in Washington, D.C. for assignment as Chief of Naval Personnel. If there is ever anything I can do for you in my official capacity, you have only to let me know. Good luck and goodbye."

After the Cape Torokina landings on November first, the HUNTER LIGGETT shuttled between Guadalcanal and Bougainville, ferrying Marine Corps and Army personnel to the landing site. On November 25th the LIGGETT received orders to proceed to the United States for repairs and crew replacement, and on the following day departed for San Francisco. We arrived in San Francisco Bay on December 29th, 1943, where most of the crew was granted thirty days leave of absence. I was ordered to report to the San Francisco District Office at the end of my leave period on January 9th. I took the Fresno bus to Ethel, Carol Ann and fifteen month old Robin, whom I was seeing for the first time. The meeting was awkward. Ethel appeared to have lost the romantic interest she had for me during the first six months of our marriage and readjustment to family life after such a long period of absence was not easy for either of us. I sensed that having left Ethel in the care of Chris and Adelheid had been a mistake. They were old-fashioned, narrow-minded, unimaginative and uninteresting. Ethel, having been brought up in a society, which regarded Scandinavian Immigrants as second-class citizens, no doubt wondered what she had done to her life by her marriage to me. I was never able to account for this change in Ethel's behavior towards me. It may to some extent have been due to my emotional immaturity, as revealed in my letters to her during my sixteen months in the South Pacific. In all the years that followed we would never regain the total communication and close companionship of our first six months of our marriage.

One might wonder why this journal is bereft of references to my family life. To begin to understand this, one must remember that I was a seaman, whose only way of providing adequately for his family was to spend ninety percent of his time apart from them. Ethel was always a good mother, an attractive and intelligent woman, whom I will always admire and cherish.

12. To what degree has he exhibited the following qualities? (See instructions in latest Bureau of Navigation subject of fitness reports.)

Intelligence (With reference to the faculty of comprehension; mental acuteness.)	Exceptionally quick-witted; keen in understanding.	Grasps essentials of a situation quickly.	Understands normal situations and conditions.	Slow of comprehension; unimaginative.
Judgment (With reference to a discriminating perception by which the values and relations of things are mentally asserted.)	Unusually keen in estimating situations and reaching sound decisions.	Can generally be depended on to make proper decisions.	Fair judgment in normal and routine things.	Frequently draws wrong conclusions.
Initiative (With reference to constructive thinking and resourcefulness; ability and intelligence to act on own responsibility.)	Exceptional in ability to think, plan, and do things without waiting to be told and instructed.	Able to plan and execute missions on his own responsibility.	Capable of performing routine duties on own responsibility.	Requires constant guidance and supervision in his work, or evades responsibilities.
Force (With reference to moral power possessed and exerted in producing results.)	Strong, dynamic.	Strong.	Effectual under normal and routine circumstances.	Less than normal.
Leadership (With reference to the faculty of directing, controlling, and influencing others in definite lines of action.)	Inspires others to a high degree by precept and example.	A very good leader.	Leads fairly well.	A poor leader.
Moral Courage (With reference to that mental quality which impels one to carry out the dictates of his conscience and convictions fearlessly.)	Exceptionally courageous.	Courageous to a high degree.	Fairly courageous.	Timid.
Cooperation (With reference to the faculty of working harmoniously with others toward the accomplishment of common duties.)	Exceptionally successful in working with others to a common end.	Works in harmony with others.	Cooperates fairly well.	Not cooperative.
Loyalty (Fidelity, faithfulness, allegiance, constancy — all with reference to a cause and to higher authority.)	Unswerving in allegiance; frank and honest in aiding and advising.	A high sense of loyalty.	Reasonably faithful in the execution of his duty.	Inclined to be disloyal.
Perseverance (With reference to maintenance of purpose or undertaking in spite of obstacles or discouragement.)	Determined, resolute.	Constant in purpose.	Fairly steady.	Inclined to vacillate.
Reactions in emergencies (With reference to the faculty of acting instinctively in a logical manner in difficult and unforeseen situations.)	Exceptionally cool-headed and logical in his actions under all conditions.	Composed and logical in his actions in difficult situations.	Fairly logical in his actions in general.	Inclined to be disconcerted.
Endurance (With reference to ability for carrying on under any and all conditions.)	Capable of standing an exceptional amount of physical hardships and strain.	Can perform his duties under trying conditions.	Of normal endurance.	Less than normal.
Industry (With reference to performance of duties in an energetic manner.)	Extremely energetic and industrious.	Thorough and energetic.	Reasonably energetic and industrious.	Indolent, lazy.
Military bearing and neatness of person and dress (With reference to dignity of demeanor, correctness of uniform, and smartness of appearance.)	Exceptional.	Very good.	Fair.	Unmilitary and untidy.

CHECK TO RIGHT OF THIS LINE CONSTITUTES AN UNSATISFACTORY REPORT

13. In comparison with other officers of his rank and approximate length of service, how would you designate this officer? Outstanding .... Above average .... Average .... Below average ....
Excellent

REMARKS

14. Is this officer professionally qualified to perform ALL the duties of his grade? Yes .... No .... If deficient in any particular, comment is required. Give in this space a clear, concise estimate of this officer's personal and military character, his fitness for promotion, and duty performed worthy of special mention, and any information which might be of value to the Department in making assignments to duty. A check opposite "No," except for inexperienced Ensigns, or a statement that performance of duty is clearly unsatisfactory constitutes an unsatisfactory report. A statement of minor deficiencies either in character or performance of duties constitutes an unfavorable report. (THIS SPACE IS NOT TO BE LEFT BLANK.)

[handwritten remarks]

15. An unsatisfactory report must have statement of officer reported on attached; an unfavorable report requires that officer reported on has been informed of his deficiencies either verbally or in writing. Has this been done? .... What improvement, if any, has been noted? _____

This officer is resourceful, calm, even-tempered, and
efficient. He is an excellent navigator, as well as
competent watch and division officer. He has done fine work
as an instructor to junior line officers, more-over, he sets
a good example. He is considered in all respects eligible for
promotion.

62-A

12. To what degree has he exhibited the following qualities? (See instructions in latest Bureau of Naval Personnel circular letter on the subject of fitness reports.)

Intelligence (With reference to the faculty of comprehension; mental acuteness.)	Exceptionally quick-witted; keen in understanding.	Grasps essentials of a situation quickly.	Understands normal situations and conditions.	Slow of comprehension; unimaginative.
Judgment (With reference to a discriminating perception by which the values and relations of things are mentally asserted.)	Unusually keen in estimating situations and reaching sound decisions.	Can generally be depended on to make proper decisions.	Fair judgment in normal and routine things.	Frequently draws wrong conclusions.
Initiative (With reference to constructive thinking and resourcefulness; ability and intelligence to act on own responsibility.)	Exceptional in ability to think, plan, and do things without waiting to be told and instructed.	Able to plan and execute missions on his own responsibility.	Capable of performing routine duties on own responsibility.	Requires constant guidance and supervision in his work, or evades responsibilities.
Force (With reference to moral power possessed and exerted in producing results.)	Strong, dynamic.	Strong.	Effectual under normal and routine circumstances.	Less than normal.
Leadership (With reference to the faculty of directing, controlling, and influencing others in definite lines of action.)	Inspires others to a high degree by precept and example.	A very good leader.	Leads fairly well.	A poor leader.
Moral Courage (With reference to that mental quality which impels one to carry out the dictates of his conscience and convictions fearlessly.)	Exceptionally courageous.	Courageous to a high degree.	Fairly courageous.	Timid.
Cooperation (With reference to the faculty of working harmoniously with others toward the accomplishment of common duties.)	Exceptionally successful in working with others to a common end.	Works in harmony with others.	Cooperates fairly well.	Not cooperative.
Loyalty (Fidelity, faithfulness, allegiance, constancy — all with reference to a cause and to higher authority.)	Unswerving in allegiance; frank and honest in aiding and advising.	A high sense of loyalty.	Reasonably faithful in the execution of his duty.	Inclined to be disloyal.
Perseverance (With reference to maintenance of purpose or undertaking in spite of obstacles or discouragement.)	Determined, resolute.	Constant in purpose.	Fairly steady.	Inclined to vacillate.
Reactions in emergencies (With reference to the faculty of acting instinctively in a logical manner in difficult and unforeseen situations.)	Exceptionally cool-headed and logical in his actions under all conditions.	Composed and logical in his actions in difficult situations.	Fairly logical in his actions in general.	Inclined to be disconcerted.
Endurance (With reference to ability for carrying on under any and all conditions.)	Capable of standing an exceptional amount of physical hardships and strain.	Can perform well his duties under trying conditions.	Of normal endurance.	Less than normal.
Industry (With reference to performance of duties in an energetic manner.)	Extremely energetic and industrious.	Thorough and energetic.	Reasonably energetic and industrious.	Indolent, lazy.
Military bearing and neatness of person and dress (With reference to dignity of demeanor, correctness of uniform, and smartness of appearance.)	Exceptional.	Very good.	Fair.	Unmilitary and untidy.

(Right margin, vertical:) CHECK TO RIGHT OF THIS LINE CONSTITUTES AN UNSATISFACTORY REPORT

13. In comparison with other officers of his rank and approximate length of service, how would you designate this officer? Outstanding _____ / Above average _____ Average _____ Below average _____
   Excellent _____

REMARKS

14. Is this officer professionally qualified to perform ALL the duties of his grade? Yes _____ No _____ If deficient in any particular, comment is required. Give in this space a clear, concise estimate of this officer's personal and military character, his fitness for promotion, and duty performed worthy of special mention, and any information which might be of value to the Department in making assignments to duty. A check opposite "No," except for inexperienced Ensigns, or a statement that performance of duty is clearly unsatisfactory constitutes an unsatisfactory report. A statement of minor deficiencies either in character or performance of duties constitutes an unfavorable report. (THIS SPACE IS NOT TO BE LEFT BLANK.)

(handwritten) This Officer is an excellent navigator and instructor for Junior Deck Officers. Excellent personal and military character. He is eligible in all respects for promotion.

This Officer is an excellent navigator and instructor for
Junior Deck Officers. Excellent personal and military
character. He is eligible in all rspects for promotion.

15. An *unsatisfactory report* must have statement of officer reported on attached; an *unfavorable report* requires that officer reported on has been informed of his deficiencies either verbally or in writing. Has this been done? _____ What improvement, if any, has been noted? _____

(Signature) _____

(Do not write in marked portion of this space)

62-B

N Form. 445
(Revised May 1943)

REPORT ON THE FITNESS OF OFFICERS

(To be submitted in accordance with Section 5 of Chapter 2, U. S. Navy Regulations, 1920, and Bureau of Naval Personnel Manual, Article C-1007)

(Before making out this report read latest Bureau of Naval Personnel circular letter on the subject of fitness reports)

The following four questions to be made out by the officer reported on:

THOMSEN, Niels Peter _____, Rank Lieut. Comdr. _____, U.S. N. C.G.
(Surname first)

Ship or
Station U.S.S. HUNTER LIGGETT _____ Period from 1 June, 1943 to 4 Jan. 1944
(Ship aviation units enter ship to which attached)

1. Regular duties NAVIGATOR - DECK COURT OFFICER

Additional duties _____
(State watch duties, both deck and engineering. After each duty insert in parenthesis number of months this reporting period)

2. Present address of wife (if married) MRS Ethel J. Thomsen, 4544 Nevada Ave, Fresno, Calif.

next of kin (if unmarried) _____

(Indicate above the best address at which the Bureau of Naval Personnel may communicate with the wife or next of kin in an emergency. The above address does not relate to the usual residence (home) which is maintained in the Bureau. See Art. 135(2), U. S. N. R., 1920.)

3. Proficiency in foreign languages, stating which ones, and ability therein Danish - 4.0
Norwegian - 3.0   Swedish - 2.5

4. My preference for next duty is—

(a) Sea Destroyer Escort - Frigate _____ Fleet Forward Combat Area
or A.K.

(b) Shore As assigned _____ Location As assigned

_____
(Signature)

Following to be made out by Reporting Officer:

5. Reporting Officer: Name R. S. Patch _____, Rank Captain _____, U.S.N. C.G.

6. Reporting officer's official status relative to officer reported on Commanding Officer

7. Employment of ship during period of this report Combat Transport in Pacific area engaged in landing Combat Teams and support.

8. Assign marks on scale of 0-4 in appropriate subdivisions given below, and any other qualification on which observation has been sufficient to justify marking.
(Staff officers to be marked with respect to required duties. Mark below 2.5 constitutes an unsatisfactory report)

Present assignment 3.5 Ability to command 3.5 As executive or division officer 3.5 As deck watch officer 3.9

In administration 3.6 Ship handling 3.7

9. Has the work of this officer been reported on either in a commendatory way or adversely during the period of this report? If so, state the subject, reference numbers, and substance of report. Clip copy to report. Comply with U. S. Navy Regulations, article 137 (11) with respect to commendatory reports. Any adverse comment constitutes an unsatisfactory report.

None

10. Considering the possible requirements in war, indicate your attitude toward having this officer under your command. Would you—
(An affirmative entry in item (4) constitutes an unsatisfactory report)

(1) Particularly desire to have him? _____ (2) Be pleased to have him? Yes . (3) Be satisfied to have him? _____

(4) Prefer not to have him? _____

11. Has he any weaknesses—mental, moral, physical, etc.—which adversely affect his efficiency? (If "Yes," give details.)
(An implied or stated defect constitutes an unsatisfactory report)

None.

[OVER]

62-C

Chapter 12

12th COAST GUARD DISTRICT

On January ninth, I boarded a Greyhound bus for San Francisco, leaving Ethel and the children, Robin and Carol in Fresno. On departure from the HUNTER LIGGETT, in filing out and submitting my fitness report to Captain Patch for my next duty assignment, I had requested sea duty on a frigate or destroyer escort in the forward combat area, so I had no inkling what my next duty assignment might be.

On arrival at the 12th Coast Guard District Headquarters, I was ushered into the presence of the District Chief of Staff, who to my pleasure and surprise, was none other than my former commanding Officer Captain Louis Perkins, USCG of the HUNTER LIGGETT, whose navigator I had been in the South Pacific. After a half hour of reminiscing about former shipmates and experiences on the HUNTER LIGGETT, he said, "Thomsen, I think we have just the job for you, providing Admiral Roach will accept a Lieutenant Commander in a position designated by the U.S. Navy as a billet for a regular Senior Coast Guard Commander, none of which are available to us at this time. Let us go in and talk to the Admiral, with whom I have already discussed the assignment briefly."

Admiral Philip Roach, U.S.C.G., one of the Coast Guard's most Senior Officers, was gruff-appearing, very short, and in his early sixties. After greeting me in a kindly manner, he said, "Captain Perkins speaks highly of your tact and organizational qualities, and recommends you for a new position requested by Admiral George H. Fort, U.S. Navy, the Commander of the Twelfth Naval District under whose command we operate. The Coast Guard has the responsibility for all coastal surveillance from San

Francisco to Santa Barbara. Because of increased activity with Navy, Army and Marine Personnel in training at Morro Bay facilities, the Navy has created the position of Commander, Local Naval Defense Forces to be combined with the duties of the Captain of the Port at our Base at Morro Bay. This position requires tact, and keeping the Senior Navy and Army Officers concerned happy and off my back. You have two weeks to move your family to Morro Bay, where quarters are available to you. Furthermore, I am not happy with the present Command situation in Morro Bay, and you have full authority to put it in order."

We arrived in Morro Bay ten days later and moved into a pleasantly located home adjacent to the Morro Bay Country Club Golf Course.

These are events of fifty years ago and I have a limited memory of my personal life experiences of that period. I do recall that family life was rewarding. Robin and Carol were very active children. So that Robin could have goat's milk, I bought a goat that was kept tethered in a field next to the house and each morning clad in full uniform, I would milk him before I left for the base. The Twelve Coast Guard Reserve Officers who comprised the Coast Guard officer complement did not greet my assuming command of the Coast Guard Base with great enthusiasm. They were enjoying military life in "old boys Coast Guard Academy pre-war fashion," with the two top priorities being an active social life with government automobiles, horseback riding on horses attached to the Base, cocktail parties and golf in full swing. I had just come from two years of the serious and realistic side of war, and did not feel at ease with the lack of military discipline, routine and dedication to the war effort.

It took three weeks to establish a military routine that I could be comfortable with.

Part of my duties consisted of a weekly personal visit and inspection of each of the Coastal Lookout Stations from Monterey to Santa Barbara. I assigned a First class seaman named Jackson as my gardener and chauffeur, and every Tuesday at 6 AM we would head North on the Coast Highway, visiting all the stations, with lunch at Monterey. I always took Carol Ann with me on those trips of inspection. On the return trip we would stop at several of the many trout streams along the highway, walk a quarter of a mile inland and fish for trout, arriving home in time for dinner.

On Fridays, Jackson and I would drive south as far as Santa Barbara, inspecting stations. At Santa Barbara I would lunch with Army and Marine Corps Officers Mess and in my capacity as Commander of Local Defense Forces, would make my weekly report. It was a great life, especially enjoyable after two years of forward area action and stress.

A few miles North of Morro Bay stood a Catholic Church, presided over by a convivial Irish Priest by the name of Father Cooney who loved to play golf and who introduced me to the game. He had probably the best cache of pre-war (rarity) whiskey in the Church kitchen cupboard, where we retired after each round - it was still a good life, but whenever I read about what was happening to the Marines at Tarawa and other Pacific invasions, I was uncomfortable.

After seven months at Morro Bay, I was overcome with an uncontrollable yearning to be assigned to some forward area battle zone, and recalled Admiral Reifsnider's final words to me when we parted at Cape Torokina. "Thomsen, if I can ever help you with your career, contact me at my next assignment, which is Chief of Naval Personnel in Washington, D.C."

I then wrote to Admiral Reifsnider, bypassing the Coast Guard. A week later, on September 18th, I received orders direct from Coast Guard Headquarters to report to the Alameda Training Station, select a crew of officers and prepare to take Command of a former Liberty Ship the USS MENKAR AK-123 on a secret mission directly under the Command of the Pacific Fleet (CINCPAC) in Honolulu. I departed two days later for the Alameda Training Base on San Francisco Bay.

"The good life" had come to an end. I was told in confidence by Captain Perkins that my bypassing of Coast Guard Headquarters by my letter to Admiral Reifsnider U.S.N. did not sit well with the Coast Guard, and after the War some chickens came home to roost in my Coast Guard career. No Academy-trained Coast Guard Officer would have made such a fatal error in his career.

See Admiral Fort, U.S. Navy comments on Admiral Roach's report on my fitness during this tour of duty.

OFFICER'S FITNESS REPORT
AVPERS-310A (REV. 8-40)

PLEASE TYPE THIS FORM
If no typewriter is available use ink but be sure all copies are legible.

NAME	(last)	(first)		RANK AND CLASSIFICATION	FILE NO.
THOMSEN	Niels	Peter		Lieut. Comdr. USCG	20760

SHIP OR STATION: Section Commander, Morro Bay, California

DATE FROM 1/5/44   DATE TO 3/30/44   PERIOD OF REPORT

DATE OF ASSIGNMENT TO PRESENT DUTY: 1/5/44

OCCASION FOR REPORT:
[ ] DETACHMENT OF OFFICER REPORTED ON
[ ] DETACHMENT OF REPORTING SENIOR
[ ] REGULAR SEMI-ANNUAL
[X] QUARTERLY
[ ] SPECIAL

2. DESCRIPTION OF DUTIES SINCE LAST FITNESS REPORT (List most recent first and describe accurately)

Section Commander, Morro Bay Section
Commander Naval Local Defense forces, Morro Section

1	44	5	1	44
1	44	3	1	44

3. IF COURSES OF INSTRUCTION WERE COMPLETED DURING PERIOD OF THIS REPORT, LIST TITLE OF COURSE, LOCATION OF SCHOOL, LENGTH OF COURSE AND DATE COMPLETED.

Are your periodicals completed for New State?
[X] Yes [ ] No [ ] Don't know

4. IF AVIATOR, INDICATE NO. OF FLIGHT HOURS LAST TWO YEARS FOR EACH TYPE AIRCRAFT
TYPE OF AIRCRAFT
NO. OF HOURS
TOTAL

5. MY PREFERENCE FOR NEXT DUTY IS:
SEA — KIND OF DUTY: As assigned — LOCATION: No preference
SHORE — KIND OF DUTY: None desired — LOCATION: No preference

6. SECTIONS 6 THROUGH 12 TO BE FILLED IN BY REPORTING OFFICER
NAME OF REPORTING OFFICER: Philip F. Roach
RANK: Commodore
OFFICIAL STATUS RELATIVE TO OFFICER REPORTED ON: Commanding Officer

IS THIS OFFICER QUALIFIED TO PERFORM ALL HIS PRESENT DUTIES? [X] YES [ ] NO
INDICATE MORE RESPONSIBLE DUTIES FOR WHICH HE IS IN TRAINING. (If none, so state): Not in training

Qualified for any duty of his grade
No physical defects

FOR WHAT DUTIES IS HE RECOMMENDED?
ASHORE: Command
AFLOAT: Any duty of his grade

7. FOR EACH FACTOR OBSERVED CHECK THE APPROPRIATE BOX...

RATING FACTORS		Not Observed	Within Bottom 10%	Within Next 70%	Within Middle 40%	Within Next Top 70%	Within Top 10%
A. SEA OR ADVANCE BASE DUTY	1. STANDING DECK WATCHES UNDERWAY?						
	2. ABILITY TO COMMAND?						
	3. PERFORMANCE IN PRESENT DUTIES AS DESCRIBED IN SECTION 2 ABOVE?						
	4. REACTIONS DURING EMERGENCIES?						
	5. PERFORMANCE AT BATTLE STATION OR IN BATTLE DUTIES?						
B. INITIATIVE AND RESPONSIBILITY	1. ASSUME RESPONSIBILITY WHEN SPECIFIC INSTRUCTIONS ARE LACKING?						✓
	2. GIVE FRANK OPINIONS WHEN ASKED OR VOLUNTEER THEM WHEN NECESSARY TO AVOID MISTAKES?						✓
	3. FOLLOW THROUGH DESPITE OBSTACLES IN CARRYING OUT RESPONSIBILITIES ASSIGNED OR ASSUMED?						✓
C. UNDERSTANDING AND SKILL	1. GRASP INSTRUCTIONS AND PLANS GIVEN TO HIM?						
	2. USE IDEAS AND SUGGESTIONS OF OTHERS?						
	3. RATE IN TECHNICAL COMPETENCE IN HIS SPECIALTY, IF ANY (Name Specialty)						
D. LEADERSHIP	1. INSPIRE SUBORDINATES TO WORK TO THE MAXIMUM OF THEIR CAPACITY?						✓
	2. EFFECTIVELY DELEGATE RESPONSIBILITY?						✓
	3. TRANSMIT ORDERS, INSTRUCTIONS, AND PLANS?						✓
	4. ORGANIZE HIS WORK AND THAT OF THOSE UNDER HIS COMMAND OR SUPERVISION?						✓
	5. MAINTAIN DISCIPLINE AMONG THOSE UNDER HIS COMMAND OR DIRECTION?						✓
E. CONDUCT AND WORK HABITS	1. ABILITY TO WORK WITH OTHERS?						✓
	2. ABILITY TO ADAPT TO CHANGING NEEDS AND CONDITIONS?						✓
	3. MILITARY CONDUCT—BEARING, DRESS, COURTESY, ETC.?						✓

8. INDICATE YOUR ATTITUDE TOWARD HAVING THIS OFFICER UNDER YOUR COMMAND. WOULD YOU: (Check one)
[ ] DEFINITELY NOT WANT HIM (UNSATISFACTORY)
[ ] PREFER NOT TO HAVE HIM (UNSATISFACTORY)
[ ] BE SATISFIED TO HAVE HIM
[ ] BE PLEASED TO HAVE HIM
[X] PARTICULARLY DESIRE HIM

9a. CONSIDERING ALL OFFICERS OF THE SAME RANK WHOSE PROFESSIONAL ABILITIES ARE KNOWN TO YOU PERSONALLY, WOULD YOU PROMOTE HIM: (Check one)
[ ] UNDER NO CIRCUMSTANCES (UNSATISFACTORY)
[ ] IF 5% WERE TO BE PROMOTED
[ ] IF 70% WERE TO BE PROMOTED
[ ] IF 30% WERE TO BE PROMOTED
[ ] IF ONLY 10% WERE TO BE PROMOTED

9b. How many Officers are included in the group used for the comparison in 9a?
[ ] 10 OR UNDER [ ] 1 TO 10 [ ] OVER

10. COMMENT IN SECTION 12 AND GIVE REFERENCE HERE TO ANY COMMENDABLE OR ADVERSE REPORTS THAT HAVE BEEN MADE ON THE OFFICER DURING THIS PERIOD.

11. HAVE YOU ANY ADVERSE COMMENTS TO MAKE REGARDING THIS OFFICER'S QUALITIES OR PERFORMANCE? [ ] YES [X] NO   If yes, explain in Section 12.
HAS HE ANY MENTAL OR MORAL WEAKNESS WHICH ADVERSELY AFFECTS HIS EFFICIENCY? [ ] YES [X] NO

Check one of these boxes—I CONSIDER THIS REPORT TO BE [X] SATISFACTORY [ ] UNSATISFACTORY

12. [handwritten narrative]
Lieut Comdr Thomsen served as Commander of the Morro Bay Section during the period covered by this report. The duties as such required very good judgment and tact as they were closely coordinated with Army and Navy activities and Army, Navy and Marine personnel were quartered, subsisted and trained at the Morro Bay Base which are his disinclination. He performed his duties in an outstanding by his manner and as far as I was concerned and Rear Admiral Ford USN personally called on me at my office in San Francisco to express his pleasure at the assistance rendered by Lieut Comdr Thomsen to the training activities at Morro Bay and the tactful and efficient manner in which he handled all activities. Problems at the base. It was a difficult situation and he handled it very well.

SIGNATURE OF OFFICER REPORTED ON (Applies only to Sections 1 through 5): [signature]
SIGNATURE OF REPORTING OFFICER: Philip F. Roach
HAVE YOU READ THE ATTACHED INSTRUCTION SHEET?

65-A   When completed remove carbon paper, forward Pages 1 & 2.   BuPers. Retain Page 3 for "Officer's Qualification Record Jacket".

He is fully qualified for promotion to next higher grade
He has a good head. When objectives are outlined
to him, he accepts the objectives as his mission
and plans and carries out the work necessary to
accomplish the mission on his own responsibility
A very good officer. *Philip H. Roach*

Lieutenant Commander Thomsen served as commander of the
MORRO BAY SECTION during the period covered by this report.
His duties as such, required very good judgement and tact as
they were closely coordinated with Army and Navy activities.
Army and Navy and Marine Personnel were quartered,
subsisted, and trained at the MORRO BAY BASE, which was his
headquarters. He performed his duties in an outstandingly
proficient manner insofar as I was concerned. Rear Admiral
Fort, U.S. Navy personally called on me at my office in
San Francisco to express his pleasure at the assistance
rendered by Lieutenant Commander Thomsen to the training
activities at Morro Bay, and the tactful and efficient
manner in which he handled all interservice problems at the
Base. It was a difficult situation, and he handled it very well
He is fully qualified for promotion to next higher grade.
He has a good head. When objectives are outlined to him, he
accepts the objectives as his mission, and plans and carries
out the work necessary to accomplish the mission on his own
responsibility. He is a very good Officer.

     Philip H. Roach
     Rear Admiral, U.S.C.G.

Report continued on ___Niels Peter Thomsen___   ___Lieut.(jg) (R)___
                            (Name)   (Rank)

                                              ___8 September, 1941.___
                                                    (Date)

REMARKS

15. To what duty do you think this officer should be assigned? Line duty on a cruising cutter or command of a smaller cutter.
                              Why? This officer has an excellent background of experienc as a seaman, is intensely interested in the service, and has had excellent training in military routine during a period of six years in the Naval Reserve.

16. Is this officer fit to perform all duties of his grade? Yes ___Yes___   No ___
     If deficient in any, comment is required.   Give a clear and concise estimate of this officer's personal and military character, including his fitness for promotion.

(This space not to be left blank.)

(Attach extra sheet if needed.)

Mr. Thomsen is an excellent watch officer, careful, and understands thoroughly the modern methods of navigation and piloting. He is thoroughly competent to perform the duties of his grade at sea. He is a very active officer, industrious to a degree where he needs restraint at times, and performs his duties rapidly and intelligently. He is strict with the crew, having a strict sense of military discipline, endeavoring to carry out regulations to the letter. He is studious, ambitious to learn new methods and to perfect himself in military matters. He is a good messmate, congenial, well educated, and can intelligently converse on a wide variety of subjects. He is qualified to perform the duties of his rank, and his retention in grade is recommended.

17. Having in mind the special fitness of this officer and the efficiency of the Coast Guard, I certify that to the best of my knowledge and belief all entries made hereon are true and without prejudice or partiality.

                                        Frank K. Johnson
                                        Frank K. Johnson
                                        Signature of reporting Officer.

Check reason for submission: Semi-annual report.....................(   )
                                Detachment of officer..................(   )
                                Detachment of reporting senior.........(X)

                                                                    327-C

ADDENDUM
ONE

LIEUTENANT COMMANDER LESLIE TOLLAKSEN, USCG

USCG CYANE

KETCHIKAN ALASKA

781-CONFIDENTIAL

COAST GUARD CUTTER

CYANE

NAVY DEPARTMENT

~~TREASURY DEPARTMENT~~

UNITED STATES COAST GUARD

Ketchikan, Alaska
24 January, 1942

From: Commanding Officer, CYANE.
To :   Commandant.

Via :   1. Lieutenant (j.g.) N. P. Thomsen, U.S.C.G.R.
           2. Senior Coast Guard Officer, Alaskan Sector,
               Thirteenth Naval District.

Subject: Fitness of Lieutenant (j.g.) N. P. Thomsen, U.S.C.G.R.

Reference: (a) Verbal Instructions, Senior Coast Guard Officer,
               Alaskan Sector, Thirteenth Naval District.
           (b) CYANE dispatch 041552 (December, 1941).

　　　1.　　　I regret that it is necessary for me to report that an
officer of my command does not measure up to the minimum requirements
of a Coast Guard officer.

　　　2.　　　I have given Lieutenant (j.g.) Niels P. Thomsen, U.S.C.G.R.,
every opportunity to enhance his prestige and have endeavored in every
way known to me to guide and instruct him.

　　　3.　　　It was thought that the seriousness of the situation had
been brought home to him when it became so aggravated that it was necessary to relieve him of duty and to confine him to his quarters for a short
period as a punishment for disobedience of orders and unwarranted assumption
of authority, the justice of which he readily admitted to Captain
F. A. Zeusler. The effect soon wore off, apparently, and the morale of
the crew became steadily worse, some of the symptoms being frequent acts
of rebellious character against Mr. Thomsen by name and a general deterioration of their spirit.

　　　4.　　　As I became better acquainted with this officer it became
necessary for me gradually to take more and more responsibility away
from him for two main reasons: First, because he could not perform properly
the particular duty, often admittedly; and second, because my trust in this
officer's reliability, loyalty and veracity became less and less, of which
he was privately advised on more than one occasion.

　　　5.　　　This is a case of the proverbial straw which broke the
camel's back -- the particular straw being of little consequence -- I had
reached, suddenly, the end of my endurance of this man's troubles.

　　　　　　　　　　　　　　　　L. B. TOLLAKSEN

Copy to SCGO, Alaskan Sect
        13th Naval Distric

781-Confidential

Ketchikan, Alaska
24 January, 1942

From: Lieutenant (j.g.) N.P.Thomsen, USCGR.
To: Commandant.

Via: Senior Coast Guard Officer, Alaskan Sector.

Subject: Fitness of Lieutenant (j.g.) N.P. Thomsen, USCGR.

Inclosure: Certified statement of events concerning suspension from duty on
             morning of 4 December, 1942

      1.   Inasmuch as the letter of which this is an indorsement so obviously
reeks of personal feelings and therefore constitutes my best defense, my first
thought was to venture no reply to the allegations contained therein. However,
the viciousness of the charges impel me to offer a short explanation on my behalf.

      2.   My relations with Lieutenant Commander Tollaksen have been absolutely
incompatible since his assignment to the CYANE last September. I have the proper
respect for rank and authority which every seafaring man knows is necessary, but
I cannot be humble towards a fellow man to the point where I must wholly surrender
my self-respect. Therein, together with my inability to carry out blindly impr-
acticable orders and "slide rule" methods of navigation in confined pilot waters,
lies the primary source of friction between Lieutenant Commander Tollaksen and
myself.

      3.   Also, under pressure from the Commanding Officer I was compelled to
apply regulations and harsh standards of discipline foreign to Alaskan service.
This brought about the unpleasantness and alleged deterioration of morale referred
to by Lieutenant Commander Tollaksen. As executive officer and navigator of the
CYANE I have been continually caught between two fires, in that Lieutenant Commander Tollaksen's belligerent and critical attitude towards the District Office often
resulted in confused policies which created endless misunderstandings involving
my duties and loyalty. Of late this strife has occasioned me untold mental strain
to such an extent that I have sometimes considered resignation as being preferable
to the CYANE.

      4.   In regards to my having been suspended from duty as a punishment for
disobedience of orders and unwarranted assumption of authority, I inclose a statement of the events of the morning of 4 December, 1941 as written immediately thereafter. In this case, I upheld Lieutenant Commander Tollaksen's action before the
Senior Coast Guard Officer because of the loyalty which I felt was due him as my
Commanding Officer, although I did feel the disciplinary action taken to be both
hasty and unjust. The taking away of my sword was itself contrary to Naval custom
and tradition, in that only in case of arrest is such action sanctioned.

      5.   I wish further to state that contrary to Lieutenant Commander Toll-
aksen's statement, I had been led to believe that my professional ability was very
satisfactory. As a matter of fact he placed such apparent confidence in my ability as a navigator in these dangerous waters, that he followed my advice unquest-
ionably. He praised my openly and required my presence on the bridge from sixteen
to eighteen hours a day, in spite of the fact that regular line officers were on
watch.

Subject: Fitness of Lieutenant (j.g.) N.P.Thomsen, USCGR.

- -

6.   I had no knowledge of my alleged deficiencies as an officer until so informed by the Chief of Staff on my arrival at the office of the Senior Coast Guard Officer on the morning of my detachment from the CYANE. My departure from the CYANE had been preceeded by a hearty handshake, a wish for my good fortune and a profession of ignorance as to the reason for my detachment by the Commanding Officer. Such insincere behavior is entirely foreign to the teachings of those from whom I have learned the codes and traditions of the sea.

7.   I request that my official record up to the unfortunate advent of Lieutenant Commander Tollaksen into my career be considered on its merits.

N.P.Thomsen

- -

SEE FOLLOWING PAGE FOR 2nd INDORSEMENT

From: Senior Coast Guard Officer, Alaskan Sector, 13th Naval
               District
To: Commandant

Subject: Fitness of Lieutenant (j.g.) N. P. Thomsen, U.S.C.G.R.

          F.   Forwarded. This office issued the orders, transferring
Lieutenant (j.g.) N. P. Thomsen from the CYANE to shore duty in connection with the District Office. Originally Lieutenant Thomsen served
on board the CEDAR. Later he was transferred to the Reserve Office, and
a short while thereafter, the CYANE needing a commissioned officer, he
was transferred to that vessel at the request of Lieutenant Commander
Johnson. It was the intention of this office to transfer Mr. Thomsen to
the HAIDA when that vessel arrived in Ketchikan, but when the matter was
discussed with the commanding officer, Commander Leslie, he requested
that his personnel situation not be disturbed and be kept frozen because,
as he stated, he had finally been able to properly assign the duties to
the various officers and they were in the process of training and he
felt that if a lieutenant (j.g.) were assigned to the vessel it would
completely disrupt the existing organization and it would be necessary
to commence anew. This office felt that this reasoning was sound, especially because of the fact that the HAIDA was proceeding on escort
duty two days later.

          2.   Upon the arrival of Lieutenant Thomsen to shore duty at
Ketchikan he was assigned immediately to serve under Lieutenant Richey
in personnel. Prior to the declaration of war, the Army requested this
office to train crash boat operators. Thirty-five men were picked from
Aviation U. S. Army to take the course. Lieutenant Richey was assigned
to take charge of this course, which he requested to last about three
months. Classes have been held daily with the exception of Saturdays
and Sundays, and theory, navigation, seamanship, signals, and rules of
the road have been expounded to these men. They are now in the process
of handling small boats. Lieutenant Thomsen was assigned to this
particular job, and since he has been handling the Army personnel he
has been complimented twice by the Army Engineer for the excellence of
instruction and also the thoroughness with which he was doing this work.
The Army personnel are very pleased with him. In addition to handling
the Army work he has been serving on boards of investigation, hull boards
and boards of survey for vessels being inducted into the service, and
his work has been most satisfactory.

          3.   Lieutenant Thomsen is a very serious minded individual.
He is what is called a slave driver when in charge of personnel. He
maintains a good vessel as an executive officer, but the morale of the
enlisted men is not what it should be because of his driving. He is a

good seaman, holding masters papers in the merchant service. He is interested in Naval and military tactics, and has taken numerous Navy courses. It is believed that his hard boiled attitude toward personnel is a matter of temperment. It is also believed that the temperment of the commanding officer, Lieutenant Commander Tollaksen, and that of Lieutenant Thomsen clashed and it is for that reason that he had the difficulties that he did with the present commanding officer. He has a habit of showing displeasure unwittingly when something is done that does not meet with his approval. A sensitive man would soon take exception to this attitude, which was the case on the CYANE. It is recommended that Lieutenant Thomsen be permanently assigned to the District Office in connection with training and with Captain of the Port duty, and that an officer of sufficient rank be assigned to the CYANE as executive officer so that in the event of sickness of the commanding officer an experienced officer will be in a position to take over the command.

F. A. ZEUGLER

Coast Guard Cutter
CYANE

4 December, 1941
0640

STATEMENT

0400, Anchored in south arm of Port Malmsbury with ample swinging room in 23 fathoms of water to 60 fathoms of starboard chain. Weather clear, sea smooth, calm. I relieved Chief Boatswain R. COWAN of the Officer of the Deck watch.

0440, Called Commanding Officer and gave condition of the weather as calm, clear, and smooth. Received verbal orders from the C.O. to start heaving anchor up at 0555 and to get under way at 0600, calling him then.

0515, Commanding Officer called bridge thru voice tube and said that the water carafe in the head was empty and to have it filled. I understood also that he wanted a drink. I sent the Q.M. aft to fill the carafe and brought it to him personally. The C.O. said he had not asked for water and was much annoyed to the extent of asking me whether or not I could understand English. He said not to awaken him until 0600. Realizing that in this cold weather he could not possibly be deressed and on the bridge by the time the vessel woulu be underway I again asked him if he wanted to get underway at six and also be called at the same time. He answered, "Yes." I then went to the bridge. As a Boatswain on the ARIADNE and as Watch Offiber on this vessel prior to the coming of the present Commanding Officer, I have on numerous occasions come to anchor or left an anchorage without the Commanding Officer on the bridge, so gave it no further thought.

0535, Vessel commenced swinging with her stern trailing in a NE direction. The weather was clear and bright moonlight and there was ample swinging room, but as the night orders stated to call the Commanding Officer is she swung with her stern in a NE direction, I called the Commanding Officer on the voice tube and informed of the vessels swinging at at the same time stated that the vessel was in no danger.

0555 Commenced heaving around and sent the Q.M. striker to call the Captain and the navigating officer, Mr. COWAN, Chief Boatswain, who was turned in with his clothes on, having had the mid-watch. As I had been reprimanded by the Captain two days previously for commencing to heave around at 0633 inste of 0630 at a previous anchorage, I was careful to commence heaving at exactly 0555 as ordered.

0559, Mr. COWAN, navigator, came on the bridge.

0603, Anchor aweigh, proceeded out of south arm with the assistance of the navigating officer. Captain not yet on the bridge, but knew that he could not have been dressed and on the bridge by this time, so being engrossed in the maneuvering of the vessel, listening to the reports from the Q.C. the fathometer and the navigating officer, I did not check on whether or not the Q.M. had called the Commanding Officer. The waters we were piloting were free of dangers and visibility was 4.0 at all times.

0606, Commanding Officer called thru the voice tube and Mr. COWAN answered. I then learned that the Q.M. had failed to call him. Some time later the Commandi Officer came on the bridge, relieved me, sent me to my room and ordered tha I place my sword in the Cabin, at the same time saying that I was suspended from duty for ten days. I retired to my room and am now making this stateme

I certify that the above is a true statement of the events which led to my suspension from duty by the Commanding Officer Lieutenant Commander T.N. TOLLAKSEN.

OFFICE OF THE INSPECTOR-IN-CHIEF

COAST GUARD HEADQUARTERS

DATE____16 February, 1942.____

MEMORANDUM FOR PERSONNEL.

Subject: THOMSEN, N. P., U.S.C.G.R., Lieutenant (j.g.); fitness of.

Reference: (a) Letter from Commanding Officer, CYANE, 24 January,1942,
              with indorsements.
        (b) Statement of Lieutenant (j.g.) N.P.Thomsen, 4 December,
             1942.

    1.   This correspondence should be referred to Tollaksen. In
fact, the reply of N. P. Thomsen, Lieutenant (j.g.), should have been
forwarded through that officer.

NORMAN B. HALL,
Inspector in Chief.

HEADQUARTERS

UN   STATES COAST GUARD

WASHINGTON

20 February, 1942

CONFIDENTIAL

From: Commandant.
To: Lieutenant Commander L. B. Tollaksen - CYANE

Subject: Lieutenant (j.g.) N. P. Thomsen, U.S.C.G.R.

Inclosure: (A) Your letter 24 January, 1942, (781 Conf);
           attached, statement of N.P.Thomsen, 4 December,1941;
           1st indorsement, Lieut.(j.g.) N.P.Thomsen, 24 January,1942
           2nd Indorsement, SCGO Alaskan Sector, 13th Naval
           District, 28 January, 1942; Memorandum, Inspector in
           Chief, 16 February, 1942.

    1.   Inclosure is referred to you for review, to afford
opportunity for you to make such supplementary comment as you may
deem appropriate.

                                    C. H. JONES
                                    By direction

71-781 Confidential

COAST GUARD CUTTER

Cyane

TREASURY DEPARTMENT

UNITED STATES COAST GUARD

6 March, 1942
Ketchikan, Alaska.

CONFIDENTIAL

From:	Lieutenant Commander L.B.Tollaksen - CYANE
To:	Commandant

Subject: Lieutenant (j.g.) N.P.Thomsen, U.S.C.G.R.

References: (a) Cyane letter 24 January,1942,(781 Conf.)
             (b) Headquarters letter 20 February,1942(P-71 Conf.)
             (c) Headquarters letter 1 September,1936,(PB-701)

Inclosure: (A) Reference (b) and attached inclosures.

1.   Inclosure (A) is returned herewith, having been reviewed in accordance with reference (b).

2.   Reference (a) was submitted as a fitness report as required upon the detachment of subject officer and was submitted in letter form because the regular form did not lend itself well to furnish-Headquarters with full understanding of this officer without supplementary sheets which then would amount to the same thing and so a letter form was thought to be more appropriate.

3.   I am astonished at the tone of the indorsements, and a little shocked. I receive the impression from them that this has somehow dropped into the category of vituperative altercation between two officers.

4.   I do not feel that the military preservation of my prestige as commanding officer, particularly in time of war, will admit any statement tending to justify the manner in which I carry out , to the best of my ability, the laws of the U.S. and the regulations of the Coast Guard and the Navy. This also seems to be the intent of paragraph (7) of reference (c).

5.   Headquarters may feel assured that all officers and men under my command are required to carry out their assigned duties as prescribed by proper authority and that all diligence is pursued in preparing them and this unit into utmost readiness to defend their country.

6.   I feel that Headquarters will have no difficulty in forming its opinion and if, as it would appear from Mr. Thomsen's ensuing promotion to Lt.(j.g.)T, Headquarters' opinion differs from mine, I consider the matter closed and my duty ended with furnishing Headquarters all necessary information to the best of my judgement.

71- 781 Confidential.

CYANE   Ketchikan, Alaska.
                                                   7 March, 1942.

CONFIDENTIAL

MEMORANDUM for: Captain C.H. Jones.

        1.   A broader base for Headquarters' opinion
would be furnished, of course, by confidential reports specifically requested from other senior regular line officers with which Mr. Thomsen has served
recently. There are only about two such officers. They are:
                Lieutenant Commander Frank Tomkiel, Chief of Staff
                Lieutenant (j.g.) J.E. Richey.
The latter has been Mr. Thomsen's immediate superior at various times during
recent months in the capacities of commanding officer, executive officer, and
district office department head.

        2.   In the light of the attitudes displayed by the
indorsements of the attached correspondence, and the fact that Mr. Thomsen
is now permanently attached to the district staff, it would appear that an
anomalistic condition exists not compatible with the best interests of the
Service and indicating the need of change in my assignment as the solution.

        3.   Because of this; because of the forced evacuation
of my family to my home in Washington, D.C.; and because of the policy expressed in Personnel Bulletin 8-42 and my three years of sea duty; it is requested that I be transferred to duty at Headquarters, preferably in radio or communications where the Service may start to get some value out of my highly
extensive (and expensive) education.

OFFICE OF THE INSPECTOR-IN-CHIEF

COAST GUARD HEADQUARTERS

DATE 21 March, 1942.

MEMORANDUM FOR   Chief Personnel Officer.

Subject: Lieutenant (j.g.) N.P. Thomsen, U.S.C.G.R.

Inclosure: (A) All correspondence and reports on
subject case.

1.   Inclosure (A) is forwarded herein for your
information.

2.   It is recommended that no further action be
taken.

NORMAN B. HALL
Inspector in Chief

The case of Lieutenant Niels P. Thomsen, USCGR, versus Lieutenant Commander Leslie B. Tollaksen, USCG, Commanding Officer U.S.C.G. Cutter CYANE.

The rebellious crew attitude referred to by Commander Tollaksen, was the result my having to carry out his "spit and polish" uniform dress policies, which had no place in inclement Alaskan weather conditions. He insisted that the crew be dressed as though the vessel were stationed in in Hawaii where he had been stationed for three years, prior to his transfer to the CYANE as punnishment for his autocratic and eccentric behavior. He was extremely unhappy at having been assigned to a vessel normally a Lieutenants billet. Commander Tollaksen was devoid of of any consideration for the feelings of men under his command. He was very ill-tempered, when in compliance with his night orders, he was awakened at night, he would verbally abuse the Quartermaster to such an extent that they dreaded being assigned to awaken him. This was undoubtedly the reason he was not awakened the second time on the morning of the fourth of December, when he confined me to my quarters for unwarranted assumption of authority by getting underway without his presence on the bridge.

Our major confrontation had come earlier, three days after war with Japan was declared, and all Japanese-owned bank accounts were frozen. The local laundry was was owned and operated by William Tatsuda, who had lived in Ketchikan for thirty years. He was a well respected businessman, who had handled the ship's laundry for many years. Commander Tollaksen had specifically ordered me not to pay the monthly laundry bill which amounted to four hundred dollars. Over the following seven days, the laundry employees would stop by the ship saying they could not be paid because of the bank restriction. I was concerned over their plight, and after some deliberation, fully realizing that the Captain would be furious, and aware of the possible consequences, I paid the account and informed him of my action. From that day forward he made my life miserable, determiined to ruin me. I had no 'quarrel with his reaction.

It was apparent from his letters what he was attempting to accomplish, and one can read between the lines of the endorsments of the District Commander and Coast Guard Headquarters what their impressions of the conflict were. The end result was the transfer of Tollaksen. He would eventually be placed out of line of promotion and retired for medical reasons. Tollaksen was a neurotic and tortured individual. He passed away long ago, and I am not comfortable in my condemnation of him.

ADDENDUM
TWO

APA-14
U.S.S. HUNTER LIGGETT

(1)

GUADALCANAL

(2)

BOUGAINVILLE

SOLOMON ISLANDS

FORCES ARRAYED FOR THE LANDING

★ ★ ★ ★

DESTROYERS

Capt. Samuel B. Brewer (ComDesron 1)

PHELPS	Lt. Cdr. Edward L. Beck
FARRAGUT	Lt. Cdr. Henry D. Rosendal
WORDEN	Lt Cdr. William G. Pogue
MacDONOUGH	Lt. Cdr. Erle V. Dennett
DALE	Lt. Cdr. Anthony L. Rorschach

Rear Adm. Thomas C. Kinkaid (Task Group 61.1.2)

CARRIER

ENTERPRISE				Capt. Arthur C. Davis
AIR GROUP 6		1	TBF-1	Lt. Cdr. Maxwell F. Leslie
VF-6		36	F4F-4	Lt. Cdr. Louis F. Bauer
		1	F4F-7	
VB-6		17	SBD-3	Lt. Ray Davis
VS-5		18	SBD-3	Lt. Turner F. Caldwell, Jr.
VT-3		14	TBF-1	Lt. Cdr. Charles M. Jett

Screen
Rear Adm. Mahon S. Tisdale in PORTLAND

BATTLESHIP
NORTH CAROLINA	Capt. George H. Fort

HEAVY CRUISER
PORTLAND	Capt. Laurance T. DuBose

LIGHT CRUISER
ATLANTA	Capt. Samuel P. Jenkins

DESTROYERS

Capt. Edward P. Sauer (ComDesron 6)

BALCH	Lt. Cdr. Harold H. Tiemroth
MAURY	Lt. Cdr. Gelzer L. Sims
GWIN	Cdr. John M. Higgins
BENHAM	Lt. Cdr. Joseph M. Worthington
GRAYSON	Lt. Cdr. Frederick J. Bell

Transport Division "D"
Capt. Ingolf N. Kiland

Capt. Pat Buchanan
Commander Transport Division 2

CRESCENT CITY (AP-40)   Capt. Ingolf N. Kiland
(Regimental Headquarters, 2d Marines, Col. John M. Arthur)
PRESIDENT HAYES (AP-39)   Cdr. Francis W. Benson
(2nd Battalion, 2nd Marines, Lt. Col. Maj. Orin K. Pressley)
PRESIDENT ADAMS (AP-38)   Cdr. C.W. Brewington
(3rd Battlaion, 2d Marines, Lt. Col. Robert G. Hunt)
ALHENA (AK-26)   Cdr. Charles B. Hunt
(3rd Battalion, 10th Marines, Lt. Col. Manly L. Curry)

Transport Group Yoke (Tulagi Transport Group) Capt. George B. Ashe

Transport Division "E" Capt. Ashe

NEVILLE (AP-16)   Capt. Carlos A. Bailey
(2nd Battlaion, 5th Marines, Lt. Col. Harold E. Rosecrans)
HEYWOOD (AP-12)   Capt. Herbert B. Knowles
(1st Parachute Battalion, Maj. Robert H. Williams,
1st Special Weapons Battalion, Maj. Robert Lucky,
and Company E, 1st Raider Battalion)
PRESIDENT JACKSON (AP-37)   Cdr. Charles W. Weitzel
(1st Battalion, 2nd Marines, Lt. Col. Robert E. Hill)
ZEILIN (AP-9)   Capt. Buchanan
(3rd Defense Battalion, Col. Robert H. Pepper)

Cdr. Hugh W. Hadley
Commander Transport Division 12

LITTLE (APD-4)   Lt. Cdr. J.B. Lofberg
(Headquarters 1st Raider Battalion, Lt. Col Merritt Edson,
and Company A, 1st Raider Battalion)
McKEAN(APD-5)   Lt. Cdr. John D. Sweeney
(Company D, 1st Raider Battalion)
GREGORY (APD-3)   Lt. Cdr. Harry F. Bauer
(Company C, 1st Raider Battalion)
CALHOUN (APD-2)   Lt. Cdr. E.C. Loughead
(Company B, 1st Raider Battalion)

The transports embarked a total of 475 landing craft divided as follows:

(a)   8 "X" type (30-foot personnel type without ramp)
(b)   303 LCP(L) (36-foot personnel without ramps, officially "T Boats" prior to 22 June 42)

(c)   116 LCV or LCPR (36-foot personnel light vehicle type with ramp, officially "TR Boats" prior to 22 June 42)

(d)   48 LCM (45-foot medium landing craft with ramp, officially called "WL lighters" prior to 22 June 42, and sometimes still called this in contemporary reports)

Fire Support Groups
Task Group 62.3
Fire Support Group L, Capt. Frederick L. Riefkohl

HEAVY CRUISERS

VINCENNES (CA-44)	Capt. Riefkohl
QUNICY (CA-39)	Capt. Samuel N. Moore
ASTORIA (CA-34)	Capt. William G. Greenman

Rear Adm. Noyes (Task Group 61.1.3)

CARRIER

WASP   Capt. Forrest P. Sherman

AIR GROUP 72	1	TBF-1	Lt. Cdr. Wallace M. Beakley
VF-71	30	F4F-4	Lt. Cdr. Courtney Shands
VS-71	15	SBD-3	Lt. Cdr. John Eldridge, Jr.
VS-72	15	SDB-3	Lt. Cdr. Ernest M. Snowden
VT-7	9	TBF-1	Lt. Henry A. Romberg
Utility	1	J2F-5	

Screen

HEAVY CRUISERS

SAN FRANCISCO	Capt. Charles H. McMorris
SALT LAKE CITY	Capt. Ernest G. Small

DESTROYERS

Capt. Robert G. Tobin (ComDesron 12)

LANG	Lt. Cdr. John L. Wilfong
STERETT	Cdr. Jesse G. Coward
AARON WARD	Lt. Cdr. Orville F. Gregor
STACK	Lt. Cdr. Alvord J. Greenacre
LAFFEY	Lt. Cdr. William E. Hank
FARENHOLT	Lt. Cdr. Eugene T. Seaward

FUELING GROUP

PLATTE	Capt. Ralph H. Henkle
CIMARRON	Cdr. Russell M. Ihrig
KASKASKIA	Cdr. Walter L. Taylor
SABINE	Capt. Houston L. Maples
KANAWHA	Cdr. Kendall S. Reed

Rear Adm. Richmond Kelly Turner
Commander Amphibious Force South Pacific (Task Force 62) in McCAWLEY

Rear Adm. V.A.C. Crutchley, RN
Commander Escort in AUSTRALIA (Task Group 62.2)

HEAVY CRUISERS

AUSTRALIA	Capt. H.B. Farncomb, RAN
CANBERRA	Capt. Frank E. Getting, RAN
CHICAGO	Capt. Howard D. Bode

LIGHT CRUISER
HOBART   Capt. H.A. Showers, RAN

DESTROYERS
Capt. Cornelius W. Flynn (ComDesron 4)

SELFRIDGE	Lt. Cdr. Carroll D. Reynolds
PATTERSON	Cdr. Frank R. Walker
RALPH TALBOT	Lt. Cdr. Joseph W. Callahan
MUGFORD	Lt. Cdr. Edward W. Young
JARVIS	Lt. Cdr. William W. Graham, Jr.
Desdiv 7	Cdr. Leonard B. Austin
BLUE	Cdr. Harold N. Williams
HELM	Lt. Cdr. Chester E. Carroll
HENLEY	Cdr. Robert H. Smith
BAGLEY	Lt. Cdr. George A. Sinclair

Transport Group X-Ray
(Guadalcanal Trtansport Group)
Capt. Lawrence F. Reifsnider
Commander Transport Divisions, South Pacific Force in HUNTER LIGGETT

APA-14
USS HUNTER LIGGETT

TRANSPORTS
Capt. Reifsnider

HUNTER LIGGETT (AP-27)   Cdr. Louis W. Perkins, USCG
(Headquarters & Service Battery 5th Battalion, 11th Marines)
FORMALHAUT (AK-22)   Cdr. J.D. Alvis
(Equipment of 1st Engineer Battalion, Maj. James G. Frazer)
BETELGEUSE (AK-28)   Cdr. Harry D. Power
(Equipment of 3rd Defense Battalion)

MEDALS AND AWARDS

★ ★ ★ ★

Decoration	Recipient
Medal of Honor	** **MUNRO**, Douglas A., SM 1/c The highest award and the only man to receive this award in the history of the United States Coast Guard!
Navy Cross Medal	** **EVANS**, Raymond J., Lt. (jg)
Silver Star Medal	** **DEXTER**, Dwight H., Commander ** **MILLER**, Harold C., BM 2/c ** **SNYDER**, Richard T., BN 1/c ** **SPARLING**, William A., BM 2/c
Legion of Merit	** **THOMSEN**, Niels P., Lieutenant **SILER,** Owen W., Admiral
Navy & Marine Corps Medal	** **PAIN**, Rodney H.H., (R) Lt (jg)
Bronze Star Medal	** **HOWARD,** Sam F. (R) BM 2/c
Navy Commendation Medal	** **BARNARD**, Philip E., C.B.M. ** **COX**, Joe M. Jr., BN 2/c ** **GENAME**, Fred J., CMM ** **KOBIALAKA**, Edmund R., Mach. ** **LYDON**, John M., Bosn. ** **MOULTON**, William H., Lieutenant ** **HENDERSON**, John, Surfman ** **VOROBEL**, Andrew, F. 2/c (R)
Silver Life Saving Medal	** **SACCO**, Joh, Mach #3
Army Commendation Medal	**HOLTZMAN**, George W., Lt. Commander
Coast Guard commendation Medal	**ROY**, Alfred J., BN 1/c
Commandants Letter of Commendation	**BRANNON**, Wilburn R., S 2/c **HENRY**, Bernard R., Lt. (jg) **SHEWBROOKS**, William W., S 2/c 09/40
Decoration Awarded by Allied Nations: **Brazil - Medalha de Campanha**	**SOUZA**, Emanuel J., CBM

The Purple Heart

** **ALCORN**, John "Red"	Killed In Action	Guadalcanal
** **CAUDILL**, John E.	Killed In Action	Munda
** **PARKER**, R.J., US Navy	Killed In Action	Guadalcanal
** **MUNRO**, Douglas A.	Killed In Action	Guadalcanal
** **STICKNEY**, Charles M.	Killed In Action	Guadalcanal

All of the Above were Awarded Posthumously

** **BURKE,** James C.	C. Pham	USS CALLAWAY	APA
** **EADY,** Joe T.	F. 1/c	USS CALLAWAY	Munda
** **ESPARZA,** Dan	F. 1/c	USS CALLAWAY	Rendova
** **GASKILL,** Alton	BM 2/c	ALHENA - AKA-9	Torpedo
** **GRAY,** Donald P.	Cox'n	Wounded at Munda	
** **HIMES,** Joseph	F. 1/c	Wounded at Munda	
** **HOWARD,** Sam F.	BM 2/c	Wounded at Vella LaVel	
** **KINDRED,** Roy C.		LST 759	
** **PARKER,** J.P.L.	Lt (jg)	Wounded at Bougainville	
** **RYCHLIK,** Bruno	F. 1/c	ALHENA - AKA-9	Torpedo
** **STETSON,** W.S.	Surf	Wounded at Guadalcanal	
** **TROCCHIO,** Frank	MoMM	Wounded at Bougainville	
** **WAGNER,** Lionel	Cox'n	Wounded at Rendova	

Vessel Statistics

** **Indicates Combat Citation**

ADDENDUM THREE

APA-14
U.S.S. HUNTER LIGGETT

UNITED STATES NAVY
BATTLE GROUP

EMPRESS BAY
BOUGAINVILLE
NOVEMBER ONE, 1943

CAPE TOROKINA LANDING

NOVEMBER 1, 1943

III AMPHIBIOUS FORCE

Rear Admiral T.S. Wilkinson in George Clymer
Transports, <u>Commodore L.F. Reifsnider in Hunter Liggett</u>
Transdiv "A" Captain A.B. Anderson

APA	PRESIDENT JACKSON	Capt. E.P. Abernethy
APA	PRESIDENT ADAMS	Capt. Felix Johnson
APA	PRESIDENT HAYES	Capt. H.C. Flanagan
APA	GEORGE CLYMER	Capt. P.R. Talbot

Transdiv "B" Captain G.B. Ashe

APA	AMERICAN LEGION	Cdr. R.C. Welles
<u>APA</u>	<u>HUNTER LIGGETT</u>	<u>Capt. R.S. Patch USCG</u>
APA	FULLER	Capt. M.E. Eaton
APA	CRESCENT CITY	Cdr. L.L. Rowe

<u>Transdiv "C" Captain H.E. Thornhill</u>

AKA	ALCHIBA	Cdr. H.R. Shaw
AKA	ALHENA	Cdr. H.W. Bradbury
AKA	LIBRA	Cdr. F.F. Ferris
AKA	TITANIA	Capt. H.E. Berger

Total of 14,321 troops carried in the transports.

Screen, Commander Ralph Earle (Comdesron 45)

Destroyers FULLAM, GUEST, BENNETT, HUDSON, ANTHONY, WADSWORTH,
TERRY, BRAINE, SIGOURNEY, CONWAY, RENSHAW

Minecraft Group, Commander Wayne R. Loud

Destroyer-Minesweepers HOPKINS, HOVEY, DORSEY, SOUTHARD
Cdr. Loud
Minelayers ADROIT, CONFLICT, DARING, ADVENT
Lt. Cdr. A.D. Curtis USNR
Four small minesweepers (YMS)

Special Minelaying Group, Lt. Cdr. J.A. Lark (C.O. Renshaw)

BREEZE, SICARD, GAMBLE

Salvage Group
Fleet Tugs APACHE and SIOUX

Cape Torokina Landing November 1, 1943

The initial landing force for Empress Augusta Bay was the 3rd Marine Division reinforced, commanded by Major General A.H. Turnage, USMC. Many subsequent echelons were floated in LSTs but the 3rd Marines went up in style in twelve lightly combat-loaded transports and cargo ships. The separate detachments proceeded by different routes to the final rendezvous, in the vain hope of preventing Japanese air snoopers from appreciating the size and importance of the movement. Transdiv "A" left Espiritu Santo October 28th and embarked Rear Admiral Wilkinson and Lieutenant General Vandegrift at "Camp Crocodile," Guadalcanal, on the evening of October 30th. Transdiv "C" embarked troops at Guadalcanal and departed, with the four minesweepers escorting, that forenoon. Transdiv "B:" with General Turnage and Commodore Reifsnider sailed from Efate October 28th. All three met on the morning of the 31st. The Commodore then assumed the duties of O.T.C., which he retained throughout the landing and unloading. Thus united, well provided with air cover by day and night, the task force approached Bougainville along the southwest coast of the Solomons. The moon was three days old.   That coast of Bougainville had been very imperfectly charted by the German Admiralty about 1890, and nobody had troubled to correct it before the war. The principal chart, with which most of the transports were furnished, placed the positions of Cape Torokina and Mutupina Point, the two extremities of Empress Augusta Bay, respectively eight and a half and nine miles southwest of their actual locations. Fortunately, the reconnaissance planes and submarine Guardfish had supplied some major corrections to the latitude of the Bay, although even they did not get the longitude right. Near the end of the approach, when the navigating officer of a transport was asked by the captain for his ship's position, he replied, "About three miles inland, Sir!"

The minesweepers that led the van found no mines but plenty of uncharted shoals and even more were subsequently discovered by the time honored method of hitting them with a ship's bottom. Fortunately, the transport area, 4,000 to 5,000 yards from the beaches, proved to be clear of obstruction. To the forces, as they approached, Empress Augusta Bay presented a magnificent but somewhat terrifying spectacle. Behind the curved sweep of the shore line, a heavy, dark green jungle, with an occasional giant tree showing a gray trunk, swept up over foothills and crumpled ridges to the cordillera which was crowned by a smoking volcano, Mount Bagana, 8,650 feet above sea level. Wreaths of cloud and mist floated halfway between the beach and the crest, over which the sun rose at about 0630. It was wilder and more majestic scenery than anyone had yet witnessed in the South Pacific, and the thought that these thick, dank jungles and mountain fastnesses were full of Japanese pleased only the most hardened hunters. Although between two and three thousand Japanese troops were deployed along the shores of Empress Augusta Bay, the actual area of the landings was defended by only 270 men, with a single 75-mm gun on Cape Torokina. But, never before in the Pacific, had a major landing been made so close to a major enemy air base as Torokina was to Rabaul. Everyone remembered what Rabaul-based ships and planes had done to Turner's amphibious force at Guadalcanal, 562 miles away; what might they not do to a landing only 210 miles away? Hence the meticulous care with which Wilkinson had planned this operation to ensure a quick getaway before the enemy could counter attack. To a veteran of the landings in Morocco less than a year earlier, or of those in Guadalcanal in August 1942, the speed and smoothness of this unloading was astonishing. Initial troop waves in several transports were rail-loaded in LCVPs instead of crawling down into them by cargo nets, and the boats shoved off right away. There was no confusion among boat waves, no landing craft milling about for hours and making the troops seasick. Clymer had all her boats in the water in 19 minutes, and her assault waves were loaded 37 minutes after the order was given. Jackson's first wave hit the beach at 0726, forty-one minutes after the transports anchored, and four minutes ahead of H-hour. Seven to eight thousand troops were taken ashore in the first wave. A light southwesterly wind was blowing. Although the ground swell was not enough to embarrass landing craft when alongside the transports, a moderate surf was breaking on the shore. Of the twelve beaches assigned, covering a front of about four miles, those east of Cape Torokina were difficult and the three northerly ones were completely unusable. Sixty-four LCVPs and 22 LCMs were stranded, partly through the inability of the crews to handle them in surf, but mostly because the beaches were so steep that landing craft could not ground for a sufficient proportion of their length to prevent broaching and swamping. The only proportion of their length to prevent broaching and swamping. The only good beaches were those behind Puruata Island; but our preliminary bombardment had not knocked out the enemy's well-concealed machine-gun nests on that island and on Cape Torokina.

Shore gunfire harassed the landing craft, sinking four of them and hitting ten others, with a loss of 70 men. Most of this damage was inflicted by the 75-mm gun of Cape Torokina, which enfiladed the west beaches. It was well emplaced in a log and sand bunker, the approach was protected by two smaller bunkers and a series of trenches manned by a score of Japanese. Calling on four Marines to assist him, Sergeant Robert A. Owens USMC placed them so as to cover the fire ports of the two small bunkers, and then charged directly into the mouth of the gun, entering its emplacement through the fire port and driving the gun crew out of the rear door, where they were shot down. Japanese in surrounding trenches concentrated their fire on this brave Marine and his body was found riddled with bullets outside the rear entrance. From the beach two narrow corridors of dry land, raised a few feet above ground-water level, led inland; there the Marines killed or drove away the small Japanese force that resisted. This area was densely wooded, giving a great advantage to the defense; but the 2nd Marine Raider Battalion had a new auxiliary for jungle work, the 1st Marine Dog Platoon. These 24 dogs, mostly Doberman Pinschers, which had been training in New Caledonia and Guadalcanal since the summer, went forward with their handlers along the jungle trails. They proved invaluable in "pointing" snipers, concealed in the underbrush and among the roots of Banyan trees, who otherwise would have waited to cut loose along prepared lanes of fire when the main column came along. By nightfall the last enemy pillbox was reduced and the initial beachhead secured.

A unique feature of the landing was derived from a happy thought of Admiral Wilkinson, to let his transports bombard Cape Torokina. When they got the word, the crews burst out cheering. Nobody had any gridded maps and most of the shots fell in the water, but it was good clean fun that boosted morale no end. The first counterattack from Rabaul came in at 0735 on D-day; 9 "Vals" and 44 "Zekes" looked like a hundred to the Marines. Last boats of the assault waves were then clearing the ships. Admiral Wilkinson ordered all transports to get under way. Commodore Reifsnider maneuvered them in the offing for two hours. The fine work of 16 planes from Munda and Vella Lavella (8 Kittyhawks, 8 P-38s) prevented all but 12 "Vals" from getting through, and their one exploit was a near-miss on Wadsworth which killed two men and wounded five. At 0930 unloading was resumed, to be again interrupted for two hours after 1300 when a second flight of about one hundred carrier planes swooped down from New Britain. They too were beautifully conned and vectored out by Lieutenant Reginald F. Dupuy's fighter-director team in Conway. Transport American Legion, aground on an uncharted shoal with Apache and Sioux attempting to haul her off, could not retire; but she was not hit and the tugs got her clear shortly.

In order to ensure fast unloading and quick getaway, Admiral Wilkinson had seen to it that the assault transports were loaded only to one-half and the assault cargo ships only to one-quarter capacity; and most of the materiel was handled in cargo nets which were not broken between the loading port and the beach. This method of light combat loading made for balance in unloading time between all holds and for easy handling, and allowed a proportionate discharge of rations, fuel and ammunition. Moreover, a good 30 percent of the ground troops were employed in unloading at the beach. So, in spite of the two interruptions and the loss of landing craft in the surf, eight of the twelve ships were completely unloaded by 1730 the same day - a record performance, accomplished (said Admiral Halsey) "in a most brilliant manner." Some 14,000 men and 6200 tons of supplies had been put ashore in eight hours' working time.

With night coming on, our fighter cover withdrew and the ships, juiciest targets the enemy had ever seen so near to his main base, lay open to air attack. In addition, strong Japanese surface forces known to be in Rabaul might attack under cover of darkness. It was imperative that all ships withdraw for the night. Accordingly, at 1800, Admiral Wilkinson ordered all twelve transports under way, and Commodore Reifsnider led them safely out through the difficult channel by which he had approached. The four partially unladen ships contained vital stores. Wilkinson, convinced by General Vandegrift that the immediate need justified their exposure to air attack next day, detached them from the main force at midnight and sent them back to Empress Augusta Bay under the Commodore in Hunter Liggett.

A scout plane then reported the sortie of Admiral Omori's cruiser force from Rabaul. Wilkinson therefore ordered Reifsnider to reverse course and resume retirement until further orders. Soon the glad news came over the radio, first of Merrill's interception of the enemy, and then of his victory. Reifsnider could return to Torokina.

ADDENDUM FOUR

USS HUNTER LIGGETT APA 14

Guadalcanal and Bougainville
Photographs

USS HUNTER LIGGETT

RANK ORG.	NAME	DATE of RANK	MOB	MPD	Cl.	REGULAR DUTIES
Captain USCG	PERKINS, Louis Waite	12/01/42	20	20	18*	Commanding
Comdr USCG	HAHN, Edward Everett, Jr.	12/01/42	3	3		Executive
LtComdr USCG	LOWREY, Searcy James	05/01/42	12	2		Gunnery Officer
LtComdr USCG	HOLTZMAN, George Whisler	10/01/42	20	20	33*	Navigator
Lieut USCG	CROTEAU, Lawrence William	06/15/42	20	2		1st Lieutenant
Lieut USCG	MOULTON, William Harris	06/15/42	20	20		Deck WO Division Officer
Lieut USCG	THOMSEN, Niels Peter	06/15/42	3	3		Assistant Navigator
Lt. (jg) USCG	HENRY, Bernhard Russell	07/17/42	20	20	40*	Deck WO Division Officer
Lt. (jg) USCG	SHANNON, Glen Joseph	06/15/42	0	0		Deck WO Asst Div Ofcr
Lt. (jg) USCGR	DICKINSON, Farleigh Stanton, Jr	10/01/42	13	13		Comm Officer Division Ofcr
Lt. (jg) USCG	FROST, Albert	10/01/42	13	13	41*	Deck WO F.C.O.& Div Ofcr
Lt. (jg) USCGR	PARKER, William James Lewis	10/01/42	13	13		Deck W.O. Asst Div Ofcr
Lt. (jg) USCGR	SILBERMAN, Samuel Joshua	10/01/42	13	13		Deck WO Aide to Ex O
Ensign USCG	GOULDEN, Paul	02/01/42	20	13		Deck WO Asst Div Ofcr
Ens E-V(G) USNR	KISTLER, John Seidel	05/05/42	5	5		Chem Warfare, FC, WO Asst Div Ofcr
Ens D-V(S) USNR	CHURCH, Robert Goodell, Jr.	04/13/42	2	2		Deck WO Asst Div Ofcr
Ensign USCG	McGARY, James Walter	06/19/42	3	3	42*	Deck WO, Div Ofcr Asst 1st Lt
Ensign USCGR	STEVENS, Charles Sidney, Jr.	06/19/42	3	3		Deck WO Asst Div Ofcr
Ens D-V(G) USNR	GREATHOUSE, James Robert	10/22/42	1	1		Deck WO Asst Div Ofcr
Ensign USN	ANDERSON, Norman Ward	02/23/42	20	6		Deck WO, Asst Div Ofcr, Asst Comm O

* US Coast Guard Academy Class

USS HUNTER LIGGETT (APA-14)

★ ★ ★ ★

The LIGGETT earned 4 battle stars on the Asiatic Area Service Medal for participating in the following operations:

Stars	Operation	Day	Month	Year
★ 1 Star	Guadalcanal-Tulagi Landings (Including First Savo)	7 - 9	August	1942
★ 1 Star	Capture and Defense of Guadalcanal	4	November	1942
★ 1 Star	Consolidation of Solomon Islands Consolidation of Southern Solomons	7	April	1943
★ 1 Star	Treasury-Bougainville Operation	1 & 13	November	1943

Vessel Statistics

Overall Length	538 Feet
Beam	72 Feet
Speed	15 Knots
Displacement	14,174 Tons

USS HUNTER LIGGETT
Decommissioned 9 March 1946

USS HUNTER LIGGETT

RANK ORG.	NAME	DATE of RANK	MOB	MPD	Cl.	REGULAR DUTIES
Carpenter USCG	JENSEN, Carl Christian	01/25/42	10	10		Asst Div Ofcr Asst 1st Lt
Lt Cmdr USCG	JONES, Willard Lemuel	12/01/42	20	11		Eng Officer
Lieut USCG	KARL, George	06/15/42	10	10		Eng WO Division Officer
Lieut USCG	PEDERSEN, Peter	01/15/42	12	12		Eng WO Division Officer
Lieut USCG	ESTES, Otis Tillman	10/01/42	20	20	40*	Std. Engineer
Lt (jg) USCG	BAHM, Carl	06/15/42	20	20		Eng WO Division Officer
Lt (JG) E-V (G) USNR	MALLORY, Harry Burton, Jr.	06/15/42	19	13		Eng WO Asst Div Ofcr
Lt (jg) USCG	McKENNA, Thomas Francis	06/15/42	13	13		Eng Rm WO Asst Div Ofcr
Lt (jg) USCG	O'HAGEN, Joseph Elliot	06/15/42	20	20		Eng WO Division Officer
Ensign USCGR	McGRATH, Joseph Eugene	11/18/42	0	0		Std Engineer
Machinist USCG	NEELY, William Vernon	10/17/41	13	13		Eng WO Asst Div Ofcr
Comdr(MC) USN	PINNER, William Ellis	01/02/42	20	20		Senior Med Ofcr
LtCmdr(MC) V-G USNR	SOURS, James Ward	10/01/42	6	6		Asst Med Ofcr Division Officer
Lt (MC) V-G USNR	WILLIAMS, Richard Jones	01/01/42	19	19		Asst Med Ofcr
Lt V-G (MC) USNR	GOLDEN, George Michael	06/22/42	15	15		Asst Med Ofcr
Lt (MC) USN	ANGEL, Alexander Steven	08/01/41	4	4		Asst Med Ofcr Asst Dental Ofcr
Lt (jg) (MC) U-G, USNR	PALMER, Paul Vincent	05/25/42	4	4		Asst Med Ofcr
LtComdr(DC) V-G, USNR	HENN, Carl George	10/01/42	20	20		Dental Officer
Lieut USCG	HUMPHREYS, Cecil Charles	06/15/42	20	10		Supply Officer
Lt (jg) USCG	HOLLAND, Arthur Carl	10/15/42	20	10		Disbursing Ofcr Asst Supply Ofcr

- **US Coast Guard Academy Class**

USS HUNTER LIGGETT

RANK ORG.	NAME	DATE RANK	MOB	MPD	Cl.	REGULAR DUTIES
Py Clerk USCG	PROFETA, Frank	07/11/41	19	19		Division Officer Asst Supply Ofcr
Py Clerk USCG	PEPPEL, Morgan John	01/21/42	10	10		Division Officer Asst Supply Ofcr
Lt (jg) ChC. V(S), USNR	REAVES, R. James Edward	05/22/42	1	1		Chaplain
Major USMCR	MILES, Jimmy Bernard	08/07/42	1	1		Transport Quartermaster

USS HUNTER LIGGETT

RANK ORG.	NAME	DATE of RANK	MOB	MPD	Cl.	REGULAR DUTIES
Captain USCG	PATCH, Roderick Stanley	12/01/42	2	2	14*	Commanding
Comdr USCG	HAHN, Jr. Edward Everett	12/01/42	9	9		Executive
Lt Comdr USCG	LOWREY, Searcy James	05/01/42	18	8		Gunnery Officer
Lieut USCG LCDR	CROTEAU, Lawrence William	06/15/42 08/01/43	26	8		1st Lieutenant
Lieut USCG LCDR	THOMSEN, Niels Peter	06/15/42 08/01/43	9	9		Navigator
Lieut USCG	SHANNON, Glenn Joseph	03/01/43	6	6		Asst Nav Div Ofcr Deck WO
Lieut USCGR	DICKINSON, JR. Farleigh Stanton	05/15/43	19	19		Comm Ofcr
Lieut USCGR	SILBERMAN, Samuel Joshua	05/15/43	19	19		Deck WO Div Ofcr Aide to Ex O
Lieut USCG	FROST, Albert	05/15/43	19	19	41*	Deck WO Division Officer
Lt (jg) USCG	JENSEN, Carl Christian	12/15/42	16	16		Asst 1st Lieut Division Officer
Lt (jg) USCGR	MINTZ, Seymour Stanley	12/31/42	1	1		Jr. Deck WO Asst Div Ofcr
Lt (jg) USCG	GOULDEN, Paul	12/31/42	26	19		Deck Boatswain Division Officer

* US Coast Guard Academy Class

USS HUNTER LIGGETT

RANK ORG.	NAME	DATE of RANK	MOB	MPD	Cl.	REGULAR DUTIES
Lt (jg) USCGR	KENLY, Farwell	05/15/43	4	4		Jr Deck WO Asst Div Ofcr
Lt (jg) USCG	McGARY, James Walter	05/15/43	9	9	42*	Asst Div Ofcr Jr Deck WO
Ensign USN	ANDERSON, Norman Ward	02/23/42	26	12		Asst Div Ofcr Asst Deck Bos'n
Ensign USCGR	NIPP, John Harold	11/25/42	1	1		Fire Control WO Jr Asst Div Ofcr
Ensign USCGR	WEANER, Gale Howard	11/25/42	1	1		Fire Control WO Div Ofcr Asst Gunn
Ensign USCGR	CONLON, Charles Patrick	12/22/42	4	4		Fire Control WO Jr Asst Div Ofcr
Ensign USCGR	DOYLE, Joseph Noel	12/22/42	4	4		Jr Deck WO Asst Div Ofcr
Ensign USCGR	FINBURY, Herbert William	12/22/42	4	4		Asst Comm Ofcr Asst Div Ofcr
Ensign USCGR	HAGOPIAN, Noriar Nishan	01/19/43	1	1		FCWO Asst Div O C/W Off Asst 1st Lt
Ensign USCGR	FITZGERALD, Gerald Aloysius	04/14/43	0	0		Fire Control WO Jr Asst Div Ofcr
Ensign USCGR	McFARLAND, John Wells	04/14/43	0	0		Radio Officer
Gunner USCGR	HETZEL, Albert Thomas	10/08/42	0	0		Asst Div Ofcr Ord Maint Ofcr
Lt Comdr USCG	WILLIAMS, Robert Nathaniel	12/01/42	2	2		Engineer Officer
Lieut USCG	ESTES, Otis Tillman	10/01/42	26	8	40*	Division Officer Engineer WO
Lieut USCG	BAHM, Carl	03/01/43	26	26		Engineer WO Division Officer
Lieut USCGR	ANDERSON, Walter Garfield	10/05/42	0	0		Engineer WO Division Officer
Lieut USCG	LUDDEN, Francis Vincent	05/15/43	4	4		Asst Eng Ofcr
Lt (jg) USCG	NEELY, William Ellis	12/15/42	19	19		Engineer WO Asst Div Ofcr
Lt (jg) USCGR	SWIFT, Marvin Glendon	10/02/42	0	0		Asst Div Ofcr Engineer WO
Ensign USCGR	McGRATH, Joseph Eugene	11/18/42	6	6		Student Engineer

* US Coast Guard Academy Class

USS HUNTER LIGGETT

ROSTER OF OFFICERS **August 1, 1943**

RANK ORG.	NAME	DATE of RANK	MOB	MPD	Cl.	REGULAR DUTIES
Machinist USCG	FITZGERALD, John Francis	03/01/43	26	5		Engineer WO Division Officer
Major USMC	McCLYMONT, Wallace Orr	07/30/41	4	4		Transport Quartermaster
LtComdr(MC) V(S) USNR	SOWERS, Bouton Franklin	03/03/42	3	3		Senior Med Ofcr
LtComdr(MC) USN	ANGEL, Alexander Steven	03/01/43	10	10		Asst Med Ofcr, Div Ofcr, Asst Dental Of
Lieut (MC) V(S) USNR	McGURL, Frank John	06/15/42	1	1		Asst Med Ofcr Asst Div Ofcr
Lieut (MC) V-G USNR	GOLDEN, George Michael	06/22/42	21	21		Asst Med Ofcr
Lieut (jg)(DC) V-G USNR	SHOVLIN, John Francis	04/24/42	2	2		Dental Officer
Lt Comdr USCG	ARMSTRONG, Louis James	12/01/42	5	5		Supply Officer
Lt (jg) USCG	AUSTIN, Joseph Robert	10/15/42				Division Officer Disbursing Officer
Lt (jg) USCG	WHITE, Thomas Simeon	10/15/42	0	0		
Lt (jg) USCG	PROFETA, Frank	12/15/42	25	25		Division Officer Commissary Ofcr
Lt (jg) USCG	PEPPEL Morgan John	12/15/42	16	16		Division Officer Temp Disb Off
Lt(jg)ChC V(S) USNR	REAVES, James Edward	05/22/42	7	7		Chaplain

- **US Coast Guard Academy Class**

LCDR GEORGE HOLTZMAN, USCG

CAPTAIN PERKINS, USCG

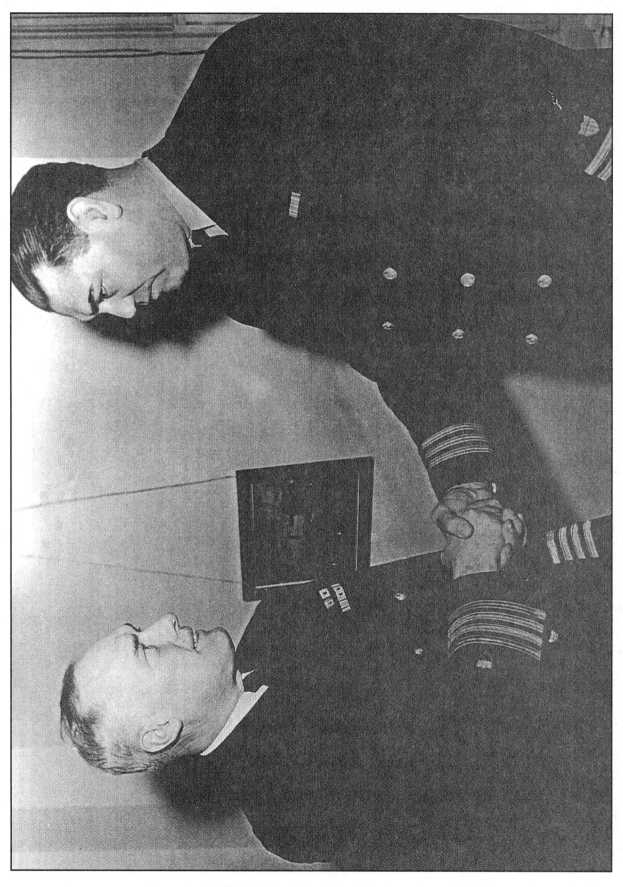

JACK DEMPSEY

CAPTAIN PERKINS

CAPTAIN PERKINS, USCG   COMMODORE H.E. THORNHILL, USN   COMMANDER E. E. HAHN, USCG

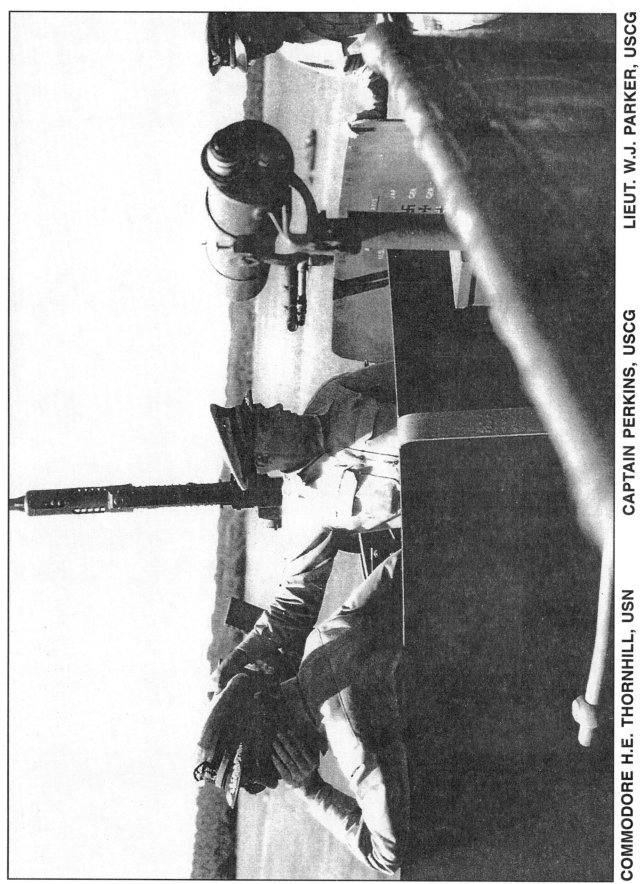

COMMODORE H.E. THORNHILL, USN

CAPTAIN PERKINS, USCG

LIEUT. W.J. PARKER, USCG

GUADALCANAL — JAP SHIP "KINGUGANA MARU"
RAN AGROUND AFTER ATTACK BY U.S. PLANES — 1942

LIEUT. CROTEAU   LCDR ARMSTRONG   CDR HAHN

"D" DAY Bougainville — Nov. 1, 1943
Empress Agusta Bay

NOVEMBER 1, 1943   EMPRESS AUGUSTA BAY BOUGAINVILLE

EMPRESS AUGUSTA BAY BOUGAINVILLE

U.S.S. HUNTER LIGGETT APA-14

164TH INFANTRY AMERICAL DIVISION DEPARTING GUADAL CANAL FOR SUVA MARCH 1, 1943

U.S. COAST GUARD

WORLD WAR TWO NAVAL EXPLOITS
A MEMOIR

BE IT REMEMBERED

MEN OF THE U.S.S. MENKAR
(AK-123)

DEDICATED TO THE MEMORY

OF

GEORGE YBARRA, SEAMAN 2ND CLASS

WHO GAVE HIS LIFE FOR HIS COUNTRY

The Song of the Menkar

By
Ray Theobald, SM 1st Class, USCGR

To Hawaii and the Marshalls,
To the Marianas, too,
Then to Guam and Morotai,
We'll sail the seas with you.

There are no waters on this earth
That we can't navigate,
We'll win this war we're fighting for,
Then see the Golden Gate.

Refrain

This is a Tribute to the Men
Who sailed across the sea,
With Captain Thomsen in command
They've all made History.

The Song of the Menkar is our Theme,
We'll sing it and believe,
That when this vessel hits the States
All hands will get thirty days leave.

To the Air of "SEMPER PARATUS."

BOOK THREE
(PLEASE TURN TO BOOK TWO PROLOGUE)

THE MEN OF THE MENKAR (AK-123)

U.S. COAST GUARD LORAN
A WORLD WAR II SECRET MISSION

U.S.S. MENKAR AK-123

THE NIGHT BEFORE CHRISTMAS
By
ROY RUSSELL, JR., S. 1ST CLASS, USCGR

'TWAS THE NIGHT BEFORE CHRISTMAS AND ALL OVER THE SHIP
THE MEN WERE THINKING ABOUT THE LENGTH OF THE TRIP;
THE STOCKINGS WERE HUNG BY THE LOCKERS WITH CARE
IN HOPES THAT ST. NICHOLAS SOON WOULD BE THERE.
SEAMEN WERE NESTLED ALL SNUG IN THEIR SACKS
WHILE VISIONS OF MR. BRADLEY MADE ACHES IN THEIR BACKS.
ALL HANDS IN THEIR SKIVVIES, IN BLANKETS DID WRAP
AND ALL SETTLED DOWN FOR A LONG WINTER'S NAP.
WHEN UP ON DECK THERE AROSE SUCH A CLATTER
I LEAPT FROM MY BUNK TO INVESTIGATE THE MATTER.
UP TO THE LADDER I FLEW LIKE A FLASH,
TRIPPED OVER DUFFY'S SHOES AND FELL WITH A CRASH!
AND THEN TO MY WONDERING EYES DID APPEAR
NOT PRANCER AND DANCER BUT A BOS'N MATE DEAR.
THE MAN WITH THE REINS SO LIVELY AND QUICK,
MORE RESEMBLED SAM HART THAN IT DID ST. NICK.
HE SPOKE NOT A WORD BUT WENT STRAIGHT TO WORK
AND SHOOK ALL THE SLEEPERS WHO WOKE WITH A JERK,
THEY SPRANG TO THE DECK AS HE GAVE A WHISTLE
AND AWAY WE FLEW LIKE THE DOWN-OF-THE-THISTLE!
'TWAS THEN MR. CHALLENGER CAME FROM UP BY THE STACK
TO TELL THE MEN TO THEIR SLEEP TO GO BACK.
THEN EXPLAINED TO THEM ALL WITH A FROWN
THAT THE COURSE HAD BEEN PLOTTED UPSIDE DOWN.
O'ER THE P.A. SYSTEM THEOBOLD SHRIEKED
    "SECURE FROM YOUR STATIONS."
VERY PROFANE WERE THE MEN'S EXCLAMATIONS
AS THEY RETURNED TO THEIR SACKS FOR MORE REST,
THE WORDS THEY USED WERE NOT WEBSTER'S BEST!
I COULD TELL MUCH MORE BUT I HAVEN'T THE TIME
BESIDES MR. PEELING, MIGHT CALL IT A CRIME.
MAY I GET MORE SACK DRILL AND MAY I SAY TO YOU,
A MERRY CHRISTMAS TO OUR SHIP AND ITS CREW.

Book Three

MEN OF THE MENKAR (AK-123)
ADDENDUM

17TH U.S. Coast Guard District
Ketchikan, Alaska

9TH Coast Guard District
Toledo, Ohio
CGC TUPELO

17TH U.S. Coast Guard District
Ketchikan, Alaska

Postscript

Author

TABLE OF CONTENTS

TABLE OF CONTENTS

ORDERS, DOCUMENTS, PHOTOGRAPHS

ORDERS, DOCUMENTS, PHOTOGRAPHS

ORDERS, DOCUMENTS, PHOTOGRAPHS

Chapter 1

US COAST GUARD
LORAN CONSTRUCTION DETACHMENT
IN THE
PACIFIC THEATER

 The Coast Guard's Construction Detachments, the major portion of which served in the combat area of the Pacific Ocean, were created for the purpose of carrying out the civil engineering work necessary to the success of the Loran program. The history of the Coast Guard Construction Detachments, therefore, is a history of the establishment of Loran stations as aids to navigation. This monograph lays greatest emphasis upon the civil engineering aspects of Loran installations, leaving to others the task of preparing a history of the electronic features of the work. This brief introductory section on the history and development of Loran serves only to lead us up to the principal features of this account.

LORAN AS AN AID TO NAVIGATION

Loran, its name compounded of the initial letters of the word - LOng RaNge Navigation, is a system whereby a vessel with suitable equipment, comparatively easy to operate, and with special charts may determine her position even when hundreds of miles from shore.

This new electronic development is a method of navigation having a long effective range. It may be used with reliability, as far as approximately 800 miles from the transmitting station in daytime and 1,400 miles at night. Loran uses a wavelength for long-range radio communications at nighttime. Its waves are reflected from the iono-sphere and follow around the earth's surface as do the familiar broadcasting waves. The speed and time of travel of these radio waves are very reliable and stable. One of the basic characteristics of the Loran system is that it uses pulse transmission, which permits measurement of the time travel of the signals.

Navigation with the aid of Loran signals has been demonstrated to be entirely practical. In this new system, an infinite number of lines of position are laced over the earth's surface by radio. To provide the necessary signals, ground stations are appro-priately located to cover the areas to be served. Two shore stations operating as a Loran "pair" lay down a set of these lines of position over a portion of the earth. By means of a Loran-receiver indicator aboard ship connected to an ordinary antenna, the navigator, selects a pair of signals, depending on the area in which he is operating. The difference in the time of travel of the radio waves from the two ground stations is measured, and the line of position is deduced from this time difference. The time difference, not the direction of the waves, is the factor that determines the line of position.

Thus, by making two or more readings on two or more pair of signals, the navi-gator may obtain his fix. The average operator requires approximately two minutes to obtain the readings that provide a line of position. A rotatable antenna is not required, and the ship, or (aircraft) does no sending. Special charts for the area served by Lo-ran, show the lines of position necessary to utilize the system. The readings taken from the receiver on board ship are plotted on the Loran Chart for the determination of the fix.

Loran does not use continuous wave radio transmission, but special types of pulsed signals. This is probably the most important electronic character of the Loran system. Pulse transmission systems make possible the measurement of time of travel of the radio signals whereas continued wave transmission is not suited to such mea-surement. Loran is not a radio direction finder system and can more properly be classed as a new system of radio distance finding. Since the speed of travel of radio waves is much more stable and reliable than any other radio wave propagation characteristics, this accounts in part for the high order of accuracy of the Loran system.

THE DEVELOPMENT OF LORAN EQUIPMENT

The radiation laboratory of the Massachusetts Institute of Technology devel-oped loran during 1941 from ideas proposed earlier. This development work was under the supervision of the National Defense Research Council.

Specialists working at MIT, the Massachusetts Institute of Technology, built experimental models of transmitting and receiving equipment, in surveying sites, in-stalled transmitters, computed tables and demonstrated the possibilities of the sys-tem. Original experiments, made in 1941, used frequencies of 2.5 to 8 megacycles with low power. The attempts to obtain the desired ground wave were unsatisfactory, but with a frequency of 2.0 megacycles the sky wave was deemed practical.

FIRST STATION BUILT

First experimental transmitting stations were located at Montauk Point, Long Island and Fenwick, Delaware, in two abandoned Coast Guard lifeboat stations. These stations operated on 1950 kilocycles, 25 pulses per second, specific pulse recurrent rate 0. Synchronization of these stations was attempted in December 1941; success was attained by January 1942, when the observer went to Bermuda to test the effectiveness of the system at long range.

The first demonstration of the use of Loran was made on 12 June 1942, with a laboratory of an LRN receiver and indicator installed on the airship K-22 during a flight south from Lakehurst along the Coast of New Jersey and Delaware to Ocean City, MD. Since only the Fenwick-Montauk Stations were in operation at the time, it was impossible to obtain fixes. Good ground wave signals were observed, however, to the two hundred mile extremity of the trip. The procedure of homing on a Loran hyperbole was used, and position-line accuracy of the system along the base line was verified.

On 4 July, 1942, the first readings from a plane were made on a laboratory built received-indicator installed in a B-24, during a test flight from Boston to Cape Sable, N.S. Good signals were received and useful data obtained on the range of the signals from stations M and F.

The first observations from a ship were made on the Coast Guard Cutter MANASQUAN during a weather cruise off Newfoundland from 18 July, to 17 July 1942. Observations of both ground and skywave signals during that period indicated a total range of 1300 nautical miles and an overlap of ground and sky coverage. The results were considered good enough to warrant the expansion of the system and it's recommendation to navigational agencies.

Experimental services was extended by the construction of a slave station at Baccaro, Nova Scotia, to operate with the double-pulsed master at Montauk Point, on specific pulse recurrent rate 2. This station was constructed during the late summer, and was placed in service on 1 October 1942, being operated by the Royal Canadian Navy.

Preliminary tables for the three rates were computed and the Radiation Laboratory during August, September, and October 1942, and were reproduced for temporary experimental use.

On 1 November 1942, a test flight was made to Bermuda in a PBY for the purpose of demonstrating the use of Loran in obtaining fixes. Representatives of the Bureau of Aeronautics, the Radiation Laboratory, Army Air Forces and other interested activities were in the flight party. The demonstration was so successful that the observers were convinced that Loran could perform an important service to the war effort. In 1942, the National Defense Research Committee started the construction of the Northwest Atlantic Loran chain, and completed it in early 1943.

COAST GUARD ASSUMES CONTROL

On 1 January 1943, the administration of Loran was officially transferred to the Navy. After a short period of test operation, the Montauk and Fenway stations were transferred from the operational cognizance of the Radiation Laboratory to that of the Coast Guard. Three stations in Nova Scotia had been transferred on 1 October 1942 to the Royal Canadian Navy. The Loran chain then stretched from Fenwick, Delaware, to Fredericksdal, Greenland. This chain provided coverage to points about 600 miles from the continental limits in the daytime and about 1,400 miles at night. This included coverage of Davis Strait. Originally no coverage was provided for the Gulf of St. Laurence. Monitor stations were established in the United States by the Coast Guard and in Canada by the Canadian Navy, as soon as the system passed from the experimental stage, early in 1943.

The Coast Guard had been directed on 31 October 1943, to establish three new stations, as follows: A single master station at Fredericksdal (Narsak), Greenland; a double slave at Battle Harbor, Labrador; and a single master at Bonavista, Newfoundland. The Radiation Laboratory, the Royal Canadian Navy and the United States Coast Guard had already done siting during the summer of 1942. Surveys were also made during November and December to establish coordinates; and in December arrangements were made by the Division of Research of the Hydrographic Office for the computation of a table for utilization of the Loran service from stations V-L, at Bonavista and Battle Harbor.

The Navy had followed the development of the system with interest, through its office of Research and inventions. The Hydrographic Office had been concerned at an early date because of the obvious necessity for the production of special tables and charts. On 13 June, 1942, Commander Gordon A. Patterson, USN (ret), Officer in charge of the Division of Research of the Hydrographic, and Mr. E.B. Collins, Senior Nautical Scientist of the Division, had met with Rear Admiral Julius A. Furer, Director of Research and Inventions, to review progress of Loran. On July 29 a conference of all interested parties was held. Progress reports given at this meeting included the following statements: Experimental stations at Montauk and Fenwick were in operation; the Canadians were building two stations in Nova Scotia (Baccaro and Deming) under the supervision of the Radiation Laboratory; sites had been chosen for stations in Newfoundland; and Greenland suggested as a possible location. On 15 August 1942, Dr. Fletcher G. Watson, then of the Radiation Laboratory visited the Hydrographic Office to exhibit sample tables prepared at the Radiation Laboratory and to report further developments.

The practicability of Loran as an aid to both surface and air navigation, and particularly its military value, having been demonstrated, through the erection of stations on the Atlantic Coast, by the Radiation Laboratory of the Massachusetts Institute of Technology, the Army and Navy assumed cognizance. The Navy became responsible for future Loran installations, and for procuring Loran receiving equipment for shipboard use. The Army took on the work of procuring Loran apparatus for use in planes. Construction and operation of new Loran stations was assigned to the Coast Guard.

While the first Loran stations were constructed and manned by personnel of the Radiation Laboratory, this organization soon realized that it had neither the experience or the personnel to construct and man a large number of such stations, especially if these were to be located beyond the confines of the United States.

To provide reliable Loran service from an isolated location, it was necessary that the units be entirely self-sustaining. From experience already gained, it was apparent that a typical station would consist of several buildings.

There was a need for a building to house the technical apparatus and the communications system, a power hut for the diesel electric generators and other parts of the power plant, and a building serving as an office and quarters for the officers, and two buildings to be used as crew's quarters, mess hall, galley, and sick bay. In addition, the antenna and ground system for Loran transmission, and receiving consisted of seven 85-foot poles, and various wires and cables. Sewage disposal arrangements, a water system and other similar items would also need to be provided.

As the rapidity with which service could be provided after a new chain of Loran stations was authorized was of utmost importance, the type of construction would be that lending itself to speedy construction. However, quick construction was not the only important feature. Reliability of service would depend on careful installation, for the replacement of parts was a difficult and time-consuming process. In addition, the crews would live for many months under conditions of extreme isolation. Extremes of climate were also to be expected for most stations would be either close to the Arctic Circle or the Equator.

There were some differences in the technical equipment of the various types of Loran stations. A double master station would have one transmitter and one timer for each "rate," with a duplicate of each of these pieces of equipment on standby service. A slave station would have one transmitter and one timer, with spares for each of these. A monitor station would require a receiver-indicator, and would have four or five of these. All types of stations would have substantially the same power requirements. The antenna and ground systems would be alike for all but the monitor stations that required less elaborate equipment of this type.

CIVIL ENGINEERING ASPECTS OF WORK

At this stage it became obvious that there was a need for a definite organization for the building and operating of Loran stations. With the experimental work completed, and with machinery already in existence through which contracts for equipment could be awarded, the problem divided itself into two major and several minor parts. Of first magnitude was the civil engineering work necessary to place such stations in effective operation in many remote and extremely isolated spots over a large portion of the world. It was obvious that this engineering work would have to be carried out at great distance from normal sources, and also that when the stations were commissioned they would have to be self-sustaining to a high degree. Where the experimental stations had been hastily constructed with the chief thought the prompt testing of the apparatus, the permanent station presented many other problems.

The civil engineering aspects of the Loran construction program were turned over to the Coast Guard's Civil Engineering Division, operating under the Engineer in Chief. This division, had a background of invaluable experience, for many of the small shore stations, lighthouses, and similar facilities of the Coast Guard had been built under the same type of conditions to be encountered in erecting Loran stations.

The second major problem was the operation and maintenance of the Loran stations once they were built. This was a two-fold task, shared by the Coast Guard's communication division and the Civil Engineering Division. Equipment strictly Loran was the responsibility of the communications engineering group, while buildings, power, and other equipment, were civil engineering matters.

The Joint Chiefs of Staff laid down a general Loran program in November 1943, to conform with anticipated military needs. This plan listed various chains of Loran stations in the forward areas, and indicated the order in which they would probably be needed. As the war progressed, the Joint Chiefs of Staff indicated which stations were most urgently needed, and thus guided the actual construction program. The Coast Guard, knowing in advance, the probably order in which chains would be needed, anticipated the individual directives and assembled material and personnel and made most of its arrangements in advance, greatly shortening the time between the receipt of orders and the on-the-air date.

In the planning of the Loran system, it was the policy to first establish chains in the bad weather areas where military operations were being conducted. On the Atlantic Coast, the first stations were in the Northeastern States, in Labrador, Newfoundland, and Greenland.

These stations provided much needed assistance to navigators in areas where celestial navigation was frequently impossible, and served the major routes of overseas traffic between the United States and Europe. In the Pacific, the first Loran stations were constructed in the Bering Sea and among the Aleutian Islands, easily classed as among the foggiest spots in the world.

FORMATION OF CONSTRUCTION DETACHMENTS

Coast Guard Headquarters developed two types of personnel for Loran work, construction detachments were formed to handle the actual construction and installation of the stations, and operating units were created to serve as the permanent crews after the stations were on-the-air. During the construction period, the operating forces were merged with those of the construction units, to expedite the building operations. The Coast Guard crew of the MENKAR, after this vessel was assigned to Loran work, also became a special group experienced in the handling of construction material between the ship and the open beaches.

Officers of all Coast Guard Construction Detachments were under the command of the Chief of the Civil Engineering Division at Headquarters, Captain Ralph R. Tinkham, USCG who directed the work and operations of the detachments through the Advanced Base Section of that division, of which his Executive, Lieutenant Commander Edward P. Wagner, USCGR, was Chief.

The fact that several Divisions of the Navy Department, as well as other Divisions of the Coast Guard were involved in planning, implementing, and finally operating the system of Loran chains, required close liaison between all these groups throughout the construction period. This was effected through representation of the various divisions and occasional conferences of their chiefs.

Lieutenant Commander Edward P. Wagner, USCGR, Executive Assistant of the Chief of the Civil Engineering Division, Coast Guard Headquarters, and Chief of its Advance Base Section, responsible for the procurement and supply for construction Detachments, and for the construction and installation of all Loran stations up to the point of final commissioning in an operating status, represented the Civil Engineering Division of the Coast Guard.

Commander Laurence M. Harding, USCG, Assistant Chief of the Communications Engineering Division Coast Guard Headquarters, represented that Division, and was responsible for the electronic equipment supplied for Loran stations.

Commander Frederick G. Wild, USCG, represented the Aids to Navigation Division Coast Guard Headquarters, responsible for operating Loran stations when placed in commission.

Lieutenant Commander Arthur F. Van Dyke, USNR, represented the office of the Chief of Naval Operations, responsible for planning Loran chains for the approval of the Joint Chiefs of Staff, and for the development of Loran apparatus.

Four Coast Guard Construction Detachments were organized as the program developed, each with a commanding officer and an executive officer, and essential field office personnel. Each detachment was further divided into three sections, each with a commanding cfficer and technical assistants, to permit simultaneous constructions of three stations in a chain of widely separated sites. All officers were civil engineers and experienced construction men, and enlisted personnel were selected for experience and skill in essential trades.

Construction Detachment A (Unit 26) was organized to complete the Bering Sea chain and to construct the Western Aleutians (Alaska) Loran chain. Subsequently transferred to the Central Pacific, this construction detachment constructed the Marshall Island chain and later performed the work of converting the previously completed Hawaiian, Phoenix and Marshall Island chains from DC to AC power.

Construction Detachment B (Unit 192) was organized to carry out work on the Atlantic Coast. It stood in readiness to extend Loran coverage in the Eastern Atlantic for European combat operations and subsequently installed new stations in Newfoundland and on the Southeast Atlantic Coast of the United States. After V-J Day this construction detachment was assigned to the construction of the United States

Pacific Coast Loran chain.

Construction Detachment C (Unit 80) built the Hawaiian chain, and the Japan chain. Construction Detachment D (Unit 211) built the Phoenix Island Chain, Palau-Morotai chain and the China Sea chain. The Command Unit of the Coast Guard Construction Detachments of the Pacific Ocean Areas (Unit 203) was organized to direct field operations of construction Detachment A, C, and D, and maintain liaison with CincPac, Commander-in-Chief Pacific, and CincPoa USN, Commander-in-Chief Pacific Ocean Area, therefore its headquarters were first at Honolulu, Hawaii, and then at Guam. Lieutenant Commander John F. Martin was the first commanding officer, and on 17 September 1944, was relieved by Lieutenant Commander (later Commander) Kenneth W. Donnell, USCGR, who completed the program in the Pacific. Construction Detachment Supply Base (Unit 290) was established at Sand Island, Honolulu.

Early in January 1945, Command Unit 203, commanded by Lieutenant Commander K.W. Donnell, USCGR, was ordered to move to Guam, and at the same time its functions were newly defined. It was made operationally responsible for the movement and operation of the three detachments, the plane, the MENKAR, the Advance Base Staging Detachment and the Charting Element. All matters of design, siting, and the supervision of construction and testing of stations in the Pacific were included.

LORAN COMMAND UNIT TRANSFERRED TO SUBIC BAY

Because of expanding Coast Guard activities in the Western Pacific, including not only the erection and maintenance of Loran stations, but other aids to navigation, and the carrying out of Marine Inspection functions, plans were made in the early part of 1945 to move the Loran Command Base to Subic Bay in the Philippines. This move was made in June 1945 on arrival of the USS MENKAR (AK-123).

LORAN ACTIVITIES TOP SECRET OR SECRET

From their inception until the close of the war Loran activities were designated as TOP SECRET or SECRET. Comparatively few persons in the Coast Guard, outside the divisions directly involved, were aware of this new electronic development and of the plans for providing coverage of a large portion of the world with these signals.

Necessary as was the secret designation of the work, it acted, many times, as a handicap, for in dealing with the multitude of military commands, the Loran construction personnel were not always able to clearly indicate the nature of their work, and thus demonstrate the need for prompt cooperation. Too, the Coast Guard's Loran personnel served throughout the entire war with no public recognition, for the very existence of this work remained largely unknown.

The rapid and accelerated installation of the U.S. Coast Guard Loran System of Navigation was one of the highest priority to the United States Airforce B-29 bombing program of the Japanese main Islands. It introduced precision bombing from high altitudes in heavy weather and periods of low visibility. Without Loran the B-29 program would have been difficult, if not impossible, to bomb from such high altitudes. It is safe to say that the use of Loran hastened the capitulation of the Japanese Empire and undoubtedly prevented the loss of countless thousands of American and Japanese lives.

Chapter 2

USS MENKAR (AK-123)

Shortly after its organization, the Loran Construction Command Unit 203 attacked the problem of expediting the delivery of Loran construction material. As one of the earliest and ever present difficulties which had been encountered in the construction of Loran stations regardless of their location, had been the securing of prompt delivery of construction equipment and its landing adjacent to the construction sites, it was apparent that a permanent solution of this problem was necessary. The securing of cargo space from other military services for comparatively small shipments had proven very unsatisfactory because of the sudden changes in schedule, re-routing, and other exigencies of ship movements beyond the control of the Coast Guard.

Too, many vessels assigned to transport Loran materials were not equipped with suitable lifting gear for the type of landing operations frequently involved. The solution of these transport problems was sought in the request for the assignment of a Victory type vessel to the Coast Guard solely for Loran work. As a result of this request the Navy Transportation Service in September, 1944 assigned to the Coast Guard the U.S.S. MENKAR (AK-123) a standard type Liberty ship, from which it would remove the Navy crew. The MENKAR was a single screw, oil burning, reciprocating engine propelled ship, having a length of 445 feet, a beam of 57 feet and a loaded draft of 23 feet.

Lieutenant Commander Niels P. Thomsen, USCG, a ship's Captain from the former Lighthouse Service which had been absorbed by the Coast Guard in 1940,

11

was selected to command the MENKAR. The balance of the ship's crew would be provided by the Coast Guard Training and Manning Station at Alameda, California, and the vessel assigned to Coast Guard Loran Command Unit 203, for the purpose of transporting Loran station gear and personnel to forward area sites. The Loran personnel on board would be the responsibility of the Commanding Officer of Unit 203. The commanding Officer of the MENKAR would be responsible for the vessel, it's boats and crew, as well as the landing of supplies and equipment above the high-water point on the landing sites. The MENKAR's Coast Guard crew would consist of sixteen Coast Guard officers, one U.S. Public Health doctor, plus 160 Coast Guard enlisted men.

The passengers would be approximately 100 to 150 Coast Guard Loran construction personnel, 120 Marines, and fifty trained police dogs and their trainers. A specified number of Marines and dogs would be assigned to each Loran station for security reasons, many of the sites being in forward areas that were subject to attack by Japanese forces. Explosive charges were also to be left at each site, so the station could be instantly destroyed in the event of enemy attack.

Op 39A-mgc
Serial 097939
(SC)A4-3/AK123-

CONFIDENTIAL

9 September, 1944

From: Chief of Naval Operations
To :   Commandant, U.S. Coast Guard

Subj: Assignment U.S.S. MENKAR (AK123) for Loran System installation.

Refs: (a) CNO conf ser 0258220 of 25 Jul '44.
        (b) Comdt Coast Guard sec ltr CG-626, 815 of 20 Jul '44 to CNO.

1. The functions of installing, operating, maintaining and supplying of U.S. Navy Loran transmitting stations were centralized in the U.S. Coast Guard by ref (a). The special type cargo vessel requested in ref (b) to expedite transportation of equipment for the rapid establishment of these installations has been designated as the U.S.S. MENKAR. This vessel is a converted Liberty ship having facilities for accommodating 50 troop officers and 1000 enlisted men on short hauls with dry cargo capacity in the holds for 288,458 cu. ft. (bale). The MENKAR will be made available at San Francisco for loading not later than 30 September.

2. The Commandant is directed to provide the necessary Coast Guard personnel to man this vessel replacing the present U.S. Navy crew. The following complement has been recommended by Bureau of Naval Personnel: 15 officers, 8 CPO's and 164 enlisted men (including 2 officers and 18 men for 2-LCM(3)'s and 2-LCVP's).

3. It is understood that passenger accommodations are desired for only 25 officers and 315 enlisted men. Therefore, by copy of this letter, Bureau of Ships is requested to authorize the removal of all troop berthing in #1 twee deck and berthing forward of frame #60 in #2 tween deck. Present berthing f 51 troop officers on port side of #3 tween deck should also be reduced to 25 and accommodations improved. Additional cargo capacity obtained in #1 and # tween decks: 70,000 cu.ft. It is desired that these alterations be expeditiously accomplished during the loading period if practicable.

4. The U.S.S. MENKAR will remain assigned to Naval Transportation Service but will be under CinCPac's operational control.

A. McGLASSON
By direction

16 SEPTEMBER 1944

162152

RESTRICTED X DIRECT LT COM NIELS P THOMSEN COTP MORRO

BAY REPORT CO MANNING SECTION WITHOUT DELAY X YOU DESIGNATE SUCH

RELIEF AS YOU CONSIDER QUALIFIED BT 162152

FROM: COMDT CG

TO: DCGO 12HHHHHHH
                  NAVDIST

Certified to be a true copy:

G. C. Fonger, Lieut., USCG

UNITED STATES COAST GUARD
San Francisco 26, Calif.

ORDER #O-791
Address Reply to
DISTRICT CAOST GUARD OFFICER
TWELFTH NAVAL DISTRICT (p)
Refer tofile CG-71-531-701

18 September, 1944

To: Lieut-Comdr Niels P. Thomsen, USCG
        COTP, Morro Bay, California

Subj: Orders; transfer; new assignment; travel

1.   In compliance with HD 162152 (SEPTEMBER, 1944) you are hereby
detached from all duties previously assigned in the 12th Naval
District. You are directed to proceed without delay to Alameda,
California and report to the CO, CG Manning Section, that place, for
assignment to duty.

2.   This order constitutes a permanent change of station from your
last permanent station to such permanent station as may be assigned
to you by the CO, CG Manning Section, Alameda, California.

3.   The travel necessary, totheexecution hereof is required by the
public interests.

4.   Mileage is allowed, chargeable against HQ travel allotment symbol
No. 051-20.

                                        /s/ S. B. JOHNSON
                                            By direction

CC¹ HQ
    FINANCE

Ind-1
COTP, Morro Bay, Calif.
18 Sept. 1944

Departed 1500 this date.

                                        /s/ NIELS P. THOMSEN

Ind-2
CGTS, MANNING SECTION
Alameda, California
19 September, 1944

1100, this date, repoted this unit for further assignment to duty. Public
quarters availa ble this date. None available for assignment to your depende

                                        /s/ J. D. ELLISON   Certified to bo a Tr
                                            By direction

                                                           G. C Forger, Lieut.
                        12-C

U. S. COAST GUARD
OFFICIAL DISPATCH

UNIT   CG BASE ALAMEDA CALIF.   DATE   23 SEPT 1944

INCOMING HEADING

C O N F I D E N T I A L   222146

TEXT

FOR ACTION COMDR EVANS O I C MANNING SECTION X DELIVER FOLLOWING ORDERS TO PCO MENKAR AK ONE TWO THREE X UPON YOUR RELIEF OF

PRESENT C O AK ONE TWO THREE ABOUT TWO SEVEN SEPT REPORT TO CINCPAC UNDER WHOSE OPERATIONAL CONTROL VESSEL WILL OPERATE AND FROM WHOM MOVEMENT ORDERS WILL BE RECEIVED

CERTIFIED TO BE A TRUE COPY:

J D Ellison

J. D. ELLISON, Lt.(jg), USCGR

OPERATOR'S RECORD   0038/BE/MN/   TIME:

                                   INITIALS OF "ACTION" OFFIC

FROM

COMMANDANT

TO (FOR ACTION)

CO CGTS ALAMEDA   RRRR

	URGENT
	PRIORIT
RRRR	ROUTIN
	DEFERR
	MAILGR
	ACKNO

TO (FOR INFORMATION)

DCGO 12ND
DCGO 14ND
CONDET 203
CINCPAC

	URGENT
	PRIORIT
	ROUTIN
	DEFERR
	MAILGR
	ACKNO

† "ACTION" OFFICER INITIAL AND RETURN ORIGINAL TO RADIOROOM, RETAINING COPY

U. S. GOVERNMENT PRINTING OFFICE   16—20203-1

U. S. COAST GUARD

OFFICIAL DISPATCH

UNIT DCGO 14TH   DATE 13 OCTOBER 1944

INCOMING HEADING

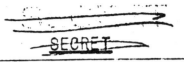

DEFERRED   132016 ·   ~~SECRET~~

TEXT

FROM CINCPAC ACTION COMFWDAREA INFO DCGO RPT DCGO FOURTEENTH
NAVDIST X USS MENKAR X MY ZERO EIGHT TWO ONE THREE FIVE X
DEPARTING PEARL FOURTEEN OCT SOA RPT SOA TWELVE KNOTS FOR
ENIWETOK VIA KWAJALEIN FOR FURTHER ROUTING TO GUAM OR SAIPAN
AS DIRECTED BY YOU X REQUEST LTCOM STOFFLE USCG AND COMDR
HERBERT USCG BE INFORMED

CC: CONDET 203
     COMDR WILD
     MRS WILKINS

RHT   TOR 2257   ND NR 144

                     TIME:
               INITIALS OF "ACTION" OFFICER

OPERATOR'S RECORD

FROM

CINCPAC

TO (FOR ACTION)	
	URGENT
	PRIORITY
	ROUTINE
COM FWDAREA	DEFERRED
	MAILGRAM
	ACKNOWLEDGE
TO (FOR INFORMATION)	URGENT
	PRIORITY
DCGO 14TH: USS MENKAR	ROUTINE
	DEFERRED
	MAILGRAM
	ACKNOWLEDGE

"ACTION" OFFICER INITIAL AND RETURN ORIGINAL TO RADIOROOM, RETAINING COPY

16—30203-1

AK-123
P17-1/00
UVM/wlm

U.S.S. MENKAR
(AK-123)

27 September 1944.

From: Lieutenant Commander Ural V. Martin, D-M, U.S.N.R.
To :   The Chief of Naval Operations.

Subj: Relieving of Command, U.S.S. MENKAR.

Ref :   (a) U.S. Navy Regulations, Article 824.
       (b) CNO ltr, Op 39A-mgc, Serial 097939, (SC)A4-3/AK-123
           of 9 September 1944.
       (c) CNO Conf. Serial 0258220 of 25 July 1944.
       (d) Comdt Coast Guard sec ltr CG-626, 815 of 20 July
           1944 to CNO.

    1.   In accordance with reference (a), I have to report having
been relieved of the command of the U.S.S. MENKAR (AK-123) by Lieutenant Commander Niels P. THOMSEN, 30634, U.S.C.G, in compliance with
reference (b).

    2.   A thorough inspection of the U.S.S. MENKAR has been made
by me in company with my relief.

    3.   The following defects were pointed out to my relief and
accounted for as indicated: NONE.

                                      Ural V. Martin,
                                      Lt. Comdr., U.S.N.R.

- -

                                      U.S.S. MENKAR (AK-123)
                                      c/o Fleet Post Office,
                                      San Francisco, Calif.
                                      27 September 1944.

    On inspection of the U.S.S. MENKAR (AK-123), I found
conditions as reported above.

                                      Niels P. Thomsen,
                                      Lt.Comdr., U.S.C.G.

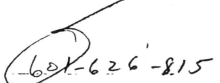

U.S.S. MENKAR
(AK-123)

San Francisco, California

28 September, 1944

To: The Commandant

Subj: USS MENKAR (AK-123); Change of Command

1.   In accordance with H/L, dated 20 July, 1944, file CG-626-815, a change of command was effected aboard this vessel at 1300, 27 September, 1944.

2.   Accordingly, the inclosure is forwarded herewith.

Incl: N. P. THOMSEN
co-Joint ltr from LtCdr U.V.
MARTIN, USNR, and LtCdr N.P.
THOMSEN, USCG, to OpNav, dated
27 September, 1944 (P17-1/00).

U. S. COAST GUARD
OFFICIAL DISPATCH

UNIT DCGO 14TH   DATE 13 OCT 1944

INCOMING HEADING

SECRET

PRIORITY - OPERATION MSG   132240   SECRET

TEXT

CINCPAC SENDS ACTION MENKAR PAREN ABLEKING ONETWOTHREE PAREN INFO

COMINCH COMSERVPAC COMTWELVE COMFOURTEEN COMTASKFOR FIVE SEVEN AN

CTF NINESIX X USCG RPT USCG FOURTEENTH NAVDIST CMA NOT AN ADEE

CMA PASS INFOR TO USCG PACAREA CODETS RPT CODETS X ALSO INFOR

COMDT CHARLIE GEORGE WASH PAREN RDO WASH PASS PAREN X REPORT

TO PORT DIRECTOR PEARL HARBOR FOR ROUTING TO ENIWETOK VIA

KWAJALEIN X ARRIVAL REPORT COMTASKFOR FIVESEVEN FOR ORDERS

CC: CONDET 203
    COMDR WILD
    MRS WILKINS

RHT TOR 0020 ND NR 147

                                              TIME:_____
OPERATOR'S RECORD   INITIALS OF "ACTION" OFFICER
FROM

.CINCPAC

TO (FOR ACTION)		
		URGENT
		PRIORITY
MENKAR		ROUTINE
		DEFERRED
		MAILGRAM
		ACKNOWLEDGE
TO (FOR INFORMATION)		URGENT
		PRIORITY
COMINCH: COMSERVPAC: COMTWELVE: COMFOURTEEN:		ROUTINE
COMTASKFOR 57: CTF 96: CONDET 203: COMMANDANT		DEFERRED
		MAILGRAM
		ACKNOWLEDGE

"ACTION" OFFICER INITIAL AND RETURN ORIGINAL TO RADIOROOM, RETAINING COPY

16—20203—1

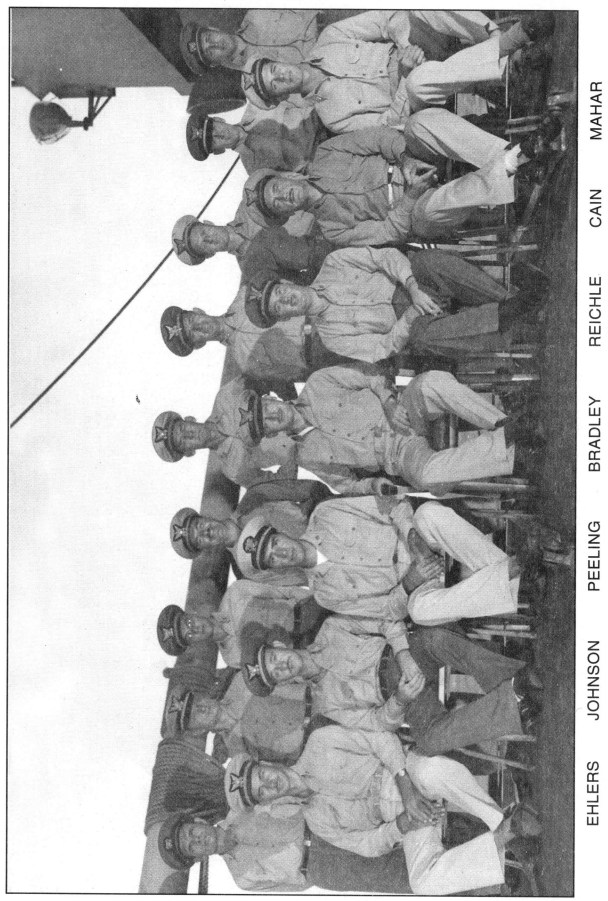

EHLERS   JOHNSON   PEELING   BRADLEY   REICHLE   CAIN   MAHAR

DOSSETT   ATWOOD   DOYLE   THOMSEN   CHALLENGER   BROWN   SKILLIN

Chapter 3

THE MEN OF THE MENKAR

 Seven months had gone by since I had returned from fourteen months in the South Pacific combat zone on the USS HUNTER LIGGETT. The Morro Bay assignment as Coast Guard Beach Patrol Commander, and Commander of Local Naval Defense Forces from Monterey to Santa Barbara was a welcome change the first few months, but once the assignment was running smoothly, I was having an uncontrollable desire for a more active wartime role, especially that while reading reports of the bloody Tarawa and Okinawa invasions I was living the good life in Morro Bay. A fine house on the grounds of the golf course, a chauffeur, a gardener, and even riding-horses at my disposal, besides being with my family, for whom I had hungered all the while on the HUNTER LIGGETT. I had to have challenges, and the excitement of the battle zone. I had to keep the faith.

I thought of Admiral Reifsnider's final words to me on the USS GEORGE CLYMER when we parted at Cape Torokina, Bougainville, on the day of the invasion. "Thomsen, if I can ever help you with your career, contact me at my next duty assignment, which is Chief of Naval Personnel at Washington, D.C.". I then wrote Admiral Reifsnider a personal letter telling him of my desire for command of a ship in the forward combat area, <u>bypassing</u> Coast Guard Headquarters.

My letter must have arrived at an opportune moment, for a week later, on 16 September, 1944 I received orders directing me to report to the Coast Guard Training and Manning Base at Alameda, California for further assignment to duty. "The Good Life" had come to an end. [1]

On arrival in the San Francisco Bay area, I reported to the Commanding Officer of the Coast Guard Manning Station at Alameda, and was assigned a room at the Bachelor Officer's quarters. The next morning I received a message directing me to report to the Chief of Staff at the Coast Guard District office in San Francisco, who was Captain Louis Perkins, under whose command I had served as navigator for over a year on the USS HUNTER LIGGETT at the invasions of Guadalcanal.

He told me that the Admiral wished to commend me personally for my work at Morro Bay, especially in my capacity as the Commander of Naval Local Defense Forces.[2] They both wished me well on my next assignment, the nature of which was not referred to, which despite the secrecy surrounding the mission, I felt they had some knowledge.

The following morning the Base Commander informed me that a converted 445 foot Liberty Class Navy cargo vessel USS MENKAR (AK-123) was expected to arrive at a railroad siding adjacent to a dock in Oakland in approximately one week. On arrival the vessel would be transferred to the Coast Guard and the Navy crew replaced with an entire Coast Guard crew. I was directed to select the MENKAR fifteen Officer complement from the Manning Base list of Officers awaiting duty assignment at the Alameda Training Station. I was told the mission was secret and not to mention the name of the vessel, or discuss any matters pertaining to the nature of the assignment of which I might have knowledge. The Chief Engineer of the vessel and the Ship's Doctor would be assigned by the Base Commander.

The Base Commander suggested that after my crew selection had been submitted to him, I should take time off to return to Morro Bay and make such arrangements as were necessary to locate my family in the San Francisco Area for at least a period of twelve months. I was informed the MENKAR would arrive at Oakland early on the morning of the 27th, and I should be prepared to board her immediately on her arrival.

I spent almost an entire day, studying the base files of Coast Guard Officers available to me. The success of the entire mission would hinge on the character and caliber of the ship's officers, and the list was discouraging to say the least. The only Coast Guard Officers with any sea experience were my first selections:

> A Chief Warrant Boatswain.
> A Chief Warrant Engineer.
> A Chief Warrant Machinist.
> A Chief Warrant Pay Clerk.
> A Warrant Boatswain.

---

[1]   My action in bypassing Coast Guard Headquarters did not sit well with the Coast Guard, as I was told in confidence by Captain Louis Perkins. After the war some chickens came home to roost in my Coast Guard career. No Academy-trained Officer would have committed such a fatal error.

[2]   I believe that Admiral Roach's interest in me may have stemmed from his having been the Admiral who pinned on my Legion of Merit decoration at the Alameda Coast Guard Base on my return from the South Pacific, plus Captain Perkin's regard for me.

U.S.S MENKAR
(AK-123)

c/o Fleet Post Office
San Francisco, California

File 781
9 October, 1944

To: The Commandant (P)

Subj: Lieutenant (jg) Prescott W.N. Gustavson, USCGR

1.   The Commanding Officer, U.S.S. Menkar (AK-123), wishes to report to HQ the unfailing devotion to duty and initiative displayed by the subject Officer in connection with the fitting out of this vessel on her present mission.

2.   In addition to assembling the cargo and the personnel for this vessel in a most efficient manner, Lieutenant Gustavson also greatly assisted the Comanding Officer inexpediting the procurement of much needed refrigeration and special cargo handling equipment. Likewise, he was instrumental in the installation of this equipment which was considered necessary for the conversion of this vessel.

3.   In this excellent performance of duty to which he was assigned, Lieutenant (jg) Gustavson exhibited administrative and executive ability far beyond that adjudged in normalcy to his rank. It is felt that his capable assistance was largely responsible for the on-schedule departure of this vessel.
                       It is requested that a copy of this letter be attached to the next fitness report submitted in the case of subject officer.

                                              Niels P. Thomsen, LCDR
                                              Commanding Officer

CC: Office of Engineering, HQ.

14-A

Address reply to:
CO, USS MENKAR (AK-123),
c/o Fleet Post Office,
San Francisco, California
Refer to file: 67-71-781

To: Lieutenant R. A. ANDERSON, USCG, Executive Officer

Subj: Deck Watch Officers; training of

1.   You are directed to immediately undertake and supervise the instruction of the deck watch officers attached to this vessel.

2.   Unless otherwise specified by the Commanding Officer, commencing at 1300 daily, classes will be held in the Wardroom seven days per week. All classes will be of at least one hour's duration and all deck watch officers will attend.

3.   The below-named officers will assist you in this instruction, each using as a reference the publications here assigned:

        Lieut. EHLERS - - - - Naval Officer's Guide (Ageton).
        Lieut. CHALLENGER - - General Tactical Instructions, USN.
        Lt(jg) SKILLIN- - - - Watch Officer's Guide.
        Lt(jg) DOSSETT- - - - General Signal Book and Mersigs.

4.   You are further instructed to report to the Commanding Officer such officers as fail to attend classes promptly or show sufficient interest.

5.   A monthly report of the progress of each officer will be made to the Commanding Officer. All subjects are to be thoroughly covered.

6.   The Commanding Officer will relieve the deck during these classes.

                   N. P. THOMSEN

The remainder were Coast Guard Reserve Officers recently become surplus to the Port Security and Beach Patrol functions of the Coast Guard. None had ever had any sea experience. Selections and assignments:

Lieutenant Skillin	First Lieutenant
Lieutenant Challenger	Navigator
Lieut. (JG) Jefferson	Division and Deck Watch Officer
Lieut. (JG) Peeling	Division and Deck Watch Officer
Lieut. (JG) Johnson	Division and Deck Watch Officer
Lieut. (JG) Cain	Division and Deck Watch Officer
Ensign Reichle	Division and Deck Watch Officer

All Officers were later assigned collateral duties.

Prior to departing Morro Bay, my Morro Bay Communications Officer Lt. (JG) Cecil Dossett, USCGR and my chauffeur, Jackson, had expressed a desire to accompany me on my next assignment. I made such a request to Captain Perkins, and they became members of the crew, Dossett as communications Officer and Jackson as Seaman. The Base Commander assigned a former Merchant Marine Engineer, Lieutenant, USCGR Brown as Chief Engineer and a Doctor Doyle, USPHS as Ship's Doctor. Fortunately, among the Enlisted ratings assigned, were a number of Chief Petty Officers, normally the backbone of any crew.

I also selected Lieutenant R.A. Anderson, USCG, a former Coast Guard Warrant Boatswain to be my Executive Officer and presented my list of officers selected to the base Commander along with their prospective duty assignments on the MENKAR. One of the functions of the Manning Section was to supply the MENKAR with the required complement of enlisted personnel. In carrying out these allocations, each of the ship's departments would be assigned Chief Petty Officers and rated men of the specialty coinciding with the department's duties, such as deck, engine-room, communication, steward, navigation and medical departments. The Division Officers, supervised by the Executive Officer, guided by the individual's service record, would then choose the men who would serve in their respective departments. All of the above would be speedily accomplished prior to the arrival of the MENKAR.

I returned to my family in Morro Bay for several days, reporting back to the Alameda Manning Station on September 26, 1944, the day before the arrival of the MENKAR from Honolulu. The MENKAR arrived at the dock in Oakland sometime late in the night. At 0800 the next day I boarded the MENKAR with my full complement of officers, each whom met with his Navy counterpart. At 1300 the Coast Guard enlisted personnel came on board and reported to their respective department heads. All Coast Guard personnel, officers and men, returned to the manning station at 1700 to report on board the MENKAR at 0800 the following day, with their seabags and belongings. On 27 September,1944 at 1500 the Transfer of Command ceremony was held, a Coast Guard crew officially in place.

The logistics and preparations essential to speeding the MENKAR on her way were mind-bogglingly complicated. I was constantly in conference with the Commanding Officer of the Loran Construction Unit, who would be in charge of all Loran personnel and equipment.

The Loran Transportation Officer, Lieutenant (JG) USCGR P.W. Gustafson, a dedicated Coast Guard Reserve Officer whose organizational talents were outstanding, and with whom I developed a fine rapport which lasted throughout my association with the Loran project. Part of my duties specified the victualling of the vessel for a ballpark figure of 400 men and 50 ravenous German Shepherds and Doberman Pinschers for a period of six months. All this to be accomplished in less than a week.

At midnight three days after taking over the vessel, a long, black, canvas-covered freight train pulled alongside the ship. Marine guards were stationed on both sides the full length of the train, and orders were issued that henceforth there would be no permissible shore leave or communication with anyone other than those on board the vessel.

Fortunately the vessel had been outfitted as a troop carrier and had berths for over 600 persons, so berthing space was not a problem. By this time we had on board a ship's crew of 160 officers and enlisted men, a Loran construction crew of over two hundred, which included technicians and U.S. Marines, plus fifty dogs with their individual trainers. Heavy trucks, tons of equipment, and countless drums of fuel oil and supplies poured on board and into the holds for the next four days. The last items to be loaded were dozens of 80 to 100 foot creosoted antenna piling to be stowed on deck.

Chapter 4

MENKAR DEPARTS

A week after taking over the vessel, we cast off from the dock, headed through the Golden Gate for Honolulu. The feeling of getting to sea, and away from the dock where we had been living in a frenzy for two weeks was exhilarating to every man on board. Even families left behind were forgotten for the moment.

The MENKAR was at last embarked on what would no doubt be the most important military mission I would ever be assigned. At this point, I had no inkling of our destination beyond Honolulu, and only a vague conception of what dangers lay ahead. The MENKAR's bridge required six deck watch officers, two on each of the three four-hour watches, 0000 to 0400, 0400 to 0800 and 0800 to 1200. We were one officer shy, so I took over the duties of Navigator, as well as standing the midnight to four A.M. deck watch, with Lieutenant Challenger. The remaining five watch officers were Jefferson, Peeling, Johnson, Cain and Reichle, none of whom had prior sea experience in any capacity. The two regular former Coast Guard Warrant Officers were literally swamped with the duties in their specialties and were unavailable for bridge duty. Fortunately, there were several experienced quartermasters and seamen available to handle signals and steer the vessel. I expected to be up and around the bridge during the night hours, and for the first four nights, I slept on a cot in the chartroom. Special night orders were posted to call me on sighting any vessel or in event of any unusual occurrence. By the time we arrived in Honolulu a week later I was more than pleased at the progress being made by all of the watch officers. Eventually they would become skilled, dedicated men, who would strive tirelessly to ensure the success of our mission. The voyage to Honolulu was uneventful.

After docking at Sand Island, I had an important personal decision to make. Were I to make that decision today, I may have made another choice. Forty-five years later I scarcely recall the faces of these fine men from whom I distanced myself for the ten months I commanded the MENKAR. My two years in the South Pacific forward combat zone had taught me that in wartime, if you wanted to stay healthy, there was no room for mistakes, no second chances. I knew my limitations when it came to the art of handling men. I could not be the charismatic commander like Captain Louis Perkins of the USS HUNTER LIGGETT, who could lead his men to superhuman accomplishments by well-chosen words of encouragement and a pat on the back, get the job done, and still be admired to a worshipful degree.

I always had an awareness of a flaw in my military stance in that beneath a confident and forceful exterior was hidden an emotional, vulnerable person, unable to demand and attain dominance and obedience to his will, except in a complete impersonal atmosphere. Taking into account the inexperience of my officers and crew, the magnitude and complicated nature of our mission, I concluded that my safest course of action would be to adopt an aloof and impersonal relationship with my officers. Therefore, on arrival at Sand Island I arranged to have our welders cut away one of the bulkheads between my quarters and an adjoining room, thereby creating a private dining room so I could take my meals alone, rather than traditionally in the wardroom with the ship and Loran unit officers. I chose this course for self-protection, and never knew my officers except to issue orders and evaluate their performances. I am saddened that I did not know them as individuals, for they were all fine men, outstanding in their dedication to the success of the mission of the MENKAR. Today, it seems unbelievable that we could have gone through so much, and have known so little of one another.

REQUIEM FOR A SAILOR

I KNOW NOT
WHAT LIES BEYOND
OR IN WHOSE CARE
I'LL BE -
BUT IT MUST END
AS IT BEGAN -
THIS WEDDING WITH THE SEA.
MY COURSE IS LAID
MY SAILS UNFURLED
AND MY HEART
IS LIGHT AND FREE -
SO SCATTER ME
OVER THE OCEAN WIDE
WHEN THE HELM
IS HARD-A-LEE.
MY DUST WILL MINGLE
WITH EACH CURLING WAVE
AND PERHAPS
I'LL A MERMAN BE
AND THERE'LL BE
SINGING AND DANCING
WITH SEA HORSES PRANCING -
AND A HAREM OF MERMAIDS
ALL TREMBLING FOR ME -
WHEN I AM CALLED
TO MY HOME IN THE SEA.

Chapter 5

MENKAR ENROUTE TO SAIPAN

Our stay at Sand Island dock in Honolulu was brief. From the time we tied up at the dock until an hour prior to our departure, the cargo winches never stopped grinding day or night. Tons of equipment crammed the holds and littered the deck. There was no shore leave, and on 15 October, 1944 we left at daylight bound for Saipan in the Marianas group of islands, a fifteen-day voyage from Honolulu.

On the same bridge deck as my cabin were the quarters of the ship's doctor, Lieutenant Commander O.B. Doyle, USPHS, and the Chief Engineer, Lieutenant B.B. Brown, USCGR. Doyle was a surgeon from Fresno, California, the San Joaquin valley town I had left on a freight train, via a bedroom window on my fourteenth birthday, so we had something in common.

He would be the only officer on the MENKAR with whom I would develop a warm and lasting friendship. The Chief Engineer a former Merchant Marine engineer, was in his late fifties, very capable and with a wealth of experience. He was a loquacious individual, and I was glad to have him on board. However, to my trained eye, having spent twenty years in the company of seagoing alcoholics of all shapes and sizes, he appeared to me as one who might have alcoholic tendencies. I would keep him under close observation. Time would tell.

The MENKAR bristled with anti-aircraft stations, with eight twin 40 millimeter Machine gun pits. The day after departure from Honolulu the top priority became gunnery drills, target practice and enemy plane recognition drills. General quarters were sounded several times daily, and there was no let up in drills. To inspire competition, I had two 40 MM gun crews manned entirely with black members of the crew. Because of the importance of the mission, the Coast Guard had placed on board a combat photographer, Charles Cook, who kept a photographic record for regular submission to the Coast Guard Engineering Department in Washington, D.C.

On 31 October, 1944, the MENKAR dropped anchor at Saipan, where on 2 November, we moved alongside a pontoon dock, only recently constructed by Navy Seabees, and unloaded a mobile Loran Unit with station personnel and equipment. This was the first case where Loran construction material was brought in by a Coast Guard ship. On 5 November, work was begun on the Saipan site and the station was ready and on the air by 16 November. The urgency of the establishment of Loran stations was dramatically demonstrated a few days later, as on the 25 November, 1944, one hundred and eleven B-29's of the 21st Bomber Command bombed Tokyo, the first bombing raid of the city since the Doolittle raid in 1942. During this period, enemy air raids were frequent. There were several dogfights close by, and two enemy planes crashed about a thousand yards away. There was also considerable danger from falling shrapnel from the American anti-aircraft fire.

On completion of the unloading of the gear for Unit 337 at Saipan, we departed for Guam, arriving there on 6 November, 1944, anchoring offshore. At Guam, or rather at a small island called Cocos Island, two miles from the town of Merizo on the South end of Guam, a station was to be built. Cocos Island was 700 feet wide and approximately 2500 feet long. It was low and sandy and covered with dense tropical growth. The first difficulty encountered was the unloading, for we were anchored well offshore in the open sea, and our relatively small boats (LCMs) had to travel a distance of three miles to the beach landing site.

As I have previously stated, the responsibility of the Captain and crew of the MENKAR was to place all Loran equipment and supplies above the high water mark, from which point the Loran Unit was responsible. After an attempt to land on the North shore, where the water was shallow, a channel that would accommodate our boats was blasted through the reefs on the South shore. This was a blessing as we could deliver our cargo without it getting wet. Good weather prevailed all during the landing operation, greatly facilitating the work. All gear was put ashore by 10 November, 1944 with the loss of only one box. This station went on the air on 27 November, 1944.

The bombers, the transport planes of the Air Transport Command, and other users of the Loran signals were usually totally unknown to the Coast Guard crews of these isolated Loran stations, and the part which Loran played became known to them only indirectly. Their view of the war was, of necessity, a narrow one, such as a morning early in December when the security guard of the Cocos Island station discovered a native canoe on the beach, and within an hour had tracked down and shot a Japanese straggler from Guam. After landing the construction material at Cocos Island, the MENKAR was ordered to Apra Harbor, 15 miles away on the west side of the Island of Guam. We sailed along the beaches where the assault landings had been made the previous July, and passed inside the Crote Peninsula on which the Japanese had built airfields, past the famous Cabras Island, from which stubborn Japanese resistance had come, and finally we anchored in the coral-studded harbor.

We arrived at Apra Harbor on 11 November, 1944, 25 days since our departure from San Francisco's Golden Gate. Considering the time of the year, the weather had been exceptionally fine. The operation had gone without a hitch, far ahead of schedule. No enemy, bombs, torpedoes or shells, and incredibly, no court-martials in our crew of over 160 men.

The passengers were all under the jurisdiction of the Commander of the Loran Unit, so their disciplinary problems were not my concern. There were a number of things about the MENKAR that were unusual which may have accounted for the harmony existing on board the vessel, such as the excitement of the mission, the conglomeration of the people on board, the dogs and their trainers, the various craftsmen, the Marines, and the fact that the ship's crew was harassed day and night with wartime drills and instructions by officers determined that their division be the most efficient at the Commanding Officer's inspection every Saturday. You can rest assured every spare moment was spent catching up on sleep.

The ship's officers, without exception, were splendid in the performance of their duties as watch and division officers. The Executive Officer, Mr. Anderson, the First Lieutenant, Mr. Skillin and Mr. Challenger were outstanding in their enthusiasm. My private dining room was a blessing. Dr. Doyle dined with me two or three times a week, and when it was possible, Anderson, Skillin, Challenger and Mr. Brown were invited individually. With the exception of Dr. Doyle, our conversations would be limited to matters connected with the operation of the vessel.

My personal attendant, Smith, took care of my meals and laundry, and kept my quarters spotless. He also looked after my fox terrier, "Boy" whom I brought with me from Morro Bay. Smith and his friends would look after "Boy" during the day, when he would frolic about the decks, making sure he did not get too close to the guard dogs and be eaten up alive.

The landing at Apra Harbor went slowly due to the delayed removal of the cargo from the narrow landing beach area. Furthermore, the entire island including the beach was strewn with wreckage remaining from the intense sea and air bombardment. Once on the beach, the cargo had to be loaded on trucks and other vehicles for a thirty mile haul along the shore road, through the town of Agana, and then inland through heavily wooded country to the Loran site at the Northern end of Guam. On 18 November, the last of the cargo had been delivered, and we received orders to proceed to Saipan, and on arrival load a Loran construction unit for delivery to the Caroline Islands. This was a routine delivery with no unusual problems, and we returned to Saipan on 5 December.

The station on Guam completed, we were ordered to pick up this group of Loran construction personnel and proceed to Ulithi, where we arrived on 13 December. After going ashore and viewing the beach landing site, it was obvious to me that landings would be possible only at high tides. The North part of the island was heavily wooded, mainly with Buka trees, some of which were four to six feet in diameter at the base. By working around the clock, we were able to complete our delivery and depart Ulithi on 15 December, with orders to proceed to Pearl Harbor, Honolulu, stopping at Eniwetok and Majuro enroute, for the purpose of transporting surplus Loran personnel and material back to Honolulu. All hands were jubilant, having had no shore leave for three months.

It should be borne in mind that the primary mission of the MENKAR was the expeditious delivery of temporary mobile Loran units capable of being on the air in a matter of days after delivery to the site of the station. Permanent installations would require a matter of weeks or months, using the materials brought out by the MENKAR on her initial voyage.

LOADING LORAN UNITS

LOUD SPEAKER ADDRESS TO CREW   **4 January, 1945**

To: Officers and men of the MENKAR

1.   The Commanding Officer congratulates and commends you upon the successful completion of our mission.

2.   Though untrained in the handling of cargo, you have, through careful handling and attention to duty, performed our task of delivering our valuable cargo without a single instance of loss or damage. You have handled this cargo on coral reefs and on beaches from the open sea in a manner which would do credit to the best of long-experienced seamen and longshoremen. You have worked cargo by day, and during enemy bombing attacks by night you have manned your battle stations in record time.

3.   There has been no liberty or recreation for you on shore during this voyage, time being of the essence. Several swimming and beach parties upon which you planned were cancelled due to the everpresent possibility of enemy attack, and of the fact that every advantage had to be taken of the good weather with which we were favored. Your cheerful acceptance of these conditions have been in true Coast Guard spirit.

4.   The Commanding Officer takes this opportunity to inform you that since commissioning by the Coast Guard, although you have been over five hundred men in close confinement on board ship for many weeks, no disciplinary action by Deck Courts has been necessary. This is as it should be, and it is the desire and hope of the Commanding Officer that on liberty ashore, you will continue to keep this spotless record unsullied.

5.   The Commanding Officer and the Coast Guard are most proud of each of you and the manner in which you have performed your duty.

6.   Men of the MENKAR, WELL DONE!

N.P. Thomsen
Lieut.Comdr. USCG
Commanding

SHIP'S OFFICERS

MERRY CHRISTMAS

Chapter 6

MENKAR ARRIVES AT HONOLULU

 The MENKAR reached Honolulu on 7 January, 1945, where we moored at the Sand Island dock. The big event was the moment when dozens of sacks of mail were delivered to the ship. Since our departure from Alameda three months earlier the ship had, because of her secret itinerary, received very little personal mail, most of it having been held at Sand Island, Honolulu. Life being what it is, not all of the mail contained good news to some crew members. Traditionally, on a ship with a normal complement of crewmen, the Captain would be the confidant of crew members with personal problems. The many operational problems and the exceptionally large number of crew members did not allow me the time to devote to this very important matter. I could devote myself to such personal problems as affected the ship's officers, but that was all I could handle. Therefore, after a month out of Alameda, I set up a counseling service headed by Doctor Doyle, Lieutenant Challenger, and the man's division officer, all intelligent, mature and compassionate people. A notice was then posted informing all hands of the aims and purposes of the counseling committee. Both Dr. Doyle and Lieut. Challenger kept me abreast of the committee's activities, especially very serious matters that might require humanitarian or executive action on my part.

I received a bundle of caring letters from Ethel, with the news that she was expecting a child in June. I was thrilled over this. I had wished for a girl, and a year earlier while on the LIGGETT in New Zealand had purchased a set of five silver napkin rings with the names of Niels, Ethel, Carol, Robin, and Tiare engraved thereon. When I was eighteen years old, and a sailor on the FOREST DREAM, I had built a small ship model of a South Sea trading schooner, which I named TIARE, a Polynesian name, which I wanted to bestow on a daughter I expected one day to have. I was certain that the baby would be girl, and be blonde-haired. Knowing Ethel's down-East family were partial to such names as Martha, Abigail, Clara, and so on, I was concerned over the name she might be given. After some deliberation, I visited the Honolulu post office and inquired as to the possibility of purchasing a twenty-five dollar war bond in the name of Tiare Marie Thomsen, to be born on June 1, 1945. I was told this was possible. I then bought such a bond, visited a local Chinese jeweler and commissioned a silver brooch and two earrings hammered into the shape of the flower named TIARE. I placed them in a small box together with one of my cards inscribed, "Hello Tiare, with the golden hair." This in turn was placed in another box, and sent to Ethel with instructions to take it with her to the hospital, and to open when Tiare was born. She was born on June 1st. I try not to think too much about the personal side of my life, and think only about what has to do with the MENKAR. In this senseless atmosphere of death and destruction in which we are engaged, one must bury all human, compassionate feelings if one is to retain his sanity.

We were told that the MENKAR would be at Sand Island for approximately one month, during which time, the vessel and her boats would undergo repair and maintenance. I was also instructed to resupply the vessel with six months of stores and other supplies, no simple task.

I was more than pleased with the performance of the ship and its crew, which I felt was up to 85 to 90 percent of what I felt was its potential. Several days after the MENKAR's arrival, I was approached by Lieutenant Challenger and Lieutenant Dossett, the Communications Officer, with the idea that inasmuch as the ship's welfare and entertainment fund now amounted to over ten thousand dollars, thoughts were floating about the ship that a large ship's party (Hawaiian style) to be held on shore would be desirable, and what was my reaction. I whole-heartedly approved of any arrangements they might decide upon, and they proceeded with arrangements for such a party, to take place the following week.

All the ship's department heads, deck, engine room, medical, stewards, and navigation were busily engaged in determining their needs for the next six months far from any source of supplies. I departed from usual procedures, by having all department heads personally present their lists for perusal, and justification, by the Executive Officer and then on my desk for approval. On the engineering department list submitted by Lieutenant Brown, the ex-merchant marine Chief Engineer of the ship, I noticed on the list a fifty gallon drum of grain alcohol. While I had no evidence, or any reason other than my initial reaction on first meeting Brown, to question this item, it bothered me and I discussed it with Doctor Doyle, who checked with his chief medical assistant, and was told that no one had reason to believe that Brown used alcohol. When I questioned Brown about the fifty gallon drum, without changing expression, and in a casual way, he told me the grain alcohol was an essential ingredient used in keeping the ship's boiler tubes clean. Not being an engineer and thus incapable of questioning his explanation, I approved the order. I was to regret this as time went on.

While on the subject of alcohol I will have to confess the following. Doctor Doyle was a very smooth, persuasive individual, who spent considerable time ashore hobnobbing with his colleagues at the Naval Supply Depot in Honolulu. One day, having lunch with me, he mentioned that his friends in the medical supply section of the Naval Base had implied that as the MENKAR would be away for a six month period, he might want to put in a request for 12 cases of whiskey for medicinal purposes, and would I approve such a request. I thought it to be a reasonable request and we divided it between my cabin lockers and his department, along with ten cases of mixers. My intention being to use it as gifts to influential individuals in the forward area in exchange for preferential treatment and attention which would be beneficial to the mission of the MENKAR in particular, and the Coast Guard generally.

The party (LUAU) turned out to be a grand affair, with the whole of the ship's crew in attendance, except for the necessary deck and engine-room department watch standers. Lieutenant Challenger and Doctor Doyle, had managed to promote a local socialite "Grand Dame" into lending her magnificent town estate grounds for the affair, as well as providing comfort facilities in several of the six bathrooms in her mansion. The spacious lawns were the site of many tables and benches, and a very large dais for dancing to a Hawaiian orchestra, complete with hula dancers. To add icing to the cake, Doyle and Challenger, with the help of our socialite hostess, had managed to procure over one hundred local young women as dancing partners.

I returned to the ship early in the evening. The next day Lieutenant Challenger, a subdued and apprehensive look on his face, reported to me that the ship's crew had become extremely boisterous as the evening wore on. Several fights had taken place in two of the mansion's bathrooms, and considerable damaged caused, such as two toilets ripped up from the floor. I directed Doyle and Challenger to call on the owner immediately, apologize, and without delay make restitution. That afternoon they returned, having concluded the incident by offering a settlement of $2,500.00, which I authorized. I took no further action, except to announce there would be no future ship-sponsored shoreside entertainment.

In a nearby spacious dock area were stored about two hundred new army jeeps awaiting transportation to units in the forward areas. The MENKAR had no ship's vehicles, so one dark and moonless night two jeeps disappeared into one of the ship's holds. Having our own transportation, not only added to the ship's amenities, but heightened the prestige of the Coast Guard, the MENKAR and its Commanding Officer.

The Commander of the Coast Guard Loran Construction Unit 203, Lieutenant Commander K.W. Donnell, USCGR, provided me with a set of navigational charts covering the itinerary of our forthcoming voyage to the forward area. He emphasized the distinct probability of sea and air attack on the MENKAR. The MENKAR sailed from Honolulu on February 10, 1945, with a full cargo of Loran equipment and construction personnel.

MY WINTER PRAYER

OH! LORD
LET ME GO BACK TO SLEEP
AND
DREAM OF ALL THE THINGS
THAT WERE
AND MIGHT HAVE BEEN -
AND IF
THAT SLEEP BE DREAMLESS
STILL I KNEEL BEFORE THEE BLESSED
SO GRATEFUL
FOR THE GIFT OF LIFE
AND
POWER TO LOVE YOU GAVE TO ME
TAKE ME HOME
SOME DAY OR NIGHT
WHEN I AM AT PEACE WITH LIFE
AND
ALL OF THOSE I LOVE -
AND
I WILL KISS THY FEET
AND COME
WITHOUT A TREMBLE
IN MY HEART -
BUT, OH LORD
WHY AM I WEEPING NOW
THIS NIGHT IN SADNESS
WAITING FOR THE DAWN
AND
THE SUN
TO LIGHT THIS LOVELY EARTH -
THROUGH WHOSE BEAUTY I HAVE STRODE
SO FLEETING
AND
SO HEEDLESS
AND
SO DRIVEN.

Thomsen

COMMANDING OFFICER MENKAR <u>LOUD SPEAKER ADDRESS</u> TO THE SHIP'S CREW AFTER DEPARTURE FROM HONOLULU 12 FEBRUARY, 1945.

MEN OF THE MENKAR:

It has been gratifying to note these past two days how happy you all seem at being once more at sea after our lengthy and tedious stay in port.

I wish to recall the last time I spoke to you many weeks ago just prior to our arrival in port. On that occasion I asked that while in port, you remember the MENKAR, your duty towards her and to your shipmates. I asked that you conduct yourself in port in the same exemplary manner that you conducted yourselves on our last mission. I am proud and happy to say to you that our perfect record of no court-martials on the MENKAR since her commissioning is still unbroken.

I am also not unmindful of the excellent manner in which you loaded and prepared the ship for sea. You worked long hours and your liberty was not all it might have been. But if you grumbled – I am not aware of it. In the past five months we have come to know each other, and it has been with extreme pleasure and satisfaction that I have watched your transition from landsmen to sailors in this short period of time. You have, each of you become a part of the MENKAR. We have a good ship, and I consider it a privilege to command so fine a crew as you. There are a few new faces among you, and to them I give our sincere welcome, and hope they will like their new home. Now, as to the future - I should like to be able to tell you more than what the work you are doing is of great importance to the war effort, but military security will not permit.

On our last voyage, although we were subject to bombing attacks on a number of occasions, it was our good fortune never to come under direct attack by enemy aircraft. It is my belief that somewhere along the path that we are now on, we will have the opportunity of first-hand combat with the planes of the enemy, and most likely when that time comes, we will be practically alone as we were on our last voyage.

We must become deadly proficient at our battle stations in the short time that lies ahead, for I can assure you from first hand knowledge that the only thing that will be of importance then, is that every man performs his duty in the most rapid and efficient manner possible. On board this ship, as on every naval vessel in time of war, the lives of all on board can rest solely in the hands of but one man. That man may be you, tonight or tomorrow, should you fail to see the wake of a torpedo in time, not to load your gun quickly, or fail to identify the foe.

We are all of us prepared to give our lives in our Country's cause, but I am not prepared to give mine because one of you goes to sleep at his post, or fails to get to his battle station on the double - anymore than you are prepared to give yours because I blunder at my station on the bridge.

For this reason we must drill long hours in the days to come, so than we can meet any eventuality with the knowledge that should we meet with disaster, it will not be us who have failed. There is no greater satisfaction than that knowledge. I have two obligations that are sacred to me. First and foremost is my duty to my country, and the success of our mission. Then I have another of which I am also forever mindful day and night - and that is to bring each of you back to those who love you and wait for your return.

Now a few words to our passengers - your interest in the MENKAR and your splendid assistance in the stowing of our cargo will make our work in the forward area much easier. This whole-hearted cooperation of yours is a fine example of separate Commands working towards a common goal, that has filled the Commanding Officer and the Officers of the MENKAR with admiration towards you.

On the MENKAR the abandon-ship stations for the crew are their battle stations. They are there to protect you from the enemy while you are abandoning a sinking ship. You will launch all the ship's rafts, and not a single man of the MENKAR will leave his battle station until you are safely away. You owe it to them to get to your abandon-ship stations as quickly as you possibly can, so that they, too, may have a fighting chance to survive.

N.P. Thomsen
Lieutenant Commander
Commanding USS MENKAR (AK-123)

Chapter 7

UNORTHODOX DISCIPLINARY POLICY

 In the February 12th address by the Commanding Officer to the ship's crew that no Deck Courts or official punishment had been meted out to any member of the crew since the vessel was manned by the Coast Guard, would normally be regarded by any Naval commander as an unbelievable statement for a Naval vessel with a crew of over 175 enlisted men and officers. But these claims are a matter of official record. My own analysis of this near phenomena is the following:

The primary reason was that 90% of the officers and enlisted men were young, inexperienced, idealistic, dedicated Coast Guard reservists. They were in some measure naive, and they were in awe of, and respected authority far more than did regular military personnel. The ship's assignment intrigued them, and they were imbued with a strong desire that the MENKAR be successful in her all-important mission, and they were proud of their individual accomplishments. The never ending variety of their duties, in the hold, on the beach, the dogs and their trainers, the Marines, the construction detachments, all added to the spice of life, as did their naivete and the prospect of probable enemy action. Another reason may have been the MENKAR's unorthodox, unofficial ship's policy in handling infractions, tension and personal problems pertaining to the ship's crew. All cases were handled by a four-man board in an unrecorded session which met in the Captain's cabin, and which consisted of the Commanding Officer, Lieutenant Commander Doyle, the ship's doctor, Lieutenant Challenger, the Navigator and the crew member's Division Officer. I know of no problems that were not solved amicably within the framework of these discussions. Another factor may have been the officers and enlisted men working side by side in the holds and on the beaches manually handling cargo.

The policy of the Commanding Officer maintaining his privacy by not intruding or having meals in the officer's wardroom, as well as otherwise disassociating himself in a personal sense from his officers may have been a factor in establishing authority.

While in Honolulu at a Sunday dinner in my quarters, during a discussion with Doyle and Challenger, I learned that many of the ship's crew members attended regular Sunday church services ashore. One thing led to another and we came to the conclusion that Sunday religious services should take place on the MENKAR, to commence after departure on our next voyage, particularly in view of Doctor Doyle's statement that many of the married crew members had confided to him their concern over the MENKAR's combat zone itinerary. It was agreed that the services should be so organized as to be acceptable to Protestants, Catholics and those of Jewish faith.

Challenger remarked that one of our deck watch officers, Lieutenant (JG) Jefferson regularly attended church services ashore, which brought him into the program. It developed that Jefferson was not only an accomplished organist, but also very enthusiastic when asked to devote himself to establishing the services. By the time the ship was ready to sail he had, with the cooperation of the church he attended, obtained a small church organ, hymn books and a supply of Bibles.

The services would commence on the first Sunday after our departure. Jefferson had secured the help of the ship's office staff, with the Chief Yeoman, Stinson, as his chief assistant. Jefferson handled the entire matter, my only contribution being that I was to conduct the initial services, after which services would be lead by crew members on a voluntary basis. Announcements consisting of a front and back page would be prepared and posted each week by the MENKAR's office staff. I could not refrain from adding a few meaningful comments on the back page of each announcement. The following two pages are copies of our inaugural service, found in a box I had not examined in over forty years.

DIVINE SERVICES

ABOARD THE

USS MENKAR (AK-123)

AT 1000

SUNDAY, 11 FEBRUARY, 1945

ORDER OF WORSHIP

1. Organ Prelude - A Bach Air and Handel's Arioso
2. Call to Worship; Prayer.
3. Hymn 72 - I Love to Tell The Story.
4. Bible Reading; Responsive Reading.
5. Sermon - Why We Pray.
6. Lord's Prayer.
7. Hymn 75 - Fight the Good Fight.
8. Organ Postlude - Marche Romaine by Gounod.

Lt.(jg) R.C. Jefferson, USCGR   Jack R. Stinson, CY, USCGR
At The Organ   At The Altar

FEBRUARY, 1945

"Brotherhood Month"

11th, Edison's Birthday   14th, St. Valentine's Day
12th, Lincoln's Birthday   22nd, Washington's Birthday

16th World Day of Prayer
Amethyst for Sincerity

Lt.CDR. N.P. Thomsen, USCG   Lt. J.A. ROOT, USCGR
Commanding Officer   Executive Officer

FIRST CHURCH SERVICES ON 11 FEBRUARY, 1945

Back Page
A PRAYER OF

<u>Jewish Faith</u> - Lord our God, God of our fathers Abraham, Isaac and Jacob, great God, all powerful and awe-inspiring, may it by Thy will that thou mayest calm the sea from its raging so that its waves may be still and thou will bring us to our destination safe and sound and without delay. For thine is supreme dominion over all. Hearken to our prayer and give heed to our heart's outpouring. Answer our prayer which at this time we off er thee. Guard us from the perils of the waves and the dangers of the waters, from tempest and storm, and grant us favoring winds.

<u>Catholic Faith</u> - God of battles, Who grantest the victory to those who put their trust in thee: mercifully hear the prayers of us, thy servants, that the evil designs of our enemies being defeated, we may praise thee with unceasing gratitude. Through Christ our Lord. Amen.

<u>Protestant Faith</u> - Keep us, our God, from all complaining and self-pity. When our work is hard, give us the strength we need to do our best. When our hearts are heavy, give us a sense of thy many blessings now and always. May our efforts and our hopes make us cheerful and serene that others may take new vigor and joy from us. Amen.

TODAYS USHERS
Donald P. LOWE, PhN2c(R), Robert W. MAUL, BM1c(R), Clarence J. RUSSELL, RM3c(R), William R. GILLEN, S1c(R), and Willard S. JENSEN, Y3c(R).

TRIBUTE TO LINCOLN
Edwin Markham
And when he fell in whirlwind, he went down as when a lordly cedar, green with boughs, goes down with a great shout upon the hills, and leaves a lonesome place against the sky.

SOCRATES SAID
"Whom, then, do I call educated? First, those who control circumstances instead of being mastered by them; those who meet all occasions manfully, and act in accordance with intelligent thinking; those who are honorable in all dealings, who treat good-naturedly persons and things that are disagreeable; and furthermore, those who hold their pleasures under control and are not overcome by misfortune; finally those who are not spoiled by success.

Vatican City was established on February, 1929

COURAGE IS AN ESSENTIAL MARK OF A CHRISTIAN

ARTIST AT WORK

CREW PETS

Chapter 8

GUAM ADVANCE BASE
COMMAND UNIT 203

With the moving of the Headquarters of the CincPac and CincPoa from Pearl Harbor to Guam at the beginning of 1945, the Coast Guard decided that Command Unit 203 should move also, as it was important to this unit that it maintain close liaison with the Navy Headquarters office. It became increasingly difficult to exercise supervision over the most recent Loran construction projects as each new chain of stations was further away from Honolulu. Plans were therefore made to transfer the command unit to new quarters at Guam and to create a new unit to handle the parts of the Loran work that would be retained at Pearl Harbor.

Early in January, 1945 Command Unit 203, commanded by Lieutenant Commander K.W. Donnell, was ordered to move to Guam, and at the same time its functions were newly defined. It was made operationally responsible to Commander in Chief, Pacific Ocean Area, and Commander in Chief, Southwest Pacific Area, and was in itself responsible for the movement and operation of the three construction detachments, the plane, the MENKAR, the Advance Base Staging Detachment, and the Charting element. All matters of design, siting, and the supervision of construction and testing of stations in the Pacific were included.

With authority granted to erect an advance base at Guam, all Construction Detachment C (Unit 80) personnel were assembled there after the completion of the Ulithi station to carry out the construction. After some difficulty in obtaining a site from the Island Commander, the work was begun. At the assigned location, dense jungle growth had to be cleared from an area approximately 400 feet by 500 feet. The first building erected was a Quonset hut, to be used as an office for the Command Unit, which would reach Guam in February. By the time this building was finished the area had been sufficiently cleared to erect pyramidal tents as quarters for the enlisted personnel of the construction force.

When construction first began, it was necessary to house the personnel of Construction Detachment C in various camps on the island, chiefly in those of Navy Seabee units. In less than a week after the area was cleared, sufficient quarters were available to house the entire unit. A mess and galley, consisting of two Quonset huts in a "T" plan and a 40 by 100 foot storage Quonset with concrete floor, were erected simultaneously. Two 20 by 40 Quonset huts for enlisted quarters, a water tower, showers, a small laundry and generator house were soon erected. Finally the carpenter shop, technicians shop, and garage were finished and the base took on the appearance of a well planned station.

About this time the effectiveness of the unit was strengthened by the assignment of new personnel. Lieutenant Albert J. Summerfield, USCG was assigned to the unit in March to supervise the electronics design, installation and testing. Lieutenant Commander Richard M. Baxter was assigned as Executive Officer at the same time. In April, Lieutenant commander Fletcher Watson, USNR, a well-known astronomer, who had been Secretary of the National Defense Research Council, under which the early Loran development had been out at the Massachusetts Institute of Technology, was assigned to the unit by the Navy Hydrographic Office to assist Lieutenant Robert D. Pomeroy in the organization of the Charting Element, one of the functions of Command Unit 203 being the issue of temporary Loran charts, which served to make the signals available immediately upon a station being announced ready for navigational purposes. These charts, which were issued to all ships and air groups having a use for them, served Loran users until such time as the Hydrographic Office of the Navy was able to distribute more permanent material.

Lieutenant Mohl, USCG, and later Lieutenant Therrell, USCG were assigned to the unit to obtain astronomical fixes at the various sites. Lieutenant Kiely was the unit's civil engineering officer until he became Commanding Officer of Unit 211.

Lieutenant John F. Hill, USCG assisted in the electronics work. Selection of sites and the making of system accuracy was a major portion of the unit's work. The control and assignment of all construction personnel of all construction kept a fair-sized office force busy seven days a week.

Lieutenant Albert J. Summerfield, USCG was awarded the Bronze Star Medal, accompanied by the following citation:

"For meritorious conduct against the enemy as electronics engineer of the Pacific Area Construction Detachment, United States Coast Guard. He was responsible for the technical aspects of the installation and operation, from the Aleutians to Australia, of the Loran stations that aided the safe navigation of air, surface and submarine forces, and contributed substantially to the early defeat of Japan. His arduous work was carried out with consistent success despite difficult and often dangerous conditions. His leadership was an inspiration to all with whom he served and his

performance of duty throughout was in keeping with the highest traditions of the Naval Service."

ANGAUR		348	Monitor
PULO ANNA		344	Double Master
Ngesebus (Pelelieu)	343	Single Slave	
MOROTAI (Pangeo)	345	Single Slave	

Built by Construction Detachment D (Unit 211)

Chapter 9

PALAU-MOROTAI LORAN CHAIN
REPLACEMENT OF MOBILE
STATIONS AUTHORIZED

 The Joint Chiefs of Staff, through the Chief of Naval Operations, on 13 January, 1945 directed the Coast Guard to proceed with the installation, operation and maintenance of three fixed Loran Stations in the Palau-Morotai Islands, to take the place of the units of Mobile Detachment Fox, which had gone on the air in this area 1 December, 1944, at Pulo Anna, Palau, and Morotai. This directive was but one more step in the advancement of Loran coverage to the Westward. This coverage already included the Philippines, where fighting was still in progress.

This new chain was to consist of a double master station at Pulo Anna Island, a single slave station in Ngesebus (Pelelieu) Island, a single slave station at Pangeo (Morotai), and a monitor on the former Japanese Island of Angaur. These stations would provide cover for the Mindanao area of the Philippines. The islands selected for the Palau-Morotai chain lay immediately to the Southwest of the Marianas, and were off to the Southeast end of the Philippine group. Morotai and Pulo Anna were only 240 and 360 miles respectively from Mindanao, the nearest of the Philippines, and a little over 500 miles from Leyte, where the first landings had eventually been made. Ngesebus (Pelelieu), and Angaur in the Palau Islands, lay to the Northeast, but about the same distance from Leyte. The importance of Loran Stations in this particular area had been so great in the planning of the military operations that the Seventh Amphibious force had made landings to secure territory for this special purpose.

The transportable units of Detachment Fox had been the best means of providing Loran service of the earliest practicable date, after the taking of the islands, but they could not be expected to supply permanent service, for the power plants were insufficient to give the greatest practicable range, and the quarters of the crew were so meager that permanent occupancy was out of the question.

Military operations against the Palau Islands had been undertaken early in September 1944, with attacks by carrier-based planes, and U.S. cruisers and destroyers. These attacks centered mainly on Pelelieu and Angaur Islands. By the middle of October, the assault phase was over. Amphibious landings at Morotai in the Halmahera Islands had taken place on 15 December, 1944, when over 50,000 troops were disembarked, and secured the island for the operation of land based planes, Loran and other purposes. In another operation, relatively small, in the same area in November, 1944 U.S. troops landed unopposed to establish radar and Loran stations on Asia and Mapia Islands as aids to future Naval operations.

This new chain of fixed Loran stations was following the northerly swing of military operations in the Pacific. Where a few months before, activities had been chiefly in the Southwest Pacific, and the principal air routes led in the general direction of Australia, action was now nearly due West of the Hawaiian Islands, and the air routes led to the Philippines. The routes of the air evacuation of medical cases were a direct indication of the location of the fighting, and those routes through the Phoenix Islands were falling into disuse and the heaviest traffic was passing through the Marianas.

The construction of permanent stations of the Palau-Morotai chain was assigned to Construction Detachment D (Unit 211) which had built the Phoenix chain. The Commanding Officer of the detachment, Lieutenant Gary S. Morgan, USCG, left Sand Island on 26 January 1945, by air, for the Palau-Morotai Islands to conduct a survey for the proposed stations, and to make necessary preliminary arrangements for the landing of the unit and its equipment at the various sites. The personnel of the detachment remained at Sand Island, where they were preparing the material, which was already arriving from the United States, until 9 January, 1945, when the entire detachment, except the Commanding Officer, boarded the MENKAR for the new station sites.

Chapter 10

MENKAR ARRIVES AT GUAM

 The trip from Sand Island to Guam was uneventful, differing only from the previous trip in that gun and general battle drills had been stepped up to the maximum levels in striving for greater proficiency. Guam was reached on 1 March, 1945, and some cargo was unloaded for Unit 203, the command unit having headquarters at the Guam base. The ship then proceeded to Ulithi and Angaur. On 6 March the MENKAR arrived at Angaur, at the Southern extremity of the Palau Islands, and began the discharge of men and equipment for the construction of the monitor station on that island, which was to be manned by Unit 346.

The principal settlement on Angaur Island was the town of Saipan on the Western shore, but this place should not be confused with the more famous Saipan Island in the Marianas. In pre-war days, the principal activity on the island was the working of phosphate deposits, for which there was a phosphate refinery. The United States was now using the island as a base for operations of land based planes. The site selected for the Loran station was on the Southern end of the island, just over a mile from the settlement. This end of the island was flat and covered with trees.

LCMs were used for the landing operation, and conditions being favorable, the unloading was completed on 7 March, 1945, only two days after arrival. Gropac 10 vehicles were used to transport the cargo directly to the site. Heavy equipment for use in raising the antenna poles was borrowed from the Army engineers.

The construction of this station was a comparatively simple matter. In addition to the necessary antennas, ground system, and communications equipment, three receiver-indicators had to be installed and tested. This work, with the exception of the communications booth, was completed by 16 March, 1945.

This station was ready for monitoring operation by 15 March at which time construction was about 30 per cent complete. Testing, adjusting, and practice operation continued until 2 April, when the unit relieved the mobile monitor station of both Loran monitoring and communication duties.

At this site there was adequate fresh water due to the abnormally large rainfall. This fresh water supply was easily tapped by sinking caissons to a depth of about six feet. The water was rendered potable by being treated with the puro-pumper with which the unit was furnished.

PELELIEU

PELELIEU

Chapter 11

NGESEBUS (PELELIEU) MATERIAL LANDED

The MENKAR next proceeded to Pelelieu Island only ten miles away, to discharge the cargo for the Ngesebus station, the northern slave of the Palau-Morotai chain. Pelelieu lay at the Southern end of the long irregular patch of reefs, constituting the Palau Islands. The station site was actually located on Ngesebus Island, a small horseshoe shaped island just North of Pelelieu, from which it was separated by a two and three-quarter mile wide channel. Unit 331, a mobile unit forming part of Detachment Fox, with Lieutenant (JG) David R. Domke, USCG, in command, was already established in Ngesebus and had been providing Loran service for about four months, having reached the island about two months after its capture. The new fixed stations were to replace this unit, and were to be built by Section 3 of Construction Detachment D, with Lieutenant (JG) John McGuire in charge.

On 9 March, 1945, the unloading at Pelelieu began and continued for five days. The cargo was unloaded from the MENKAR into LCMs and landed on the beach, from which it was trucked to a storage area adjacent to the port. Here it was reloaded into DUKW's for transportation to Ngesebus. Equipment too heavy for the DUKW's, such as generators and refrigerators, was hauled across the shallow channel on a trailer towed by a bulldozer. This hauling had to be done at low tide, and with the lowest tides then occurring between 2300 and 0100, the difficulties of night work were encountered. Ngesebus Island was "Beach Crimson" of invasion days, and on it had been a 3,000 foot Japanese air strip. All cargo had reached the station site by March 14th, and by this time, a camp was also established. The bulldozer dug a pit in the soft sand and struck brackish water at a depth of only five feet. This provided enough water for showers and for the evaporator, which could make 150 gallons of fresh water an hour. A screened-in hospital tent made a very satisfactory galley and mess hall.

The Ngesebus site was a very difficult one on which to install a Loran ground system and erect poles. To seaward to the West, the coral dropped off abruptly 20 feet to a coral shelf, awash at high tide. To the Northwest, there was a sand beach only 174 feet from the vertical radiator, and to the Northeast and east was a jagged coral ridge covered by a tangled mass of vines and underbrush. The ridge rose steeply from a line about ten feet back of the proposed location of the equipment hut. Only to the South could 300 feet of clear ground be found for the radials. The major difficulty in erecting the 75 foot creosoted poles of the fixed station was arranging the guys so that they would not conflict with the existing guys of the mobile unit's antenna, which went out in four directions, and also place the pole so that it could be raised.

The carpenters began work on the equipment hut and the power hut. As soon as the pole gang had erected the vertical radiator and two of the six poles, the technicians began the installation of the ground system. The poles were raised by slipping the butt down in the slot next to the hole and having the "cherry picker" in line with the pole behind the hole. Sand bags placed on the tail of the "cherry picker" kept it from turning over as the cable was taken up on the winch with the boom fully extended. In pulling the power cables from the power hut to the equipment hut, it was necessary to use all personnel, both construction and manning, and space them five to ten feet apart along a trail blazed over the ridge and down the intervening hollow. Obstacles to the placing of the ground system were three tents occupied by Army and Marine Corps personnel responsible for the defense of the sector. Rather than move the tents, the ground wires were run under them and buried.

The site of the Quonset huts of the fixed station was on the Eastern side of the ridge behind the equipment hut, where were already located the tents of the mobile unit. All these tents had to be moved to make room for the Quonset huts.

Installation of technical equipment was started on 21 March, at which time the inside screening of the timer room had been erected and soldered. The installation of timers, transmitters, and associated equipment inside the equipment hut was completed by March 24th. By this time the power cables had been laid, and power was applied to the transmitters and timers. By 27 March, installation of the antenna and tuning units, coaxial lines and receiving antenna ground system had been completed. In spite of many difficulties, the station was ready to go on the air 28 March, fourteen days after the last of the material reached the site. Previous to that date the transmitters, and timers had been thoroughly dried out and the tubes given over 24 hours "baking." Timers were adjusted to the proper frequency and rate. both transmitters had been adjusted and tested on internal and external dummy loads for 12 hours or more.

At 0345, 28 March, power was applied to the antenna of the new fixed station, and the mobile Unit 311 ceased transmission. The change from a mobile Loran transmitting station to a fixed station was accomplished with no interruption to the service. As the fixed station went on the air the mobile unit went off, but remained on standby while final tuning adjustments were made. When the transmissions of the fixed station proved to be stable, the mobile unit ceased operation. Immediately the gear to the mobile unit was prepared for shipment, and the trucks left the site. This and the other mobile Fox Stations were picked up by the MENKAR between 29 May, and 27 June, and were taken to the sites already chosen for them in the West Philippines.

With the fixed station on the air, all hands turned to completing the various station buildings and facilities, which included the living quarters and the galley. A storage hut was erected next to the power hut, forming one side of the "U." North of the crew's quarters was the officers' quarters. A concrete rainwater cistern was built behind the galley, along with a pumphouse and an elevated tower for the two 3000-gallon tanks. From the elevated tower, could be seen during the invasion of the Japanese Island to the North, the men going ashore, the bombers blasting the targets, and fighters strafing installations. At night the two red lights on the top of the vertical radiator were used as a range for the coast artillery to shell the Japanese positions.

Ngesebus and Kongaru were the Northernmost islands held by the American forces, some of the Japanese islands being only a stone's throw away, and Babelthaup only a little further Northeast. On dark nights when the tide was low, the Japanese could wade across the shallow coral shelf to the American held islands. When these islands were in Allied hands, the Loran personnel felt more secure in their isolated position.

The routing of the MENKAR, since its assignment to the Coast Guard as a Loran ship, was entirely in the hands of the Commanding officer of the Loran Command Unit (Unit 203) under whose direction all this construction work was being performed. To the landing of the large quantities of construction material, and its transportation from the open beaches to the station sites, Command Unit 203 had organized a special beach landing party, consisting of officers and men who had already gained valuable experience in this unusual type of work. This beach landing detail traveled on board the MENKAR, and performed or supervised the landing operation once the cargoes were landed on the beach.

41

Chapter 12

PULO ANNA OPERATION

9 MARCH 1945 TO 14 MARCH 1945
PULO ANNA LANDINGS

 Immediately after unloading cargo at Pelelieu, the MENKAR had been ordered to Pulo Anna, reaching there on 9 March, 1945. Pulo Anna was a palm-studded island 200 miles Southwest of Angaur and Pelelieu, approximately 900 yards long and 500 yards wide, completely encircled by a coral reef 200 yards from the beach. We had been informed of the possibility of air or submarine attack while lying off the island, so a special attention was given to radar scanning and bridge lookout. At the time the MENKAR arrived, a moderately Northeasterly wind was blowing and the sea with six to twelve foot crests was breaking on the reef. There was also a heavy cross swell both from the North and East. These adverse conditions made the discharging of cargo seem particularly difficult to attempt. However, the longer the vessel remained at the island, the more likely it was subject to detection by Japanese reconnaissance planes. A DUKW from the island came alongside to take the beachmaster, the ship's First Lieutenant, Lieutenant Skillin, and his assistants ashore to survey the conditions. The Commanding Officer of the MENKAR was advised that the present condition of sea and weather had prevailed for some time, and would probably continue. Lieutenant Skillin reported that there were no openings in the reef, and that boats could cross the reefs only at high water, but some construction materials could be passed manually over the reef.

Given the urgency of the situation, and the unlikelihood of more favorable weather conditions, the Commanding Officer of the MENKAR decided to proceed with the unloading of the ship's cargo in spite of the difficulties. The first cargo to leave the ship reached the beach at 1500, together with the beach working party of 50 men and five officers. Unloading was continued until 2000. The beach working party then returned on board, the ship's LCM and LCVP (landing crafts) stood off the island throughout the night, as did the MENKAR. Because of the great depth of water the MENKAR could not anchor at any time during the unloading operation.

The following day, discharging operations began at 0600, and continued throughout the day. There were only two high tides during the day when the reef could be crossed, at 0600 and 1800. At other times of the day supplies had to be brought to the edge of the reef, removed from the barges, transferred across the reef into a DUKW or trailer and towed to the beach for discharging. On 12 March, 1945, work again began at 0600. This was a particularly difficult day for landing operations due to heavy swells and cross seas. It was almost impossible for the boats to come alongside the MENKAR without being damaged, and the discharging of cargo from the ship into them was extremely difficult. However the work continued until 2115.

On 13 March, 1945 work was continued as before. By this time the landing craft were beginning to show the effects of their arduous task. Much damage had been done to propellers and rudders by crossing the coral reef. One LCVP had been greatly damaged by being smashed against the ship's side, and had to be beached and a survey held. At 2100 the beach working party returned to the ship. At 0600 on 14 March,1945 work was continued, and at 1930 discharging operations were completed and the LCM returned to the MENKAR with all ship's personnel. From this point on the entire project was in the hands of the construction detachment.

COMMANDING OFFICER

LIEUT. SKILLIN BEACH MASTER

44-B

REEF PULO ANNA

BEACH PULO ANNA

44-D

PULO ANNA

PULO ANNA

MENKAR – OPEN SEA

MENKAR

MENKAR

PULO ANNA

ON GUARD.   DAMAGED LCVP

PULO ANNA

COMMANDING OFFICER

USS MENKAR (AK-123)
File: 601

16 March, 1945

CONFIDENTIAL

From: Lieutenant J.T. Challenger, USCGR, Navigator
To: Commanding Officer

Subj: Pulo Anna Operations, 10 to 14 March, 1945, inclusive

1.   In accordance with Commanding Officer's directive dated 15
March, 1945, file 601, the following report is hereby submitted.

2.   On 10 March, 1945, at 1000, we stood off Pulo Anna Island
wih a DUKW from the Island alongside for the ship's beachmaster
and his assistants to go ashore and survey landing conditions.
Pulo Anna is an island approximately 900 yards long and 500 yards
wide with a reef entirely surrounding the island and standing out
200 yards from the beach. A moderate Northeasterly wind was
prevalent and a sea of approximately six to twelve foot crest was
breaking on the reef. There was also a heavy cross swell both
from the North and East. These adverse conditions made the discharging of our cargo seem particularly difficult to attempt,
The Commanding Officer was advised by the island Commander that
these conditions had been prevalent for some time. It was decided
to begin discharging our cargo in spite of these difficulties.

3.   At 1115 we began lowering boats into the water so the
operation of discharging our cargo could commence. The first
load of cargo departed the ship at 1500 together with a beach
working party of fifty men and ten officers. Officers and men
worked side by side in the handling of cargo. The remaining
officers and ship's crew were working in the holds, discharging
gear. It was necessary for the Commanding Officer to remain on
the bridge and conn the ship at all times during the unloading
operations. There was no possibility of anchoring the ship.

4.   At 1600 the herring-bone gear on winch #1 was damaged
while in the process of of lifting a 1½ ton carryall. This made
it necessary to place in effect a "jury rig" to winch #3 on hold
#2. Unloading was then continued after a short delay until 2000.
At 2100 the beach working party returned on board, and the LCM
and the LCVP stood off the island throughout the night, as did
the MENKAR, the navigator and another watch officer conning the
ship throughout the night. It was presumed that we may have been
sighted lying off the island by enemy patrol plane, in which
event submarine or air attack was highly probably. To keep the
crew alert a general quarters drill was held at 2300.

4.   On 11 March, 1945, discharging operations began at 0600 and continued throughout the day. Due to only two high tides during the day, which made it possible for boats to reach the beach, best results were acheived approximately at 1800 when the tides were highest. Only at this time was it possible for cargo to be discharged directly upon the beach. At all other times of the day supplies were loaded into the DUKW or trailer, moved over the reef by hand and into the DUKW or trailer on the other side of the reef to be towed ashore. At 1950 the beach working party returned to the ship, and the same procedure as the previous night was followed.

6.   On 12 March, 1945, our work again began at 0600. This was a particularly difficult day for our operations due to heavy swells and cross sea. It was almost impossible for the boats to come alongside without being banged about and the discharging of cargo from the ship into small boats was extremely difficult. Work continued during the day and at 2115 the beach working party returned to the ship. Due to the sea and swell conditions, it was almost an hour before all hands were safely on board.

7.   On 13 March, 1945, work was continued as before. By this time the landing craft were beginning to show the effects of their arduous task. Most of the damage was caused to propellors and rudders due to scraping on coral while crossing the reef. One LCVP suffered severely by being smashed against the ship's side and had to be beached and a board of survey held. At 2100 the beach working party returned on board, leaving two officers and a signalman to spend the night on the island so as to be able to supervise the unloading of one LCM which had been trapped inside the reef.

8.   On 14 March, 1945, operations were continued at 0600 and proceeded throughout the day. At 1930 the LCM returned with all hands and the barges were hoisted on board. Discharging operations were completed.

9.   Much difficulty was encountered due to the nature of the cargo being unloaded. Cargo consisted of commissary supplies, various sizes of crates, quonset hut material, drums of fuel, and highly delicate electronic equipment. The latter was especially difficult in handling as extra precaution had to be exercised as the material was not replaceable. Only when weight or bulk demanded, was mechanical gear employed on this type of equipment. Whenever possible, this tpe of gear was handled by hand so as to insure safe delivery.

10.   In the opinion of this writer this almost impossible operation was handled with extreme efficiency and with particularly satifactory results. Damage to cargo was negligible and no serious injury, except a broken leg, resulted to any of the ship's company. That there were no fatal injuries on the landing crafts being loaded at the ship's side was short of a miracle. All hands can feel justly proud that this job, which would have been immediately refused by experienced longshoremen, had been successfully completed.

J.T. Challenger
Lieutenant, USCGR

Chapter 13

MOROTAI PANGEO OPERATION

17 MARCH 1945 TO 25 MARCH 1945

At the conclusion of each Loran installation, all participating officers were required to submit a report on their assessment of the landing operation. Each officer was encouraged to be completely candid in their observations.

The next landing operations were conducted at Morotai. One of the two single slave stations of this chain was to be built on this mountainous, jungle-covered island about fifty miles long. The site selected for this station was on the Northeast end of the island, close to the village of Pangeo river, fifty miles North of the Naval Base. Mobile Unit 333 was already in operation there, and was to be relieved by a fixed station known as Unit 345.

Plans were made to have the MENKAR land the cargo there as she had landed the Pulo Anna material. While the preliminary layouts were being made there were torrential downpours, and roads were impassable except to trucks that pulled themselves from tree to tree by winch. All navigational information indicated that due to swells and high breakers on the shallow beach, landing by other than native canoes was considered to be impractical and highly dangerous.

MENKAR ARRIVES AT PANGEO

Friday morning, 16 March, 1945, the MENKAR reached the Naval Base at the South end of the island of Morotai. Here arrangements were made for two LCT's (landing craft tanks), that were then unloading supplies for an Army garrison force at a native village on the island, to meet the MENKAR the following day at Pangeo cove to assist in landing cargo. Landing conditions at this site were very poor even in the most favorable weather, due to direct exposure to the open sea and the high breaking surf on the shallow beach.

Chapter 14

SECRET DAILY REPORT ON THE (PANGEO) NORTH MOROTAI OPERATION

TOP SECRET

In this report, troubles and natural oppositions are briefly related as they affect activities. It should be borne in mind that throughout this operation enemy airfields were within one hour's flying time, and constant gun watches had to be maintained. No friendly air coverage was present at any time.

17 MARCH, 1945

At 1300 the USS MENKAR (AK-123) stood in towards the coast of Northeast Morotai, and anchored in Pangeo Cove, approximately four hundred (400) yards from the beach in twenty-three (23) fathoms of water over a sandy bottom. As no charts of the cove were available, soundings around the ship and throughout the cove were taken immediately. There was a moderate offshore breeze. The sky was overcast with intermittent rain squalls moving through the cove. A current set from the North held the vessel in the trough of a long Northeasterly ground swell. A heavy surf was breaking in all parts of the cove.

By 1400 the ship's three LCMs had been lowered, and were ready to receive cargo. Although the ship was kept headed into the swells, she was far from steady, and difficulty in putting the LCMs over the side was experienced. The first LCM was loaded with the beach working parties, along with one tractor without a blade attachment. The second LCM contained a concrete mixer and a trackson crane. The lowering of this heavy equipment was a delicate task even with the ship headed into the swells. On striking the beach, both barges broached. The heights of the breakers on the beach were estimated at approximately eight (8) feet. It was evident that LCMs would be unable to retract from this beach solely under their own power. The rolling equipment in these LCMs was landed and taken to higher ground off the beach. The tractor now ashore was not equipped with a blade attachment, and therefore could not be of any assistance in launching the LCMs. To compound the bleak situation, the mud on the road leading down to the beach from the site was over two feet deep, and the rain was coming down in a solid deluge without any letup.

For the next few hours the personnel on the beach did little but sit and look in discouragement at the stranded barges and pounding surf. Some sat under the palms and tried to imagine transporting an entire Loran station through this mud and jungle to the Loran site. Many natives congregated on the beach, apparently oblivious to the continual downpour. Communications were set up with the ship, and at 1630 the third LCM, loaded with a second tractor and a blade attachment, broached on the beach, true to precedent. The second tractor was run on to the beach, the blade attachment was unloaded and assembled on the tractor. The beach parties with the assistance of this tractor spent the next several hours clearing the area above the beach for cargo storage. The three LCMs assisted by steadying lines and launched by the tractor, were then sent out through the surf. With the exception of one man, who remained on the beach to man the tractor, all hands were back on board at 2015.

It was decided that evening that the risk involved in attempting to unload Loran cargo on Pangeo beach in LCMs under the existing beach conditions was too great. It was the opinion that larger landing craft should be used. Consequently it was planned that at daybreak we would return to Southern Morotai, load our cargo into LCT's in the calm of the anchorage there, and return to Pangeo. Our LCMs remained in the water all during the night with instructions to come alongside at daybreak for hoisting. During our few hours here we had been thoroughly impressed with the operational difficulties in store for us.

18 MARCH, 1945

It rained continuously. At 0600 the ship's LCMs came alongside for hoisting. There was a heavy squall and no amount of maneuvering could entirely eliminate the rolling and pitching of the ship. While hoisting the after LCM, one of our young seaman, George Ybarra, Seaman 2nd class, while in the routine performance of his duties was crushed, and instantly killed. At 0730 we departed from Pangeo Cove and at 1300 anchored in the bay at Southern Morotai. Arrangements for the funeral of the deceased seaman were made. He was buried with full military honors at 1700 in the Army Cemetery. A priest of his own faith administered the last rites.
The service of two Navy LCT's was secured for the Pangeo operation. The LCT Captains were familiar with the beach conditions at Pangeo, and were reluctant to accept the assignment. Many excuses were advanced, such as engine trouble, ramp trouble, and the non-feasibility of landing on the beach. The two LCT's assigned

USS MENKAR (AK-123)
c/o Fleet Post off
San Francisco, Calif.
20 March, 1945

Mr and Mrs Roque Ybarra
14753 Blythe Street
Van Nuys, California

My dear Mr and Mrs Ybarra:

While I offer you my deepest sympathy I know mere words from
me cannot console you in your grief over the loss of your
son George. I can only tell you of his life with us on the
MENKAR, and the manner of his passing from this earth.

Amongst the crew of every ship there are always some men whose
eagerness and interest in their allotted duties bring the
eye of their Commanding Officer upon them. Your son George,
was one of these. He was extremly happy on the MENKAR, and
among his effects was found a request that he be retained in
the permanent Coast Guard after the war's end. George was
one of our orignal crew who joined the MENKAR last September
in San Francisco. He came on board as a mess attendant, and
along with his friend Hernandez took care of the officer's
quarters and wardroom.

These boys had their hearts set on a transfer to the seaman
branch on board ship, and in the early part of January as a
reward for work well done, they were transferred to the deck
department as seamen second class. George was an alert and
willing worker and was assigned as a member of a boat crew.
He was proud and happy in his work. On an early Sunday
morning, 18 March, 1945, while earnestly and ably performing
his duty he was accidentally struck by a heavy object. He
never knew nor felt the approach of death, which was
instantaneous. As he was struck he fell into the water, and
although the ship was far from shore and the ptopellers
turning over, two members of the crew leapt overboard fully
clothed and brought him back to the ship. This in some
measure will reveal to you the regard in which your son was
held by his shipmates.

The ship immediately set sail for a port some sixty miles
distant. That morning the Commanding Officer, together with
your son's comrades held a divine service on board ship in
his behalf. At five P.M. on that same afternoon your son
left his ship, wrapped in the colors of his country, and was
buried with full military honors in consecrated ground. He
lies in a beautiful cemetery on the Island of Morotai in the
Netherlands East Indies. His closest friends were his pall-
bearers, and his Commanding Officer and as many of the crew
of officers and men as could be spared, accompanied him to
his last resting place.

A Catholic Priest, Father Stamn, administered the last rites. Your son was a religious boy, and I never failed to see him at divine services on board ship each Sunday. Photographs of your son's resting place, of his departure from the ship, and of Father Stamn were taken and are being sent to you. The flag which covered him on his last journey, the flag for which he gave his life, is in my possession. My home is in California, and when I return I shall bring to you personally this flag together with a picture of his ship. Should you change your address kindly notify me at my presnt station.

The officers and men of the MENKAR desire that a part of their regard for your son be expressed in masses to be said for the eternal peace of his soul. We enclose for this purpose the sum of two hundred and sixty ($260.00), all entirely unsolicited and voluntarily contributed by his shipmates. Should you wish to use this money to perpetuate the memory of your son in any other manner, that is our wish also.

I am deeply grieved.

You have lost a son and I have lost one of my crew, whose life, which was in my keeping, was also dear to me, his Commanding Officer.

Sincerely,

Niels P. Thomsen,
Lieutenant Commander
U.S. Coast Guard

were openly unenthusiastic, although the Commanding Officer of the Naval Base and all Port and Cargo Authorities were most cooperative. The status of the LCT's was somewhat complicated as they were attached to a Navy Command who had moved ahead into the Philippines leaving the senior of the three LCT Captains in direct operational control. Their usual assignments were transporting freight about the bay and to small Army posts on the island. It later proved that their hesitancy in accepting our assignment was most justified in that their experience was wholly inadequate for a beach operation such as Pangeo.

19 MARCH, 1945

<u>It rained heavily throughout the day</u>. The first LCT arrived alongside at 0830, and was loaded at 1405. Its cargo consisted of stores, technical gear, and tents (the latter being used to cover the cargo from rain). This LCT load was over-estimated by the LCT Captain at one hundred twenty (120) tons, while actually it had only 80 tons on board. At 2100 this LCT returned to the ship and requested to be lightened, the Captain claiming he was overloaded and listing heavily. Upon investigation by the Commanding Officer of the MENKAR, a slight list of two degrees was found. However, approximately two tons of cargo were then removed as a gesture to maintain harmony. Throughout the operation the Captains of the LCT's were humored and handled with kid gloves, and every attempt to instill them with self-confidence was made.

20 MARCH, 1945 (MY 38TH BIRTHDAY)

<u>It rained continuously</u>. The second LCT came alongside at 0100, being 12 hours late. This LCT completed loading at 0630, taking on board only 60 tons, which consisted mainly of heavy items, such as metal Quonset material, heavy pieces of technical equipment, bundles of plywood and lumber. Three armed guards were assigned to each LCT to safeguard the Loran equipment enroute to Pangeo. At 0700 both LCT's departed for Pangeo. One of our three LCMs being assigned to the Loran unit there was left behind. Prior to getting underway our escort vessel took on water and fuel from the MENKAR, and at 1100 we departed for Pangeo Cove.

At 1755 we anchored as before in Pangeo Cove and immediately lowered our two LCMs in a heavy Northerly swell. The beach conditions did not appear to have improved. A 6x6 dual wheel truck was lowered into one LCM and an Athey trailer was lowered into another. The trailer was in turn loaded with an 8,800 pound evaporator. These two LCMs made the beach and their position was held fairly well by mooring lines and tackles rigged to coconut palms despite the seven foot surf. The truck was run onto the beach with ease, but the heavily-laden Athey trailer gave difficulty owing to its top-heaviness.

Both LCMs broached several times before they could be launched and it was 2000 before the beach parties were heading back to the ship in heavy rain and darkness. However, much had been accomplished, and we felt confident of our ability to safely land our cargo here. The Commanding Officer of the MENKAR was ashore overseeing the operation. A conference was held with the Captains of the LCT's, and it was agreed that they were to land in the morning as soon as the beach parties were ashore.

21 MARCH, 1945

It was raining heavily at 0700 when an 80-man working party was sent to the beach. At 0735 we commenced loading our two LCMs with cargo from the ship's holds.

It soon became apparent that landing upon a beach under such conditions as existed here at Pangeo, was a new experience to these Navy LCT Captains. The timidity of the first LCT in making the approach delayed his getting on the beach until 0935. Despite mooring lines the ship swung out in the surf, and the LCT Captain refused to slack his stern anchor cable and come closer in. After a few moments the LCT backed off for another approach. Four faint-hearted approaches were made without success, following which, the LCT moved out into the cove and anchored.

During this interval one of the ship's LCMs landed on the beach and unloaded two sleds of general cargo. While unloading the LCM, the trackson crane took "aboard" a large sea, which immobilized this piece of equipment. This crane was dragged off the beach, and after several hours was again in commission.

The Commanding Officer of the MENKAR came into the beach with the next LCM load to direct the unloading of the LCT's. After some persuasion by the Commanding Officer of the MENKAR, the LCT came in once more and made a partially successful landing. This time she lowered her ramp, and the Athey trailer was backed into the LCT. The LCT was being tossed about considerably and as the tractor was towing a trailer load of vital equipment out of the LCT, it took a sea and stalled in approximately three feet of water. The other tractor, which was engaged in cutting a road through the jungle to the Loran site, was sent for and soon arrived to tow the disabled tractor and trailer off the beach. The surf was increasing and all four four-inch mooring lines made fast to the bow of the LCT, suddenly parted. The LCT backed off the beach once again. This time the Captain of the LCT asserted hat he was "through" with this beach. In defense of these Navy LCT Captains, it can be said that they were young and inexperienced, and their timidity and reluctance to risk their vessels, as they believed, was understandable. However, this cargo had to be put ashore regardless of necessary risks to equipment involved. The Captain of the LCT then refused to attempt another landing. The Commanding Officer of the MENKAR boarded the LCT, and after an hour of persuasion, the original LCT Captain finally agreed to make one more attempt to land. It was suggested to the LCT that the next landing be made several hours later on at high tide. The Commanding Officer of the MENKAR then had two heavy four-inch diameter mooring lines and several heavy tackles brought ashore from the ship. As the LCT touched the beach, a heavy mooring line was fastened to the bits on each bow of the LCT and heavy tackles made fast from these mooring lines to trees on the beach. A heavy wire was then made fast to the bow of the LCT. On the other end of the cable was a 15 ton tractor. As the tractor hove the LCT onto the beach, crews of men manned the tackles on the 4" lines. There were protests from the Captain of the LCT, but before he could take any action, the reluctant LCT, was "Shanghaied" on the ebbing tide and he had no choice but to remain on the beach until the next high tide.

Discharging of the LCT then resumed. The day's progress amounted to a complete unloading of the LCT plus three loads by LCM. A dispatch to the Commander of the Naval Base at South Morotai requesting the loan of two LCMs was sent that evening.

This hectic day on the beach was climaxed by near disaster shortly after, when the LCM on the beach attempted to return to the ship. The surf had increased considerably in the afternoon and the height of breakers was approximately eight feet. As the LCM was being launched, a large breaker threw her on her beam ends, sweeping overboard four men, including the Commanding Officer of the MENKAR. All these men were drawn under the LCM by the strong undertow. The Commanding Officer of the MENKAR was knocked momentarily unconscious and was rescued by the quick action of two of the other men. The only casualties in this accident were bruises and one man suffering from a wrenched back. The LCM was straightened out on the beach and successfully launched.

22 MARCH, 1945

It was raining heavily as the beach party arrived on the beach at 0705. The surf had subsided somewhat and throughout the day the higher breakers averaged only about six feet. Work progressed splendidly on the beach all day. Six LCM loads were landed, and with our improved methods of mooring lines, there was no serious broaching. Truck transfer of cargo from the beach to the construction site was halted after two laborious trips with light loads. Later in the day the mud on the road to the site reached a depth of two feet and transportation to the site came to a standstill. The cargo accumulated rapidly on the beach, and had to be moved by Athey trailer and tractor from the beach landing site to even higher ground.

Materials reaching the beach today consisted mainly of miscellaneous boxes or wire reels, which could be manually carried or rolled out. In some instances 1,200 pound boxes were laid on bars and carried by sixteen men.

Both LCT's remained at anchor today, one loaded and the other empty of cargo. The Senior Officer in charge of the two LCT's flatly refused to permit the loaded LCT to land and discharge our cargo.
This action compelled the Commanding Officer of the MENKAR to send a dispatch to the Commander of the Morotai Naval Base requesting operational control and full responsibility for landing the LCT's:

Commanding Officer, USS MENKAR (AK-123), Confidential Dispatch, 220430 (March, 1945) to Commander Naval Base, Southern Morotai.

PASS TO ARMY GEORGE FOUR PORT DIRECTOR FROM COMMANDING OFFICER MENKAR X BEACH CONDITIONS EXCELLENT FOR LANDING BY LCT RPT LCT X **OFFICERS IN CHARGE CONSIDERED INCOMPETENT DUE TO INEXPERIENCE X IN VIEW OF HIGH PRIORITY OF CARGO THIS OFFICER REQUESTS COMPLETE RESPONSIBILITY AND AUTHORITY TO LAND REMAINING LCT RPT LCT X** REMAINDER OF CARGO ON BOARD BEING DISCHARGED BY LCM RPT LCM X **INFO TO CINCPAC AND COMPAC AREA CONDETS COAST GUARD**.

In the opinion of the Commanding Officer of the MENKAR, the re-handling of our cargo under existing weather conditions would be taking an unnecessary risk. At 1600 in response to the Commanding Officer's previous request, the three LCMs from Southern Morotai reported to the ship for duty. The beach party left for the ship at 1800.

23 MARCH, 1945

It rained heavily as the beach party left for the beach at 0700. The surf remained comparatively light all day, breakers averaging about five feet. The progress made on the beach was the best yet. In the early forenoon the rain stopped. It became very hot and all hands on the beach were considerably annoyed by myriads of insects. The climate is extremely enervating and the men are quickly fatigued. During the day trucks were winched up to the construction site with light loads. Several heavy trailer loads also made their way to the site. One of the three borrowed LCMs flooded her engine room, and was disabled in the surf. It was pushed and towed off the beach, taken to the ship, pumped out and reloaded. As no answer to the Commanding Officer of the MENKAR's dispatch had yet been received, it was decided to commence the transferring of the cargo from the LCT into the LCMs in order that the operation not be delayed. The LCT's cargo consisted mainly of large bundles of building materials. These bundles were dismantled and manually transferred into the LCMs. When no cargo remained which could be manually handled, the LCT was taken alongside the ship and the remaining cargo, consisting mostly of large boxes of technical equipment, was taken back on board the MENKAR, and later transferred into LCMs. Materials put on the beach today were as follows: 600 sacks of cement, 275 drums of fuel, considerable bundles of plywood, eight poles 75 feet long, and a quantity of boxed cargo. That evening the ship's two LCMs were hoisted on board for repairs. As the ship had to be darkened, a hatch tent was placed over them on deck, and the engineers worked on them throughout the night.

24 MARCH, 1945

Promising weather characterized the early morning and it was substantially cooler. The LCMs were lowered at daybreak and at 0750, left for the beach, loaded and with the beach parties. The surf was moderate. considerable cargo was landed on the beach this morning and when not unloading LCMs, the beach parties were busy moving cargo to dryer ground. Three trucks with medium loads made it to the site during the day. A good deal of work was done on improving the road and in making a new one. Some cargo was dragged straight up the cliff and near the landing by means of a winch and "A" frame. Both LCMs had to be taken aboard again to be repaired during the night. The three borrowed LCMs from southern Morotai were all damaged and of little further use. They departed for southern Morotai at 1400.

At 1600 the commanding Officer of the Naval Base at Southern Morotai arrived by crash boat and granted the Commanding Officer of the MENKAR full operational control over the LCT's. This authority, while appreciated, arrived too late to be of value, since the cargo was already ashore. He had heard from CINCPAC.

25 MARCH, 1945

This day was clear and a trifle cooler. The swell appeared to have moderated to some extent. At 0700 the LCMs were lowered. Relatively little cargo remained to be taken from the ship, and as the tractors were still in use constructing the new road, the beach parties did not go ashore until 0900. Part of the crew had remained ashore and worked on the road during the night. Rain during the last thirty-six (36) hours having been very light, the prospects of getting cargo to the site today looked promising. Heavy pieces of cargo were put ashore this morning. These were placed in Athey trailers in the LCMs alongside the ship. They consisted of an evaporator weighing 8,800 pounds; three generators weighing 5,900 pounds each; and two refrigerators weighing 5,300 pounds each. These trailer loads were taken directly to the site as they landed on the beach. Oil drums, oxygen bottles, dynamite, and small arms ammunition were also put ashore. A favorable surf condition, combined with the speedy cargo to handle, accounted for the rapid progress during the morning hours. Very few breakers were over five feet high when the barges first hit the beach, although further down the cove they appeared larger.

Upon departure of the MENKAR, the construction detachment continued moving the cargo to the station site. After two days of comparatively light rain, the roads were suitable for trucks, and two trucks loaded with lumber made the site with the assistance of a winch, up the steepest grade. The surf was increasing during the morning, and at noon the breakers were six feet. This is a heavy break here, and it is fortunate that the last LCM load hit the beach at 1230. About 1330 a heavy downpour occurred, converting the road again into a quagmire.

In the next two and one half hours of rain, the tractor, now no longer needed to handle LCMs, made three trips to the site with the Athey trailers carrying heavy loads. The Commanding Officer of the MENKAR made the last trip to the site to witness the transfer of the last of the heavy cargo from the beach.

There now remained on the beach only such cargo as could be easily handled by the construction crew remaining behind. One tractor, the trackson crane, and one Athey trailer, were taken back on board ship. At 1800 the MENKAR weighed anchor, hoisted her LCMs and stood out of Pangeo cove, and every man on the MENKAR breathed a sigh of relief, and fervently expressed the hope that he never see this cove again.

MOROTAI BEACH   LCM (LANDING CRAFT MEDIUM)

MOROTAI

MOROTAI

L.C.V.P. (LANDING CRAFT VEHICLE)

CRANE UNLOADING FROM LCM

LCM CRANE   TRACTOR AND ATHEY WAGON

LCT BEING *SHANGHIED* BY TRACTOR

54-G

MOORING LCT

UNLOADING LCT

C.O.

LCT

ROAD TO LORAN SITE

ROAD TO LORAN SITE

ROAD TO LORAN SITE

MANHANDLING 1400 LB. CRATE

Address reply to:
CO, USS MENKAR (AK-123)
c/o Fleet Post Office
San Francisco, California
Refer to file: F15/S82

24 March, 1945

C-O-N-F-I-D-E-N-T-I-A-

To: H.H. Harrison, CDMDR. USN, Commander US Naval Base, Morotai

Subj: Three LCM's under your command, in charge of ChBosn
        H. W. Gehring, USN.

1. Three LCM's from your command, in charge of ChBosun
   Gehring reported to this vesel for duty at Pangeo at
   1700, 22 March, 1945.

2. For the past two days these LCM's have been landing the
   MENKAR's cargo upon the beach at Pangeo in an excellence
   performance of seamanship. The cooperation extended to us
   by ChBosun Gehring, USN, of your command is example of
   two commands striving for a common goal.

3. The beach conditions were extremely difficult and I
   regret that all three of your LCM's were slightly
   damaged. I assure you that it was unavoidable, and that
   the craft were ably handled by their coxswains.

4. Due to the refusal of the LCT to land upon the beach,
   it was necessary to transfer the cargo from the LCT
   to the LCM's for discharge on the beach. This delayed us
   considerably.

5. This officer again expresses his appreciation of your
   substantial cooperation.

                              N.P. Thomsen, LCDR, USCG
                              Commanding, USS MENKAR

Address reply to:
CO USS MENKAR (AK-123)
% Fleet Post Office
San Francisco, California
Refer to file 601

5 April, 1945

S-E-C-R-E-T

To: COMMANDANT (O) (OAN) (ECV)

Subj: Northern Morotai (Pangeo) operation; report on

1.   The three (3) enclosures constitute the report on subject operation.

2.   Our satisfaction over the success of this operation was clouded by the accidental death of one of our number in the line of duty.

3.   The type of duty being performed by the MENKAR is characteristically Coast Guard as apart from normal wartime activities. The training in seamanship here is invaluable to the postwar Coast Guard, and should be retained within the service if possible.

4.   It is recommended that six regular Coast Guard Ensigns be assigned to the MENKAR, replacing reserve officers on whom this training is lost insofar as the Coast Guard is concerned.

5.   It may be of interest to the Coast Guard that with an average daily complement of 400 Coast Guard personnel, there have been no deck or summary court-martials on board during this first six months of operation in the forward area.

N.P. Thomsèn, LCDR
U.S. Coast Guard

Encls:
1. Daily report of North Morotai
   operation, 17 to 25 March, 1945.
2. USS MENKAR Confidential Dispatch,
   220430 (March), 1945.
3. Photographs of subject operation.

CC: (less inclosure #3)
HQ (OAN)
    (ECV)

26 March, 1945

<u>**LOUD SPEAKER ADDRESS**</u>

MEN OF THE MENKAR!

Again you leave behind you a task well done. It was one, which many would have considered impossible, as we have reason to know. You can be proud, as I am, of the MEN of the MENKAR's performance on that rugged, boiling strip of beach that we have newly left behind us. A beach which I am sure none of us ever wish to see again. Sadly, Our satisfaction is clouded by the tragic death in line of duty of one of our comrades whose sacrifice we will always remember.

Your reward is not contained in these words I utter here, but in the satisfaction within each of you in the knowledge of a job nobly accomplished. Each of you is aware of what his personal contribution to the success of our mission consists of. Therein lies your reward. It is my belief that only the Coast Guard could have done what we did at _____.[1]

I know you must be weary and exhausted from your efforts. For the next four days it is planned that only necessary work will be performed after 1200 hours. In other words, your next four afternoons will be your own.

I am bursting with pride over your accomplishments at _____.

N.P. Thomsen
Lt. Comdr., USCG
Commanding

---

[1] The mission being secret, the location of the ship was never revealed to the crew.

Chapter 15

BEACH ORGANIZATION

The First Lieutenant of the ship is also the Beachmaster. He is in constant touch with, and directly responsible to, the Commanding Officer of the MENKAR, for getting the cargo out of the LCMs and to a safe point above high water. Under the Beachmaster are two officers. The first of these officers is in charge of mooring the LCMs and he is responsible to the Beachmaster for holding the LCMs in position with mooring lines and tractor.

The Second Officer arranges for the efficient placement and stacking of materials on any available drained ground, and he directs the crew assigned to that task. The beach parties are divided into groups of ten men each, with an aggressive petty officer in charge of each group. This makes for greater mobility of personnel, and also encourages competition and pride in accomplishment between the groups. All men are versed in the importance of Loran cargo and the care with which it must be handled. A certain amount of idealism and Coast Guard pride must be instilled into this type of an operation. Officers and men must work side by side both on board ship and on the beach during these operations.

Next there is the "Beach Landing Party" whose functions as part of the Construction Detachment is to transport the cargo from above the high water mark to the site of Loran construction. A Construction Detachment Officer, known as the "Beach Landing Officer" directs these men. The title of this officer and his party is misleading, as they have no connection with the landing of the cargo, that being the sole responsibility of the MENKAR. It is the policy of the MENKAR after the cargo is landed, to assist in the movement of cargo to the site, as the entire Loran program is a Coast Guard Mission. It is difficult at times to explain to men who are not seamen, there must be no delay in discharging the landing craft and getting them off the beach as quickly as possible. A landing, once begun, especially in these regions, must be carried to a conclusion as speedily as possible, since the threat of adverse weather and enemy action is always present.

Chapter 16

THE BEACH

The greatest obstacle at Pangeo was the bad surf. For direct reference to the "High seas and rollers" and the currents mentioned in this report, of sailing directions for New Guinea. Weather comments concerning Northern Morotai Island, prove interesting. There is no mention of this cove in any navigational publication at our disposal.

The heavy ground swell came in nearly parallel to the landing beach. There was no especially strong current close to the shore line. With the five foot range of tide, the distance from the high to the low water line was fifteen or twenty yards. [1] The beach was of black volcanic sand, hard and even. Unlike a shingle or stony beach, the returning waves traveled rapidly and solidly out again. The steepness of the beach gave rise to very steep breakers which broke close in and sometimes fell on the bare sand. The breakers ran from a minimum of four feet to a maximum of ten feet. This made hard going for small barges such as the LCMs carried by the MENKAR. It is suggested that when a Loran site is selected more complete study be given to the landing conditions, not only as they appear at the time of selection, but during the unfavorable weather periods. An experienced seaman, familiar with the problems of beach landings should most certainly be a member of the group selecting the Loran site. This particular operation came close to being impossible, as theoretically only native outrigger canoes can land in Pangeo Cove during the period of North and Northeasterly swells.

-N.P. Thomsen, LCDR, USCG

---

[1]   Photographic supplement to this report illustrates this well.

LORAN STATION COMMENTS

The task of hauling the gear consumed much time. Trucks ruined the road for even tractor use, so they were not used, making the tractor and Athey wagon the only available transportation. Only two or three trips a day could be made, even after a new road had been built. The tractor, which the MENKAR had left behind, had a very poor clutch, and required constant care and repair.

Construction of the station went well after the hauling was completed. A very fortunate break in the weather aided materially although the heat was very tiring. No clearing was necessary, but all holes for hoisting antenna poles, cisterns, and septic tank, had to be blasted out of solid coral. This presented no small problem due to the fact that mobile Detachment Fox was set up at the same location, and concussion and flying debris had to be kept under control. There was no aggregate for mixing cement, and sand alone had to be used.

There were a number of complications in the building of this, as well as other stations of the chain. The mobile unit in this case, was so situated as to be in the direct path of the power cables and conduit, necessitating various bends to avoid conflict. The emergency antenna pole, located to the South of the main tower, was in the center of the equipment of the mobile unit. Raising this pole was deferred until the mobile unit moved out. Installation of the electrical equipment was started on 22 March, and with the exception of the communications equipment, was completed by 31 March. A small item, typical of this type of construction work, with the nearest source of supply hundreds of miles away, was the lack of angular fittings, bands, and junction boxes among the electrical supplies.

These, as a consequence, had to be made on the job by cutting and brazing available stock. When the manning personnel of Unit 345 arrived on 7 April, 1945, the equipment hut was erected and the inside screening of the timer room was almost completed. One emergency antenna pole and the remote receiving pole were up. The unpacking and installation was started the next day.

The main vertical pieces of the steel vertical radiator were missing, and it was necessary to use the emergency antenna. Installation and wiring inside the hut was completed on 12 April, and the exterior conduits, coaxial lines and tuning units were installed and connected by 13 April. Power was available late on 12 April and was immediately applied to the equipment. A 24 hour filament baking period and a twelve hour period of operation under dummy load was accomplished by 14 April. With the exception of several bad tubes there was no trouble with the transmitter, and the timers were in equally good condition.

On 14 April, mobile unit 333 went off the air, and their antenna was easily lowered, as it crossed at right angles below the permanent station antenna. The emergency antenna, previously fabricated in accordance with Headquarters' drawings was then raised. The 58 foot download was too long to permit hauling up tightly due to the antenna poles being erected on sloping ground, and the seaward pole being approximately eight feet lower than the other pole. Three feet was cut from the downlead and the antenna, all indications being that the length of the antenna was excessive. Continuous lowering, cutting, resplicing, and hoisting was necessary for a period of more than four hours. On 15 April, tuning was accomplished and the perfect match was obtained. The length at this time was 50 feet in the downlead, including the lead-in and 43 feet each side of the center in the flat top. The fixed station, rate 4-H-7 was on the air on 28 April, just 14 days after the arrival of the material at the site.

The other permanent transmitting stations were also built adjacent to the operating mobile stations and were put on the air with little or no interruption of service. Mobile Detachment Fox turned over the Palau-Morotai chain to Unit 211 on 24 April, 1945, all the permanent stations then being ready for regular operation. The mobile stations then were to be moved to the Western Philippines, supplying service at points where permanent stations were never built. The chain was commissioned on 22 June, 1945.

A small Army force close by maintained a perimeter against the Japanese forces in the interior of the island. These Japanese were in a bad way, but were being occasionally reinforced by troops from a large Japanese base on Halmahera twelve miles away. The construction detachment personnel, upon completion of the Morotai station, were picked up by the USS MENKAR, along with Mobile Detachments Fox and Mike to debark at Guam for transportation later to the Philippine Islands.

Chapter 17

MENKAR PREPARES FOR IWO JIMA

The MENKAR proceeded to Pelelieu on 29 March, 1945 where it took on cargo and Loran personnel for Guam, arriving there on 3 April. Between this period and 12 April, the MENKAR shuttled Loran Cargo and personnel between Saipan and Guam. While at Guam on 10 April, orders were received to prepare to load mobile Loran equipment for installation on the island of Iwo Jima, and I was advised that major enemy action was a distinct probability. Special identification classes were set up for deck officers, gun crews and lookouts, concentrating on rapidly identifying every type of enemy plane.

Two days before the date of our departure, on the 13th of April, 1945 the Secretary of the Navy issued a priority ALNAV announcing the death of Franklin Delano Roosevelt, the President of the United States.

JAPAN LORAN CHAIN

IWO JIMA	Kanoke Iwa	348	Double Master
TOKYO	O Shima	349	Single Slave
OKINAWA	Ichi Hanare	350	Single Slave

BUILT BY
Construction Detachment C (Unit 80)

With the assaults on Iwo Jima and Okinawa well underway, the time was approaching when the network of Loran Stations could be expanded further in the general direction of Japan. New stations would provide navigational aids for the bombers which were concentrating on the main islands of the Japanese Empire, and were also a part of the plan for providing this same service for the amphibious assault on Japan, preparations which were being made at the time of the abrupt capitulation of Japan.

Iwo Jima, 700 miles South of Tokyo, and Okinawa, approximately the same distance Southwest of that city, were satisfactory locations for Loran stations, and plans were made for installing equipment there. A third station, to complete the chain, would be erected at some point in the vicinity of Tokyo, when this became possible. This proposed chain became known as the Japanese Loran chain. Siting surveys of Iwo Jima and Okinawa were made long before the islands were secured, and the Coast Guard parties carrying out this work were on more than one occasion under fire. This chain was to consist of a double master at Iwo Jima, a single slave at Okinawa, and a single slave at Tokyo. The "Tokyo" station eventually was located on O Shima, an Island in the entrance to Tokyo Bay.

62

Heading: FROM: SECNAV
ACTN: ALNAV #67   PRIORITY

I HAVE THE SAD DUTY OF ANNOUNCING TO THE NAVAL SERVICE THE
DEATH OF FRANKLIN DELANO ROOSEVELT COMMA THE PRESIDENT OF THE
UNITED STATES COMMA WHICH OCCURRED ON TWELVE APRIL X THE
WORLD HAS LOST A CHAMPION OF DEMOCRACY WHO CAN ILL BE SPARED
BY OUR COUNTRY AND THE ALLIED CAUSE X THE NAVY WHICH HE SO
DEARLY LOVED CAN PAY NO BETTER TRIBUTE TO HIS MEMORY THAN TO
CARRY ON IN THE TRADITION OF WHICH HE WAS SO PROUD X COLORS
SHALL BE DISPLAYED AT HALF MAST FOR THIRTY DAYS BEGINNING 0800
THIRTEEN APRIL WEST LONGITUDE DATE INSOFAR AS WAR OPERATIONS
PERMIT X MEMORIAL SERVICES SHALL BE HELD ON THE DAY OF THE
FUNERAL TO BE ANNOUNCED LATER AT ALL YARDS AND STATIONS AND ON
BOARD ALL VESSELS OF THE NAVY COMMA WAR OPERATIONS PERMITTING
X WEARING OF MOURNING BADGES AND FIRING OF SALUTES WILL BE
DISPENSED WITH IN VIEW OF WAR CONDITIONS X JAMES FORRESTAL

ACTION

From: SECNAV	Prec. P	System J FOX	Time of R ⁴418	Supv. BY	WU JD	CWO	No.
Action: ALNAV					Release		
Info:					Date (GCT) 13 APRIL 45		

PT	EXEC.	COMM.	NAV.	GUN.	ENG.	MED.	OOD	SUPPLY	1stLT.	YEO.	TROOP CO.			

MEMORIAL SERVICE
U.S.S. MENKAR (AK-123)
1000, SUNDAY, 15 APRIL, 1945.

"Burden-bearers are we all, Great and small—"

Organ Prelude - "Adagio from First Sonata"
Mendelssohn

Opening Hymn - "Faith of Our Fathers"

The Call To Worship

Memorial Hymn - "Rock of Ages, Cleft for Me"

Responsive Reading - "The Lord Our Shepherd"

Doxology
"The Old Hundredth"

Meditation

The Lord's Prayer

The Navy Hymn - "Eternal Father, Strong to Save"

Benediction
For Inner Peace

Patriotic Hymn - "Battle Hymn of the Republic"

Organ Postlude - "National Echoes"
(An Arrangement)

L. M. BARRACLOUGH, Leader   R. C. JEFFERSON, Organist

N. P. THOMSEN,
Lieutenant Commander, USCG,
Commanding

J. A. ROOT,
Lieutenant, USCGR,
Executive

/Born - 30 January, 1882/
FRANKLIN DELANO ROOSEVELT
/Died - 12 April, 1945/

62-B

Dear Lord and Father of mankind, forgive our feverish ways!
Reclothe us in our rightful mind, in purer lives Thy service find,
in deeper reverence, praise.

In simple trust like theirs who heard, beside the Syrian sea, the
gracious calling of the Lord, let us, like them, without a word,
rise up and follow Thee.

Drop Thy still dews of quietness, till all our strivings cease:
take from our souls the strain and stress, and let our ordered
lives confess the beauty of Thy peace.

Breathe through the heats of our desire Thy coolness and Thy balm;
let sense be dumb, let flesh retire; speak through the earthquake
wind and fire, O still, small voice of calm. Amen.
                         -- John G. Whittier.

Program quotation from "Burden-Bearers" by John Oxenham.

"Almighty God,with whom do live the spirits of those who depart
hence in the Lord and with whom the souls of the faithful, after
they are delivered from the burden of the flesh, are in joy and
felicity; We give Thee thanks for the good examples of all those
Thy servants, who, having finished their course in faith, do now
rest from their labors. Amen."

Religion is the art of being, and of doing, good: to be an adept in
it is to become just, truthful, sincere, self-denying, gentle,
forbearing, pure in word and thought and deed. And the school for
learning this art is not the closet but the world-- not some
hallowed spot where religion is taught and proficients, when dully
trained, are sent forth into the world, - but the world itself -
the coarse, profane, common world, with its cares and temptations,
its rivalries and competitions, its hourly ever recurring trials of
temper and character.   --John Caird.

"For the trust reposed in me I will return the courage and the
devotion that befit the time. I can do no less. We face the arduous
days that lie before us in the warm courage of national unity; with
the clear consciousness of seeking old and precious moral values;
with the clean satisfaction that comes from the stern performance
of duty by old and young alike. We aim at the assurance of a
rounded and permanent national life. We do not distrust the future
of essential democracy."   --Franklin Delano Roosevelt.

O God, the King of righteousness, lead us, we pray thee, in ways of
justice and peace; inspire us to break down all tyranny and
oppression, to gain for every man his due reward, and from every
man his due service; that each may live and for all and all may
care for each, in Jesus Christ our Lord. Amen.

Come unto me, all ye that labour and are heavy laden, and I will
give you rest.   (Matthew 11:28)

DIVINE SERVICES

COMMANDING OFFICER'S LOUD SPEAKER ADDRESS TO SHIP'S CREW

17 April, 1945

MEN OF THE MENKAR!!

Shortly after our departure from Honolulu several months ago I spoke to you at considerable length on the nature of this voyage. At that time I told you somewhere, sometime, we could expect action against the planes of the enemy. I stressed the importance of your battle efficiency, and we spent many weeks of training for what now lies ahead. In my opinion you became very proficient at your battle stations.

Since that time we have been constantly engaged in beach landing and construction activities. We have had little time for the thought of battle, as the likelihood of direct enemy action seemed remote.

I have been extremely lenient with many of you as regards your shortcomings in respect to wartime discipline, and the proper and specific performance of your duties as men-of-warsmen during these past weeks. This was partially because of the nature of your duties during that time, and also because I felt that when the time should come that enemy action was a distinct probability, I could count on you to do your part as splendidly as you have done it on the beaches, in the surf, and in the ship's holds.

The time is now here. You are no longer winchmen or long-shoremen on a construction vessel. You have only to observe the number and firepower of our escorts, and to look in the sky above you, to realize that we are embarked on a dangerous mission. After sunrise tomorrow enemy air attack by torpedo and fighter planes is highly probable. Our chances of reaching our destination un-disturbed by enemy activity are perhaps fifty per cent, more or less.

Henceforth you will remain fully clad at all times, so that you may have some protection against flash burns from bombs or shellfire.

You will man your battle stations on the double.

Those of you who stand lookout watches will remember the hundreds of men who sleep soundly below decks because of their faith in the manner in which you are doing your duty.

You will observe every regulation and command to the letter.

Should you neglect your duty in the slightest degree, a quick and severe punishment awaits you.

As is the custom for vessels of the United States Navy when going into battle, a copy of "Rocks and Shoals," Article four (4) Articles for the Government of the United States Navy is being posted alongside a transcript of this address.

Now a word to our passengers –

The abandon-ship stations of the crew of the MENKAR are their battle stations, so that they can protect you while you are abandoning a burning or sinking ship. They will not leave the MENKAR until you are safely away. Give them a fighting chance by getting to your abandon ship stations on the double.

N.P. Thomsen
Lt. Comdr., USCG
Commanding

USS MENKAR (AK-123) "ROCKS AND SHOALS" 17 April, 1945

Article 4, Articles for the Government of the United States Navy

The punishment of death, or such other punishment as a court-martial may adjudge, may be inflicted on any person in the Naval service.

1. Who makes, or attempts to make, or unites with any mutiny or mutinous assembly, or, being witness to or present at any mutiny, does not do his utmost to suppress it: or knowing of any mutinous assembly or of any intended mutiny, does not immediately communicate his knowledge to his superior or commanding officer;
2. Or disobeys the lawful orders of his superior officers;
3. Or strikes or assaults, or attempts to strike or assault, his superior officer while executing the duties of his office;
4. Or gives any intelligence to, or holds or entertains any intercourse with an enemy or rebel, without leave from the President, the Secretary of the Navy, the Commander in Chief of the Fleet, the Commander of the Squadron, or, in case of a vessel acting singly, from his commanding officer;
5. Or receives any message or letter from an enemy or rebel, or, being aware of the unlawful reception of such message or letter, fails to take the earliest opportunity to inform his superior or commanding officer thereof;
6. Or, in time of war, deserts or entices others to desert;
7. Or, in time of war, deserts or betrays his trust, or entices others to desert or betray their trust;
8. Or sleeps upon his watch;
9. Or leaves his station before being regularly relieved;
10. Or intentionally or willfully suffers any vessel of the Navy to be stranded, or runs upon rocks or shoals; or improperly or maliciously or willfully injures any vessel of the Navy, or any part of her tackle, armament, or equipment, whereby the safety of the vessel is hazarded or the lives of the crew exposed to danger;
11. Or, unlawfully sets on fire, or otherwise unlawfully destroys, any public property not at the time in possession of the enemy, pirate, or rebel;
12. Or, strikes or attempts to strike the flag to the enemy, to an enemy or rebel, without proper authority, or, when engaged in

battle, treacherously yields or in want of courage cries for quarter;

13. Or, in time of battle, displays cowardice, negligence, or disaffection, or withdraws from or keeps out of danger to which he should expose himself;

14. Or, in time of battle, deserts his duty or station, or entices others to do so;

15. Or does not properly observe the orders of his commanding officer, and use his utmost exertions to carry them into execution, when ordered to prepare or join in, or when actually engaged in, battle, or in sight of the enemy;

16. Or, being in command of a fleet, squadron, or vessel acting singly, neglects, when an engagement is probable, or when an armed vessel of an enemy, or rebel is in sight, to prepare and clear his ship or ships for action;

17. Or, does not, upon signal for battle, use his utmost exertions to join in battle;

18. Or, fails to encourage in his own person, his inferior officers and men to fight courageously;

19. Or, does not do his utmost to overtake and capture or destroy any vessel which it is his duty to encounter;

20. Or, does not afford all practical relief and assistance to vessels belonging to the United States or their allies when engaged in battle.

21. A summary court-martial may disrate any rated person for incompetency.

Posted this date: 17 April, 1945 USS MENKAR (AK-123)

USS MENKAR (AK-123)
File: 600

MORNING ORDERS FOR THURSDAY, 19 APRIL, 1945.

0350—Relieve the Watch. cont'
0545—Call Bugler.
0545—Scott, BM2c, call Warren, S1c,
    and Negrin, MM2c.
0600—Sound Reveille.
0630—Muster all Divisions.
0700—Pipe down mess for Ship's Crew
    and Watch Standers only.
0750—Relieve the Watch.
0800—Ship's Co, turn to. Pipe down
    mess for Troops.
0830—Sick Call.
0900—Troops turn to.
1100—Reveille for Mid Watch.

1130—Pipe down mess for Ship's Crew
    and Watch Standers only.
1150—Relieve the Watch.
1230—Pipe down mess for Troops.
1300—Troops turn to.
1550—Relieve the Watch.
1630—Pipe down mess for Ship's Crew
    and Watch Standers only.
1730—Pipe down mess for Troops.
1945—Evening Reports Amidships.
2200—Tatoo
2205—Taps.
2350—Relieve the Watch.

SPECIAL ORDERS AND NOTES
for the attention of all hands

1. Troop Personnel will obey Ship's Order and stay forward of the Deck House.
2. Water hours are as follows: 0600—0630, 0800—0820, 1115—1215, and, 1600—1645.
3. Unauthorized Personnel not allowed on #3 Deck House.
4. Any light not in use should be turned off. When the ship has been darkened all hatches leading into light locks are to be secured with at least one dog. Remember that the showing of light of any kind during the blackout period is a menace to the safety of all hands.
5. Unauthorized tampering with fire equipment is considered a very serious offense. The safety of the ship, yourself, and your shipmates may depend on their proper working order.
6. The following personnel changes have been made: (a) VIAYRA, Miguel (677-087), StM2c (r), transferred from Div-2 to Div-5 and assigned to Wardroom Galley. (b) SZYMANSKI, Joseph (663-982), StM2c (R), transferred from Wardroom Galley to Ship's Cook striker. (c) Strike the following names from Division Two Rosters: BUCKLER, BM2c, and ANDERSON, BM1c. (d) Rating of BARTLETT, Manuel C. (7012-307 Div-4, changed from CM3c, to MM3c. (B). (e) Rating of JOHNSTON, Thomas G. (597-503), Div-5, changed from SSML3c(R) to SSML2c(R). (f) The attention of all hands is called to a memorandum from the Commanding Officer which has been posted on the Wardroom, Post Office, and Mess Deck Bulletin Boards and regarding recent reductions in rating by disciplinary action.
7. Genoral Information: Laundry only for: Lts(jg), MAHAR, DOSSETT, JOHNSON, JEFFERSON, HACKETT, Ship's Cooks and Mess Cooks. (2). All hands are reminded that Ship's Order No. 11 directs that a shirt or undershirt shall be worn to Mess and to Divine Service. (3) At 0630 Petty Officers, all divisions, will muster their Divisions in the following places: Div-1 muster port side #2 hatch. Div-2 muster #5 hatch. Div-3 muster port side #3 hatch. Div-4 muster sttd side #3 hatch. Div-5 muster port side of the boat deck.

J. A. ROOT,
Lieutenant, USCGR,
Executive Officer.

Copy to: All Staterooms,
Sr. Troop Officer, BltnBds,
Post Office, Navigator, OOD,
CCStd, BM, CMAA, Steward, File.

62-I

Chapter 18

IWO JIMA

15 APRIL, 1945 TO 24 APRIL, 1945

 The MENKAR departed in convoy from Saipan to the island of Iwo Jima. On approaching Iwo Jima the MENKAR detached itself from the convoy and proceeded to Kangoku Iwa, the island selected for the Loran installation.

20 APRIL, 1945

At 1430 the USS MENKAR (AK-123) dropped anchor in the straits between Kangoku Iwa Island and Iwo Jima in twenty-two fathoms of water, approximately four hundred yards from the East side of Kangoku Iwa. From available navigation charts this was selected as the most advantageous anchorage for the discharging of cargo. This anchorage is some distance outside of the protective anti-torpedo nets forming the main harbor at Iwo Jima and presented a definite hazard in the form of enemy submarine activity. Also, being only 700 miles from Tokyo, enemy air activity was a possibility, and gun watches were maintained accordingly.

Kangoku Iwa lies one and one-quarter miles from the center of Iwo Jima Island in the volcano group. It is approximately six hundred feet long and two hundred feet wide at its widest part. It rises out of the water not more than thirty feet at its highest point. Of its total area only a portion thereof is useable due to its structure. This structure consists solely of rock formation, rocks ranging in size from six feet in diameter down to the size of a man's fist, with the majority of rocks about one foot in diameter. There is no sand on the beach. Rocks extend from the waters edge to the crest of the island. Between Kangoku Iwa and Iwo Jima a current of two knots runs in a Southerly direction. Prevailing winds are from the East, and with medium force winds it is impossible to make landings at Kangoku Iwa.

Our LCVP was immediately lowered over the side, and the Commanding Officer of the MENKAR, accompanied by the ship's beach officers, went ashore on Kangoku Iwa to survey and inspect the Island, its beaches and approaches, in order to determine what advantages and disadvantages confronted the discharging operation. A small cove on the Eastern side near the South end of the island was selected, as affording the best protection, and the least obstructions for our LCM tank lighters.

Upon return of the Commanding Officer of the MENKAR, it was decided that advantage would be taken of the good weather prevailing to clear the beach of the obstacles and send ashore our heavy working equipment, which would consist of two (2) bulldozers complete with blades, a trackson crane (cherry picker), and two steel rock sleds. A working party of fifty-four men (54) was sent ashore to clear large boulders and obstructive parts of damaged Japanese landing craft from the shallow water adjacent to the beach, and to level the restricted area of the cove we planned to land our LCMs on.

The first LCM to go ashore brought one bulldozer with blade attached, together with lines for holding the LCMs head to the beach. A second bulldozer was sent ashore to be used in rock leveling operations. The trackson crane and lines were also sent ashore, along with the two rock sleds. These were the last pieces of equipment to be transported ashore before operations were discontinued because of approaching darkness. The beach party returned to the ship at 1830. On board the MENKAR the vessel was readied for the next days' unloading from holds one, two and three. Hatches were opened, booms rigged, lines checked, and decks cleared.

This evening the Commanding Officer held a critique with his officers, and organization plans and operational methods for the ensuing day were laid out. Officers and men were assigned specific phases of the unloading operation, on the ship and on the beach. A limited general quarters lookout and gun crew watch was designated to preclude a surprise enemy attack. It was agreed that the unloading operation should proceed at an unprecedented speed in order to take advantage of the existing good weather.

21 APRIL, 1945

The sky is overcast, wind is moderate. The swells coming in from the Northwest are gentle, and the surf is breaking light. A limited sky lookout and anti-aircraft general quarters is in place. Discharging operations were begun at daybreak. Eighty (80) men were sent ashore. Forty ship's company were assigned to unload and store the cargo on the beach. The remainder were Loran personnel. The first LCM hit the beach at 0730 with cargo consisting of commissary supplies, and large boxes of construction material. Tarpaulins were sent from the ship, and as the commissary supplies were landed and stored, they were covered for protection in the event of rain.

One bulldozer was used continuously to clear large areas of boulders and obstructive rocks. It was planned to store all cargo of like nature in separate areas to facilitate future handling and construction operations.

The next several LCMs to hit the beach landed more lumber and supplies, which were piled on sleds and towed by tractor to the site. At 1129 miscellaneous material began to go ashore. The wind was from the North and the surf commencing to break heavily. The Commanding officer of the MENKAR came ashore to supervise and arrange for better methods of securing the LCMs to the beach, so as to alleviate the necessity of running the LCM engines while in the shoal rock-filled waters. Wheels and shafts of the LCMs could easily be damaged under these conditions, and it is of great importance that they be kept in good working order. For the remainder of the day operations progressed satisfactorily. At 1800 the last load of the day reached the beach with two heavy 300 pound reefers. After these were set up, all hands returned to the ship.

22 APRIL, 1945

Discharging operations began at daybreak. Weather is again good, with sky overcast and a fresh wind from the North. The sea is moderate with a light surf on the beach. The first LCM ashore landed an evaporating unit and a cement mixer. The rest of the day was taken up with unloading miscellaneous cargo and dragging long ninety foot creosoted piling to be used for poles for the antennas. All hands returned to the ship at 1930. Excellent progress made.

23 APRIL, 1945

Weather fair. Heavy overcast with threat of rain. Wind strong from the Northeast. The swell is rolling parallel to the beach with a two or three foot surf breaking on the beach. Unloading operations commenced at daybreak. The cargo of cement is to go ashore today. In the unloading plan it was decided to limit the number of bags in a sling to twenty. This was done having in mind that the trackson crane (cherry picker) can take these nets of cement from the barge and move them directly to the storage site. This would alleviate handling the bags twice by hand. This was found to greatly speed the operation. The LCMs brought ashore five hundred (500) drums of assorted gasoline, fuel oil and kerosene. These drums were unloaded and rolled up the beach on a long line of boards from the LCMs to the storage site. At 1700 the Kangoku mission was completed and the crew returned to the ship. This operation has been routinely and expeditiously performed.

24 APRIL, 1945

1300, USS MENKAR departed Iwo Jima as Flag and Commodore of a three merchant ship convoy bound for Saipan.

NOTE: The landing beach at Iwo Jima was the most unfavorable of all the

Loran sites in the Western Pacific. The operation would have been extremely difficult, had we not experienced such favorable weather during the entire stay of the MENKAR. Actual construction on the site started on 24 April, 1945. No vertical radiator was received with the gear, but two 110-foot vertical antenna poles formed by splicing two 90-foot poles with two 45-foot poles. The station was ready to go on the air as a master station on 5 May, 1945, at which time the various buildings and facilities were about fifty per cent complete. However, it could not be put into operation until its paired station at Okinawa was completed.

BOMBER COMMAND COMMENTS

The following are excerpts from comments received by the Iwo Jima station from the Air Force: Major Reineck, Senior Wing Navigator, 73rd Wing, 21st Bomber Command, "Loran service has been instituted more rapidly than we ever expected. Our navigators have been using it for several weeks, and find that it is the best available means of fixing their position. We find that the signals have been picked up well North of Tokyo and far beyond our target range."

Captain Johnson, Radar Officer, 73rd Wing, 21st Bomber Command, "Our navigators have been using your signals to great advantage. On several occasions we have managed to bring a plane back with Loran when all other means have failed. There is no doubt that you have saved us several planes and many men. Your service will be appreciated more when the rain squall season covers this area, as it will be the only means of navigation."

Lieutenants Dolkaro and Ashton, Radar and Loran Maintenance, 73rd Wing, 21st Bomber Command, "The system of Loran service has been accepted by all our navigators. All that remains is that we keep the sets in repair, and that you keep the signals on twenty-four hours a day."

Chapter 19

OKINAWA OPERATION

At 0600 the USS MENKAR departed Iwo Jima for Saipan, arriving in Saipan on 27 April, 1945, loaded Loran equipment and personnel and on 5 May, departed for Okinawa.

USS MENKAR (AK-123)
Lieutenant Commander Niels P. Thomsen,
USCG Commanding

<u>SECRET DAILY REPORT</u>
<u>OF THE (ICHI HANARE) OKINAWA OPERATION</u>

This report, covering the day to day events encountered in the Ichi Hanare (Okinawa) operation starts from 5 May, 1945, the day the MENKAR joined the convoy and departed Saipan Harbor for Okinawa Island. This is deemed necessary in order to describe events preceding and following the actual discharging of cargo which makes up the Coast Guard Loran station on Ichi Hanare Island.

SUCCESSIVE DAILY EVENTS

5 MAY 1945

Departed Saipan Harbor at 0645 in convoy bound for Okinawa Island, in Ryukyu Retta, 325 miles South of the Japanese mainland. At 1100 changed course upon orders from the convoy Commodore. Recognition of Japanese suicide planes is being particularly stressed in the classes being held daily.

This evening held practice "general quarters" and "prepare to abandon ship" drill in order to acquaint the passengers with their various stations, and instruct them how to handle themselves in the event of an emergency. Continuous tracking drills held by gun crews.

6 MAY, 1945

Underway, destination Okinawa Island. General quarters was sounded at 1830. Held fire and tracking drills, secured from general quarters at 1845.

7 MAY, 1945

Underway for Okinawa Island. All gun crews, lookouts, and the bridge gang are being trained in the recognition of definite Japanese suicide planes. A Recognition Team consisting of one commissioned officer and five enlisted men who are best versed in Japanese suicide planes, have been under training for three months. This group has been given special training beyond that given in the semi-daily recognition classes. One officer, Lieutenant (JG) Dossett, USCGR, especially adaptable, has been released from all duty except recognition of enemy aircraft.

8 MAY, 1945

Underway for Okinawa Island. At 1143 received instructions from Convoy Commodore to alter course.

General quarters was called at 1845, this time the Convoy Commodore directed all ships in the convoy to hold morning and evening general quarters.

9 MAY, 1945

Underway for Okinawa Island. At 1200 we received word from the Convoy Commodore to change course. General quarters was sounded at 1845. At 1855 a floating mine was sighted as being off our starboard bow. The mine was sighted by one of the escort vessels, which followed it through the convoy and then destroyed it.

At 2018 the general alarm was sounded as depth charge detonations indicated possible submarine attack. These charges were being fired by two of our escorts astern of the MENKAR. The escorts evaluated the situation as a positive submarine contact and made a number of depth charge runs on the target. At 2020 we received word from the Convoy Commodore to make a 45 degree emergency turn to starboard. It was a very bright moonlight night. At 2045 word was received over our TBY radio from the vessel astern of us in the convoy, that they had sighted a torpedo wake approaching their port side. Signal was then given by the Convoy Commodore to make another 45 degree turn to port to avoid direct submarine torpedo attack on the convoy. Repeated depth charge attacks were made on the submarine until 2120 when the escort reported that the contact had been lost. Escorts spent the next half hour in an attempt to re-establish contact. Later, in a message from the escort Commodore, it was indicated that the counter attack on the enemy submarine had been highly successful.

10 MAY, 1945

This vessel departed from the Saipan-Okinawa convoy at 0630, approximately forty miles off Okinawa, as we were to make the Eastern side of the Island. Land was sighted at 1130, and we were standing in to our destination of Chimu Wan Harbor at 1300. After receiving anchorage instructions from the Port Director we anchored in 23 fathoms of water one and one-half miles North of Ichi Hanare Island our LCVP was lowered into the water, and the Commanding Officer of the USS MENKAR (AK-123) with the Navigating Officer and Communications Officer, visited the Port Director's Office on board a Naval vessel, in order to obtain information relative to defense and warning in regard to enemy air attacks, of which there were considerable. We requested and received the assignment of two LCI's (landing craft infantry) for making a smoke screen cover for the MENKAR, and to supplement our own anti-aircraft power in the event of a low level attack.

The Commanding Officer then surveyed and inspected the beaches, selecting the one to the Southward end of Ichi Hanare as the most appropriate due to it's offered protection, and the availability of the semblance of a road which would facilitate moving of the cargo to the site chosen for the Loran station. Upon his return to the vessel, the Commanding Officer made necessary preparations for the defense of the vessel, had the decks cleared and holds open for the ensuing days of cargo operations.

As was to be expected, enemy aircraft were reported over the area five times during the night, making it necessary to call all hands to battle stations each time.

DESCRIPTION OF ICHI HANARE ISLAND

Ichi Hanare Island forms the South side of the entrance to Chimu Wan Harbor and anchorage. It lies due East of and approximately two miles from Okinawa Island. Ichi Hanare is two miles long and one mile wide, and rises from 200 to 300 feet above the water. It is covered by a heavy growth of trees, shrubbery and grass. There is a native village of over 500 inhabitants on the island. There are two sand beaches on the Northwest or leeward side of the island which are ideally suited for landing craft. The one towards the Southwest end of the island was better because it is in a cove, well protected on two sides, and gives us a landing area of over one hundred yards. Our tank lighters (LCMs) can beach and retract without assistance. During this operation the weather and sea conditions were good. The winds were from the Northeast, East and Southeast, there was no rain, and the temperature was in the middle seventies, making for ideal working conditions.

11 MAY, 1945

All hands turned to at sunrise with our beach working party and Loran Construction Detachment being ferried ashore at 0630. The discharging operations commenced at 0730 when the first LCM with a truck and trackson swing crane (cherry picker) hit the beach. Other heavy equipment, namely bulldozers, and the Athey wagon were put ashore immediately. Cargo holds one and four are being worked simultaneously with the two LCMs carrying cargo to the beach. Evaporators, compressors, and miscellaneous cargo were worked until 1100, when it was decided that the MENKAR could be moved much closer to the beach so that discharging could be speeded up by cutting down, by over a mile, the distance it was necessary for the LCMs to run. Also, the vessel would blend more easily into the shoreline after dark in the event of air attack. This was done as the working of cargo continued. Lumber, Quonset material, and commissary items were put ashore during the remainder of the day.

Discontinued work an hour before sunset in order to prepare for anti-aircraft defense and safety of the ship in case of attack. Three air raids approached our area after dark, and general quarters sounded each time.

12 MAY, 1945

The crew did not appear to be affected by having been to battle stations three times during the night. Unloading began at sunrise with cement, lumber and generators being put ashore. The cargo was not piling up on the beach as feared, because a good road was made and the truck and Athey trailer could move the cargo to the Loran site very rapidly even though the site was over a mile away from the beach proper. Late this afternoon gasoline and diesel oil in 55-gallon steel drums were unloaded from number one hold. Due to the large amount of gasoline and diesel oil to be delivered to this Unit, this operation had to be continued the following day. Operations were discontinued at 1815. General quarters was called at 1915, as our radio watch received warning of enemy aircraft approaching the immediate vicinity. Shortly thereafter, heavy anti-aircraft fire was observed in the Northeast, the direction from which the attack was approaching. Word was received that the attacking planes had split up, and two sections were now attacking from the North and East respectively. The attacking force from the North was of little importance to us at the time of the report, because our immediate main concern became the attack approaching from the

East, as we were anchored off a point of land which extended East of Okinawa.

After the passing of four or five minutes, heavy anti-aircraft fire was again observed near us to the North. It was then, only seconds later, when we distinctly heard the sound of aircraft approaching from the East over Ichi Hanare island coming in over the forward part of the MENKAR. The shore batteries and vessels opened fire. The attacking plane dropped a stick of four bombs which straddled the MENKAR, then veered sharply to the South, followed by a rapid succession of heavy anti-aircraft fire which ostensibly broke up the attack, because the plane, or planes did not attempt a second attack.

No serious damage was incurred by the MENKAR even though many bomb fragments were found on our decks. One member of the crew, Koeber, F.E., BM 1/C, USCG, an ammunition loader on gun #43, was injured when a bomb fragment entered his left hand just above the thumb joint. His injury required medical attention, as it was necessary to take three stitches in the flesh. Koeber is being recommended for the purple heart. Later on, anti-aircraft fire was observed moving over Okinawa from the South, as the attacking planes departed from our immediate vicinity. The "ALL CLEAR" was sounded, and we secured from general quarters at 2030.

14 MAY, 1945

As the enemy no doubt has our position well spotted, we will attempt to complete discharging today and leave our present anchorage for an anchorage not quite so isolated. Discharging operations were continued by unloading Gasoline and diesel oil drums from number one hold. These drums are rolled out of the LCMs by hand and on to the beach, where they are lined up in rows of ten each. Sets of chime hooks or barrel hooks are then attached and the bulldozer drags all ten up the incline from the beach to a position above the high tide line. This method is used when the shore above the beach is too steep for rolling barrels by hand. It is anticipated that we will complete discharging operations at 1400 and prepare to leave for Katchin Wan Harbor.

Our discharging operations are stopped for two hours as the starboard winch has broken down. As this is being repaired, our LCMs are returning the ship's operating gear from the beach, and the vessel is made ready for the fifteen mile trip to Katchin Wan Harbor. Now that we have been spotted by the enemy, we do not desire to remain in our present area for another night.

At 1345 our winch is operating again and discharging is proceeding satisfactorily. Unloading ceased at 1700. The LCMs are hoisted on board. The LCVP is left for the Loran Unit, and we are standing out of Chimu Wan harbor at 1730, this assignment completed.

We arrived at Katchin Wan Harbor at 1900 without incident. The Port Director assigned us to berth-178, however due to a warning that enemy aircraft were approaching and the fact that a heavy cover of defense smoke was being laid over the harbor, further maneuvering was impossible. It was therefore necessary to drop our anchor while still several hundred yards from our designated berth. The night passed without incident.

15 MAY, 1945

Early this morning we moved to our assigned anchorage. The Commanding Officer checked with SOPA (Senior Officer Present Afloat) and the Port Director regarding information relative to our departure in Convoy to Saipan. These sources provided a negative response.

The day was spent in repairing broken and worn out deck equipment, booms, rigging and winches. This is a task to be performed after each operation. We have received word that our next mission will be to transport two entire Loran Units and accompanying personnel. Except for the First Lieutenant's Division, which is engaged in planning and preparing for the next assignment, such as measuring lower holds, between decks and topside to handle the heavy machinery and mobile equipment.

Because of the lack of rest due to constant general quarters activities the past several nights, and the prospect of continued enemy raids, the crew was granted a two day of rest, performing only essential duties.

16 MAY, 1945

We are still anchored in Katchin Wan harbor awaiting sailing orders. Today we checked over all fire fighting equipment to assure ourselves of its proper operation in the event of possible enemy air attack. A few repairs were found necessary and made. Lieutenant Dossett, our recognition officer kept his Aircraft Recognition team in session most of the day. This evening we were called to general quarters three times upon receiving reports of enemy aircraft in our area. Anti-aircraft fire was observed to the North and East. Enemy aircraft were reported approaching from the North and West. During the first thirty minutes of general quarters, only scattered anti-aircraft fire was observed around the area. Then suddenly, eight or ten searchlight batteries flashed on and caught two enemy planes etched against the black sky. They were flying at approximately 12,000 feet above the airstrip three miles from our anchorage. Anti-aircraft bursts around them were numerous as they dropped their bomb loads. The attack continued for thirty seconds. No enemy aircraft were observed as being shot down. We secured from general quarters at 0430.

17 MAY, 1945

We continued waiting for information relative to our sailing orders. Work as mentioned on the 15th and 16th of May was continued. The Commanding Officer, after consulting with the ship's officers, decided to move our anchorage slightly out of the smoke defense area for the reason that ship's crew are uncomfortable in a position of not being able to defend themselves in the event of attack. A move of

U.S.S. MENKAR

Heading:

ENEMY AIR ATTACKS IS EMINENT FROM WEST TONINGH TAKE
APPROPRIATE ACTION

From: COMMANDER TASK FORCE 31	Prec.	System	Time of	Supv. BY	WU BY	CWO	No.
Action: ALL NXX VESSELS OKINAWA AREA					Release		
Info:					Date (GCT) MAY 15, 1945		

CAPT.	EXEC.	COMM.	NAV.	GUN.	ENG.	MED.	OOD	SUPPLY	1stLT.	YEO.	TROOP CO.			

several hundred yards outside the smoke area was then made.

Again this evening we were summoned to our battle stations on two separate occasions as enemy aircraft are again reported in our area. No action took place. We secured from general quarters at 0020.

18 MAY, 1945

We are anchored in Katchin Wan harbor, Okinawa, waiting for sailing orders. We were called to general quarters 0230 and manned our battle stations without incident until 0315 when all clear was sounded. The ship's crew, happy to be anchored outside of the smoke defense zone and once again breathing fresh air.

At 1945 a report of "enemy air attack imminent" brought us to our battle stations "on the double." At 1948 a plane was reported by our after gun watch as bearing 210 degrees relative, at a position of 25 degrees. It was at first tentatively identified as a Japanese "VAL" by our specially trained recognition lookouts, who had the craft sighted in their binoculars framed against the clear twilight sky. All guns that could bear began tracking. When the plane reached 160 degrees relative at an angle of 20 degrees, it was positively identified a Japanese "Oscar" by the bridge recognition team.

Anti-aircraft firing conditions were solely under the command of the Army Air Command on Okinawa and two conditions were in effect: (CONDITION "RED" MEANT FIRE AT WILL and CONDITION GREEN FRIENDLY PLANES IN THE AIR, MEANT HOLD FIRE). The control being condition GREEN the order was not given at this time.

However, when the plane reached 100 degrees relative, at a range of 800 yards, it banked to the left and dove directly towards the MENKAR the order to open fire was given and all our starboard batteries, including the forward and after twin forties opened fire. Many bursts were seen to explode on the plane. The plane disintegrated and struck the water alongside the merchant ship "URIAH ROSE" off our starboard bow, about 300 yards distant. We commenced firing at 1948 and fired for approximately forty seconds. During that period we expended 441 rounds of 20 millimeter and 150 rounds of 40 millimeter ammunition.

At 2015 the MENKAR received a message over the TBS from the Commanding General Command Post, for the Commanding Officer of the MENKAR to report at 0800 to the Command Center to explain the MENKAR's violation of condition GREEN, a message which created considerable concern, not only to the Commanding Officer, but to the gun crews, concerned over the possibility of perhaps having shot down a friendly aircraft. None of the ship's crew could sleep peacefully that night. [4]

---

[4] This was the second time in World War Two this officer challenged Authority: The Admiral on the bridge of the USS HUNTER LIGGETT at Empress Augusta Bay at Bougainville 1 November, 1943 and orders of the Army Commanding General at Okinawa.

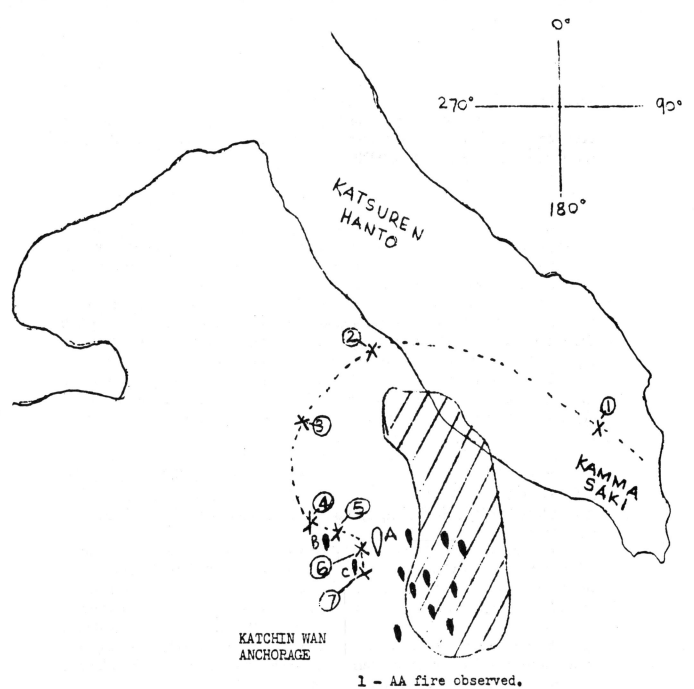

KATSUREN HANTO

KAMMA SAKI

KATCHIN WAN
ANCHORAGE

1 - AA fire observed.
2 - AA fire and plane observed -
    commenced tracking.
3 - Positively identified as "Oscar",
    still tracking.
4 - Plane turned directly towards ship -
    commenced firing.
5 - Plane being hit by 40 and 20mms.
6 - Plane disintegrates.
7 - Plane crashes in water.

A - MENKAR.
B - LST # 670.
C - "URIAH ROSE".

SMOKE AREA

Scale = |————————|
        1000 yds.

73-A

Address reply to:
Commanding Officer,
USS MENKAR (AK-123)
c/o Fleet Post Office,
San Francisco, California

22 May, 1945

SECRET

To: THE COMMANDANT (O)

Subj: Ichi Hanare (Okinawa) operation; report of

1.   The enclosed reports and photographs constitute the
report on subject operation. The landing conditions at Ichi
Hanare were excellent and the unloading of the cargo and
transportation to the site were completed without incident.

2.   The highlights of this operation were contributed by the
enemy and were as follows;

       (a) Attack upon the convoy by submarine on the night of
           10 May, 1945.

       (b) Straddling of the ship by a stick of bombs on the
           evening 13 May, 1945, which resulted in a minor
           shrapnel injury to one of the gun crew.

       (3) An attempted ramming attack by an enemy plane on the
           evening of 18 May, 1945. This plane was disintegrated
           by our anti-aircraft fire when within 300 yards from
           the ship.

3.   A copy of the action report covering the incident of 18
        May, 1945, is enclosed.

                                    N. P. Thomsen
                                    Lieutenant Commander, USCG
                                    Commanding USS MENKAR

Enclosures:
    (A) Operation report
    (B) Photographs
    (C) Action report of 18, May, 1945

CC: (OAN) Less enclosures (B) and (C)
    (ECV) Less enclosures (B) and (C)

19 MAY, 1945

At 0500 the "URIAH ROSE" reported that parts of the downed plane were scattered about her decks and that examination showed the plane to definitely be of Japanese manufacture. An unmistakable sense of relief flooded over the entire ship, particularly over the Commanding Officer, who, along with his navigator, Lieutenant Challenger, USCGR, were taken by LCVP to the "URIAH ROSE" where they collected two envelopes of small Japanese-marked, molten plane parts. Not fully trusting the Army Command Center, one envelope was taken to the Senior Naval Officer Afloat (SOPA), and the second envelope was delivered to the Army Command Center ashore at 0730. No comments were made by the Army Command Post Center regarding the firing violation.

On 22 May, 1945 the MENKAR departed Okinawa, joining an escorted convoy to Guam. Several days were spent in Guam loading Loran cargo before departing for Subic Bay in the Philippines, reaching Subic Bay on 10 June, 1945.

DR. DOYLE   SEAMAN   COMBAT PHOTOGRAPHER SMITH
CO   LIEUT. BROWN

OKINAWA

74-B

74-C

74-D

74-E

Chapter 20

SUBIC BAY ENGINEERING BASE

Because of Coast Guard activities in the Western Pacific, including not only the erection and maintenance of Loran stations, but the maintenance of other aids to navigation, and the carrying out of Marine Inspection functions, plans were made in 1945 for erecting an engineering base in the Philippines. The islands had been recaptured in actions beginning in December, 1944, and the scene was altering rapidly. The Bataan Peninsula was no longer being bitterly contested by the slowly retreating line of the Japanese forces. The Marivelas Mountains and the more Northerly Natib Mountains were free of Japanese. The Naval Base at Olongapo on Subic Bay, just to the Northwest of the Bataan Peninsula, was again in American hands. Activities were being rapidly expanded.

PHILIPPINE ISLANDS - SUBIC BAY

On 10 June, 1945 the MENKAR arrived at Subic Bay in the Philippine Islands. My first act was to report to the Port Director for mooring instructions and receive a berth assignment, to which we shifted as soon as I returned to the ship. When we had moored to the dock, the first person on board was Commander K.W. Donnell, USCGR, Commanding Officer of the Loran Construction project, with the MENKAR's mail. Commander Donnell and I repaired to my cabin to discuss our next assignment. He informed me that the Island of Lubang, approximately 100 miles South of Manila would be our next assignment, and that he hoped the MENKAR could be prepared to start taking on cargo the following day and be ready to depart Subic Bay on or about the 15th, five days hence. This date was agreed upon, and the following day cargo began pouring into the holds of the ship.

For the past two months I had been having severe pains in my back under my shoulder blades, the same pains I had experienced on the USS HUNTER LIGGETT at Guadalcanal in the Solomon Islands, and which had been diagnosed as a gall bladder problem. I had also lost over twenty pounds in the last nine months since taking command of the MENKAR, and felt that perhaps it was time for me to be relieved, and would he convey my desire to Coast Guard Headquarters. He agreed to take the matter up with Commander Evans at the Twelfth Coast Guard District. I also wrote a letter to Lieutenant Gustafson, USCGR a friend in the engineering Loran Section in Washington, D.C. with whom I was regularly corresponding. Up to now I had been like a small boy at a party who was having a good time and did not want to go home, but finally I was worn out and ready to go to bed.

Commander Donnell estimated that the Lubang operation would take three or four weeks, after which the MENKAR would return to Subic Bay for further orders. At the Port Director's office I had been informed that by order of the Army Commanding General of the area there could be no shore leave for the ship's crew.

The Philippine Steward who had been taking care of me and of my quarters mentioned to me that he and three other Filipinos mess attendants had families living in the foothills and mountains some forty miles from Subic Bay, whom they had not seen or heard from for over four years. I had to tell them that the policy of no shore leave was not my decision, but an order from the Army General in Command of the area. I did however, tell them that I would sleep on the problem and let them know in the morning. In the morning I called all four of them to my cabin, where I informed them that there was no way that I could give an official leave of absence or allow them ashore, but if they were to agree to certain conditions, and give me their solemn word of honor that they would do exactly what I would instruct them to do, I would, at a some risk to myself, arrange for them to visit with their families unofficially.

I would issue them written orders to report to the Loran Detachment Base on the outskirts of Subic Bay. That would get them out of the Naval Base where the ship was moored. They would find someone they could trust to leave their uniforms with, and get into some form of civilian clothes, take off into the hills and visit with their uncles, aunts, cousins, and in two cases their parents and grandparents. They would not go near any cities, and in three weeks they were to be on the dock in Subic Bay to rejoin the MENKAR. If they were picked up by the shore police and detained, they would be charged with being AWOL (absent without official leave) and take the consequences of possible punishment. They were to destroy the letter I had written them, as I would deny having given them permission to leave the ship. We shook hands, and they went on their way.

In my reports I have said little or nothing about the ship's engineering department, headed by Lieutenant B.B. Brown, USCGR, a former Merchant Marine Chief Engineer, to whom I referred to briefly during our last stay in Honolulu some months ago in connection with a fifty gallon drum of grain alcohol that was ordered by the engineering department in Honolulu.

The Chief Engineer, Brown, was fortunate in that he had a number of remarkable talented and hardworking regular Coast Guard Warrant Machinists and Chief Machinist Mates, plus a Chief Warrant Machinist. They kept everything in the engine-room running as smooth as clockwork under the watchful eye of Lieutenant Brown. However, about six weeks after leaving Honolulu, I noticed that Mr. Brown, whose quarters were adjacent to my cabin and the Doctor's quarters on the upper deck, had on a number of occasions appeared unsteady on his feet, and once when I spoke to him in passing I thought his speech was slurred. I mentioned my concern to Doctor Doyle, who admitted he had similar concerns about Brown, but had not wanted to disturb me with his suspicions. I had no doubt about the source of the alcohol.

I knew that something had to be done about Brown's drinking. It was a problem filled with complications. Not only was he important to the MENKAR, but I liked him and he was important to me as a person. I had become emotionally involved, just what I had promised myself at the beginning of this voyage I would not allow to happen with the ship's officers. Because of our similar background in the Merchant Marine, a bond did exist between me and Brown that was difficult to ignore. Having spent twenty years in the Merchant Marine as a Sailor, an Officer and a Shipmaster, I had learned how to live with alcoholics.

It is traditional in the Merchant Service for the Ship's Captain and the Chief Engineer, due to their dependency on one another, to enjoy a close, almost equal social and working relationship on board ship, which in peacetime, Brown and I would have enjoyed. Because of my policy of adhering to an impersonal relationship with all of my officers, this camaraderie had been denied to Brown. He was in his late fifties, twenty years older than his fellow officers in the wardroom, all young college graduates with whom, like myself, he had little or nothing in common, except to ensure the success of the wartime mission of the MENKAR. Furthermore, he was a good engineer and a father figure to his young engine room crew, all of whom regarded him with fondness. It would have been injudicious, if not tragic, were he to be relieved of duty and his stature diminished in the eyes of his men.

Doctor Doyle told me that beginning with the Iwo Jima and Okinawa operations, Brown had appeared tense and under strain, and he had mentioned several times that if a ship came under attack by bombs or torpedoes the engine room crews rarely survived. I let several days pass by before I invited Brown to my cabin for dinner. After our meal I went straight to the matter at hand. I said, "Brown, I know you have been drinking for some time and I know from where you are getting it."

Mr. Brown, with some embarrassment, admitted he had been drinking for some weeks, but never on his watch in the engine room, or before going on watch. He was being very frank and honest. He told me he had been drinking alcohol from the fifty gallon drum, carrying it to his room in some two-ounce opaque, cold cream jars that he kept in his medicine cabinet and usually drank before going to bed. Before he left my cabin, he promised me that he would limit his drinking to one two-ounce jar per day.

I never upbraided him, threatened him or raised my voice. I think he understood that I was his friend, and he never broke his promise.

COMMANDING OFFICER MENKAR
and
PHILIPPINE ARMY LIEUTENANT ARTURO RINALDO
HAVING A COLD DRINK ASHORE IN LUBANG

LUBANG

LUBANG

LUBANG

Chapter 21

LUBANG ISLAND OPERATION

15 JUNE, 1945 TO 4 JULY, 1945

 The MENKAR departed Subic Bay on 15 June, 1945 for the tiny island of Lubang, approximately 100 miles from Manila, where we were to install a Loran station on a point of land about one mile from the village. No charts of the Bay were available, so we proceeded cautiously into the center of the bay, and anchored in 20 fathoms. While lowering our LCMs and our LCVP into the water we could see crowds of villagers lining the shore, all waving hats and flags, and holding up their hands making "V" signs with their fingers. Lieutenant Skillin was instructed to survey and take soundings on one side of the bay, which was heavily wooded up to the shoreline. He reported ten fathoms with a mud bottom close to the shore. As a possible protection against enemy air attack about which we had been warned, we hove anchor and moved to within about forty yards of the beach in ten fathoms of water, and with the aid of the LCMs anchored the vessel bow and stern parallel to the beach. I then sent 120 men ashore to cut down bushes and branches of trees which were tied and draped on the rigging, masts, and on the decks so the ship would blend in with the shore. About fifty villagers joined our crew to help in cutting and gathering brush. Our battle stations were manned and ready 24 hours a day by rotating gun crews.

After we had completed our final mooring, our LCVP brought out to the ship a Philippine Army Lieutenant who was in charge of the village. With him was the Priest of the local Catholic church, the only stone structure in the village. They welcomed us and informed us that we were the first vessel, other than fishing boats and small patrol launches that had come to the island since the routing of the Japanese who had dominated the island for years.

The Priest said the village had been without wheat flour for several years. It so happened that the MENKAR had on board a large quantity of flour, surplus to the ship's needs. The supply officer reported approximately one thousand sacks in the hold. Five hundred sacks were then officially surveyed as showing signs of mold, and were delivered to the church for distribution by the Priest to the villagers.

A square mile of open grassy plain lay between the site of the MENKAR's anchorage and the edge of the village. The following morning I set out for the proposed Loran site in our jeep, accompanied by Dr Doyle, Lieutenant Skillin, and the officer in charge of the Loran construction detachment. As we drove across the grassy plain we passed a wan-looking, half-naked Japanese soldier with a rope around his neck, being led by a local person, with a group of shouting children following close behind. I was later told by the Philippine Army Lieutenant that such incidents were routine, occurring two or three times a week.

As we reached the edge of the village, scores of people clustered about and followed our jeep, showing "V" signs with their fingers and shouting "Viva Americanos." We felt as General McArthur must have felt when he walked ashore on Philippine soil at Leyte. The village consisted of a solitary street with all the houses built of bamboo with thatched roofs, and elevated on poles ten to fifteen feet above the ground. All the verandas were filled with people, waving and cheering. Word of the wheat distribution by the church must already have penetrated the village. The parade continued all the way to the Loran site, one-half mile beyond the village.

Shortly after reaching the Loran site, the Army Lieutenant joined us, and I invited him to lunch with me on the MENKAR. I found him to be an intelligent and caring person, whose functional duties were comparable to that of a Town Mayor administering the affairs of the Community, except that he had greater authority. His name was Arturo Rinaldo.

Over lunch in my cabin, with Doctor Doyle as my other guest, we went into considerable detail on how we would arrange for liberty and recreation for a crew of over three hundred men during our stay. We agreed that the crew were to be allowed ashore in groups of not over one hundred at any one time, and that a midnight curfew would be in effect. At least four of the ship's officers or Chief Petty officers would be on police duty on shore at all times. Lieutenant Rinaldo said that many long awaited weddings, postponed because of the Japanese occupation, would be taking place during our stay, with four or five dances to be held weekly. He indicated that all of the ship's crew would be welcome to attend the festivities.

At 0800 the following day discharging of cargo commenced and LCMs were plying to and fro between the ship and the beach, where cargo was piling up. Lieutenant Rinaldo showed up later in the day, came out to the ship and conveyed to myself and Doctor Doyle, an invitation to lunch with Father Palermo the next day, which we happily accepted. At this luncheon I was asked by Father Palermo if it would be possible for Doctor Doyle to pay a visit to the local medical clinic to discuss some medical problems with the Head Nurse in charge of the clinic, there being no doctor on the island at the present time, a request that Doctor Doyle was only too pleased to grant. As it turned out he wound up holding a daily clinical session the entire time of the ship's stay in Lubang.

26 JUNE, 1945

We have been in Lubang for ten days, and it has been a glorious experience for everyone on board the MENKAR. The weather has been very good, cloudless skies and cool sea breezes day and night. The unloading and work at the site has been going well. This is the only assignment we have had that we wish would not end too soon. There has been a holiday atmosphere ashore and afloat here in Lubang ever since our arrival. Every day there have been weddings, with dances each night. This is an island of unworldly, lovely, warm-hearted people. The church has a great influence in the community, a fountain of high moral standards of behavior. The people have taken the crew of the ship into their hearts. There has not been one unpleasant incident since our arrival. I should have mentioned earlier that by agreement between me and Lieutenant Rinaldo, alcoholic beverages have not been available, either to the ship's crew or to the local people during our stay.

There have been a number of humorous incidents. After the first crew liberty, it was reported that some of the crew were taking ashore commissary food items, emptying sugar bowls, salt shakers etc. So a notice prohibiting this conduct was posted, plus a watch set on the gangway. Then the crew began taking ashore their personal clothing items, plus anything they could purchase at the ship's store as gifts for their friends ashore, which of course I could do nothing about.

I had become quite friendly with Lieutenant Arturo Rinaldo, who would have dinner with Doctor Doyle and me on the ship frequently, and later escort me, Doctor Doyle and Lieutenant Challenger to the evening dances ashore. Through Arturo the villagers knew I collected seashells, and whenever I passed through the village someone would hand me a cigar box of lovely shells, which I have to this day, including the cigar boxes.

An especially amusing incident occurred during the first week of our stay. It was usual for me, together with several officers to go ashore every forenoon to see how operations were progressing at the Loran site. One day while driving along the one main street, always slowly, there being so many children running about, when pots of water cascaded down on us from every house we passed. We were dismayed, wondering what we might have done, or what had transpired to change the attitude of the local people towards us, especially when the Doctor remarked that the containers they were using appeared to be chamber pots. We were most gratified and relieved later to learn that it was a Philippine custom to throw water on their friends on the morning of "Saint John the Baptist day."

DRAGGING 20 MILES TO THE SHORE OF PALAWAN

C.O.

3 JULY, 1945

Our operation at Lubang is completed. All of the MENKAR's crew are saddened that we must depart from this quiet, peaceful island of lovely, friendly people. As a parting gift from the villagers, Arturo presented me with five local handmade knives with wooden sheaths that are used to harvest crops and cut grass. The ship's store reported that the store shelves were bare, not a cigarette, cigar or piece of candy left, and not a sailor with more than one undershirt or an extra pair of socks in his seabag. The ship's crew have been working all day and dancing until midnight every third night and are exhausted. They leave many friends behind.

The Officer in Charge of the Loran construction detachment has relayed instructions from Commander Donnell, which are very sketchy. I have been ordered to proceed to a certain location which gives me only a latitude and longitude position somewhere on the West Coast of the Island of Palawan, three or four hundred miles South of Manila, where I would be contacted by a Loran Officer.

ISLAND OF PALAWAN

On examining an antique chart of the Island of Palawan I noted that for fifty miles in each direction of the position given, as well as twenty miles from the shore, the chart was completely blank. No soundings, no nautical information of any kind. Nor did the pilot books have any information. I was told that every day a friendly plane would appear, circle over the ship, and perhaps make an air drop with instructions. I was warned of possible enemy air attack and was to maintain complete radio silence.

The MENKAR departed from Lubang on the morning of the fourth of July, arriving several days later at a "run in position" twenty miles off the coast of Palawan Island. Having no knowledge as to the depth of the waters, or what marine hazards such as rocks or coral reefs might lie in the path of the ship as she headed in towards the coast I put two LCMs over the side, stringing a line weighted with ten links of anchor chain in the middle, we moved towards the coast at five knots with the two LCMs sweeping a path a quarter of a mile ahead of the ship.

This procedure brought us to within a mile of the shore, where we anchored in twenty fathoms. By using binoculars we could see several radio towers on a point ashore. This was a tense moment. Shortly after we anchored a small launch came out, bringing the Officer in Charge of the Loran station who requested permission to take a number of boxes of electronic equipment from the hold to be delivered ashore by our LCVP. He also brought two Loran personnel to be transported to Subic Bay, and two Loran replacements went ashore. In less than two hours the LCVP returned to the ship and was hoisted on board.

At daylight the following day we hove anchor, and departed from Palawan Island with the two LCMs sweeping ahead for the first twenty miles, when we hoisted our LCMs and set our course for Subic Bay. I was never told, and never asked for any information concerning this trip to Palawan. I can only surmise that it was an isolated Loran station at a highly secret location.

On 7 July 1945, the MENKAR dropped her anchor in Subic Bay and I made my routine visit to the Port Director's office for mooring instructions. Shortly after tying up at the dock, the Commanding Officer of the Loran Detachment came on board bringing the ship's mail. Over a cup of coffee Commander Donnell informed me that as soon as the Loran cargo remaining on board was discharged, we were to proceed to Sand Island, Honolulu via a stop at Guam.

During the noon hour our four "AWOL" Filipino stewards reported on board, having delayed their return for several hours after our arrival as they had been instructed, so as not to invite attention from Port Authorities. Their "leave" had been happy and uneventful, and they were laden with homemade gifts from their relatives, such as woven mats, which after fifty years, are still in my possession.

The ship's crew were overjoyed and excited over our sailing orders. As for me, I looked forward to a relaxing two weeks of uneventful ocean cruising in calm, Pacific Ocean waters. I had mixed feelings; the turn of events had left me with an emotional let down. I was tired, physically and mentally.

LIFE

WE CANNOT QUELL
THE RAGING SEAS
OR DECREE
WHAT WINDS WILL BLOW
NOR WILL THE SET
OF OUR SAILS
AND THE TRIM
OF OUR JIB
DETERMINE THE WAY WE GO.

FOR SOME OF US
ITS AN EASY REACH
WITH A WIND
THAT IS FLOWING FREE
AND FOR WHOM
THERE IS ALWAYS
A FLOODING TIDE
AND THE RUSH
OF A FOLLOWING SEA.

BUT FOR MOST OF US
IT'S A TACK
OR A WEAR
AGAINST THE WIND
AND THE TIDE
AND SOME OF US
NEVER REACH OUR GOALS
AS WE RUN AGROUND
ON HIDDEN SHOALS.

THOUGH OUR ARMS
GROW WEARY
AND THE NIGHT IS LONG
AND WE HAVE KEPT OUR HANDS
ON THE TILLER STRONG
WE MAY NEVER MAKE
THE PORT OF OUR DREAMS
OR ATTAIN
OUR HEART'S DESIRE.

Chapter 22

ENROUTE TO HONOLULU

Our stop in Guam was brief, and the trip to Honolulu was smooth uneventful, fair-weather voyage. We arrived in Honolulu on 22 July, 1945, moored at Sand Island, all of us speculating on our next assignment. The mail was interesting. I learned that Ethel had given birth to a baby girl. She had been born on the date I had written on the war bond, and she had been given the name "Tiare Marie". I also received orders to turn over the Command of the MENKAR to a new Commanding Officer, Lieutenant Commander Jens Krestensen, and to report to Alameda for further assignment to duty. These orders had been issued three weeks earlier at my request to Commander Donnell. This was what I had hoped for, and was anxious to be on my way. However, two days later, on 14 August, 1945 orders were received by the MENKAR to proceed to Seattle, Washington for overhaul at the Puget Sound Navy Yard. This was a blow to me, as I would have liked to have taken the MENKAR to Seattle, and the voyage would have been restful. I could not complain, having been granted my request.

I departed Honolulu by Military Air Transport for Oakland, California at 0900 on 27 July, 1945, arriving at Oakland Airport at 0015 28 July, 1945, back to where I had departed with the MENKAR ten months earlier. I telephoned the manning station at Alameda and was given permission to spend the weekend at my home in San Francisco, and to report to the manning station on Monday. It was a happy reunion with Ethel and the children. Carol Ann was eight, Robin almost three, and Tiare was two months old. I had been away for ten months. On Monday I reported to Commander Evans, USCG at the Manning Station and received twenty days leave until 22 August. On 13 August, 1945, my orders originally issued on 3 July, were amended, ordering me to report to Ketchikan, Alaska for permanent duty, the very assignment I had requested in the hope of spending some time in a quiet environment free from stress and strain. This was not to be.

AFTERMATH

THE STORM HAS PASSED
THE SEA IS CALM
AND DISTANT SHORES I SEE
AND LIKE A WILD BIRD WINGING HOME
SO FLY MY THOUGHTS TO THEE.

THOU ART THE HAVEN OF MY DREAMS
THOUGH I HAVE WANDERED FAR
A LIGHT THAT SHINES
FOR ERE IT SEEMS
AN UNEXTINGUISHED STAR.

Chapter 23

17TH COAST GUARD DISTRICT

KETCHIKAN, ALASKA

 Two days later, on 15 August, 1945, the Japanese Empire surrendered. On 22 August, the day my leave expired, a dispatch was received from the 17th Coast Guard District in Ketchikan requesting to know when I would be reporting for duty, and the 12th District Commander directed me to report to Ketchikan immediately. I departed Oakland by Military Air Transport to Seattle, and by Alaska Steamship to Ketchikan, Alaska, reporting to the Coast Guard District Headquarters in Ketchikan at 0900 30 August, 1945. I was to make arrangements for my family to follow as soon as authorized transportation could be granted.

Admiral Norman H. Leslie, USCG was the 17th District Commander. We had met once in 1942 when he was Captain of the USCG Cutter HAIDA, and I a Lieutenant attached to Admiral Zeusler's staff. Admiral Leslie told me he had inquired about me of Admiral Zeusler, presently stationed as District Commander of the 13th Coast Guard District in Seattle, and on his recommendation was appointing me as his District Personnel Officer, and Chief Demobilization Officer, to handle the discharge of 3,000 Coast Guard Reserve Officers, Spars and enlisted men clamoring to be released from Military Service.

Admiral Leslie said that though I was junior in rank to most of the regular commissioned officers on his staff, they were all either Coast Guard Academy classmates or friends, and he wanted a Personnel Officer who would be impervious to outside influences, and that I would hold that position on his Staff only as long as he was assured that all decisions pertaining to duty assignments were made by me alone.

After a week in the personnel officer it became apparent why Admiral Leslie had been so concerned over the personnel department. Several desks in my office were stacked with requests and demands from hundreds of Coast Guard Reservists expecting immediate release from military service. Alaska being such a vast, isolated area, coupled with the Coast Guard's responsibility for essential maintenance of aids to navigation and inherent transportation difficulties presented many obstacles. Many duty stations in remote areas required replacements with regular Coast Guard personnel before changes could be effected.

Every ship arriving from the lower "Forty-Eight" brought to Ketchikan regular Coast Guard personnel for duty assignment. When the man's service record arrived at my desk (and I personally reviewed every record, especially prior duty assignments), I had a number of assignment options; an isolated lighthouse station for twelve months, a ship away for three to six months, a ship away for a week or ten days. Most assignments meant separation from one's family if he happened to have one. I could also assign him to shore duty at the Coast Guard Base, where not only would he be at home with his family, but also be entitled to extra monetary compensation for quarters and subsistence for himself and his dependents. I felt that the only fair method of determining assignments should be the man's service record, with some considered differentiation accorded to married men with families. Another determination would be a man coming from sea duty would have preference over a man coming from shore duty. Knowing there would be problems, I wrote down the policy I planned to follow, and laid it before the Admiral, who gave his approval.

To point out the nature of the problem facing me I will cite one of the first incidents which did not endear me to a number of fellow senior officers on the staff. One morning, the day after a passenger ship had brought in a group of regular enlisted men as replacements I received a telephone call from the Base Engineering Officer, considerably my senior and a classmate of the District Operations Officer. He said, "Thomsen, two Chief Machinist Mates arrived on the boat yesterday, one is named Olson, and the other is named Barton. I know Barton, who has been in to see me, and I want to make certain that he gets assigned to me at the base."

The following day I interviewed both men and examined their service records. Barton's record revealed that he had spent the past seven years on shore duty at various Coast Guard facilities. He had excellent marks, and it was obvious why the Base Engineer had requested Barton to be assigned to his department. Barton knew how to work the system. Olson, the other Chief Machinist Mate, had a wife and four children, and had just completed four years of sea duty. He was not an aggressive individual, never once imagining that he might acquire shore duty, and would be grateful if he were assigned to a ship that occasionally docked in Ketchikan. My course of action was clear. I assigned Barton to one of the Coast Guard ships headed for the Bering Sea and Olson to the Coast Guard Base. Within an hour I received the expected phone call from the Base Engineer. "Thomsen, you sent me the wrong man."

I said, "Who reported." He came back with Olson's name, and I replied, "Sorry, but Olson was due for shore duty in accordance with District policy."

Twenty minutes later, his classmate, Commander Fred Schreiber, USCG, the District Operations Officer, came into my office saying he wished to discuss the assignment. I told him he would have to speak to the Admiral. In my first ten days in office I had made two personal antagonists who years later from seats of power, would exact a penalty for my not having played the game. I was fortunate in that I was serving under two outstanding men for whom I had an undying admiration and respect, the District Commander, Admiral Leslie, USCG and his Chief of Staff, Captain Fritsche, USCG, both of the old school, men like Admiral Louis Perkins, Admiral Zeusler, Admiral Roach, and Captain Patch, just to name a few Coast Guard Officers under whom I have had the privilege of serving. Each man was an epitome of the high moral principles that characterize an Officer and a Gentleman.

I had asked to be assigned to Alaska and had visualized a quiet, peaceful existence where I could regain my health and the twenty pounds I had lost while on the MENKAR. As far as stress and strain were concerned I had gone from the frying pan into the fire. The work load and problems were unimaginable, far greater than any I had experienced in the forward areas. My family was not due for at least a month and I lived at the Bachelors Officers Quarters (BOQ). After the first ten days I would check in at the infirmary each Friday evening at the Coast Guard Base, pull down the blinds and remain there in a darkened room until Monday morning. I was having the pains I suffered on the HUNTER LIGGETT at Guadalcanal and on the MENKAR, which the local Ketchikan doctor kept diagnosing as gall bladder pains.

In due time Ethel and the children arrived in Ketchikan on the Alaska Steamship Company's passenger vessel BARANOFF and we settled down in a house on a hillside overlooking the City of Ketchikan, a few minutes walk from the Federal Building which housed the Coast Guard District offices. Together with my family, and a line of work that challenged me daily, this was probably one of the most contented periods of my life. The first six months of the demobilization program were demanding, replacing hundreds of Coast Guard Reserve personnel with regular Coast Guard officers and enlisted men on ships and remote Alaskan duty stations. My medical problems subsided and I was soon back to my normal weight. In 1947, I received a letter from Coast Guard Headquarters stating that the Secretary of the Treasury, acting on the recommendation of a personnel board, had determined that I would retain temporary commissioned status in my present rank of Lieutenant Commander, which I accepted.

As the daughter of a pioneer Alaskan family in Ketchikan, where she had been reared, Ethel wearied of the continual rainfall and expressed a desire to leave Alaska at the end of my two-year Alaskan duty assignment. Never having served in the Great Lakes Area I requested a transfer to sea duty in the Ninth Coast Guard District in Cleveland, Ohio. So in the fall of 1947 I received orders to proceed to Toledo, Ohio to take command of the USCG TUPELO, a cutter tender stationed at Bayview Park

Coast Guard Base. We arranged to purchase and pick up an automobile in Seattle and requested thirty days leave enroute. My two years as District Personnel Officer under the command of Admiral Norman H. Leslie, USCG had been the most rewarding, satisfying and pleasurable duty assignments in my Coast Guard career. To my sorrow I would never meet either of these two outstanding people again. Both Admiral Leslie, USCG and Captain H.E. Fritsche, USCG died of heart attacks in their early fifties.

MY LEGACY

NO TOWERING CASTLES
HAVE I BUILT
IN THE TIME ALLOTTED ME
NOR HAVE I LAUNCHED
A THOUSAND SHIPS
TO SAIL UPON THE SEA
AND NOWHERE
IS MY NAME ENGRAVED
FOR ALL MANKIND TO SEE.

SO AT THE APPOINTED TIME
WHAT WILL MY MEASURE BE

I WOULD BELIEVE
THAT IF IN THE DARK
OF NIGHT
ONE BEING I HAVE LOVED
WOULD SHED A TEAR FOR ME
AND SO DEAR LORD
I HUMBLY PRAY
THAT THIS MAY BE
MY LEGACY.

(last)	(first)	(middle)	RANK AND CLASSIFICATION	FILE NO.
THOMSEN	Niels	Peter	Lieut.Comdr., USCG	30611

STAFF, ODCGO, 17ND

DATE FROM 9-30-45 DATE TO 3-31-46

District Personnel Officer, ODCGO, 17ND

None

SEA — KIND — No preference LOCATION Pacific Coast
SHORT — KIND — Personnel - M'l LOCATION Pacific Coast

NAME OF REPORTING OFFICER NORMAN H. LESLIE Commodore, USCG DCGO, 17ND

None

Qualified for any line duty of his rank. Physical condition reported satisfactory.

Any line duty

RATING FACTORS	Not Observed	Within Bottom 10%	Within Next 20%	Within Middle 40%	Within Next 20%	Within Top 10%
1 ASSUME RESPONSIBILITY WHEN SPECIFIC INSTRUCTIONS ARE LACKING?					X	
2 GIVE FRANK OPINIONS WHEN ASKED OR VOLUNTEER THEM WHEN NECESSARY TO AVOID MISTAKES?					X	
3 FOLLOW THROUGH DESPITE OBSTACLES IN CARRYING OUT RESPONSIBILITIES ASSIGNED OR ASSUMED?					X	
1 GRASP INSTRUCTIONS AND PLANS GIVEN TO HIM?					X	
2 USE IDEAS AND SUGGESTIONS OF OTHERS?					X	
3 RATE IN TECHNICAL COMPETENCE IN HIS SPECIALTY IF ANY?						
1 INSPIRE SUBORDINATES TO WORK TO THE MAXIMUM OF THEIR CAPACITY?					X	
2 EFFECTIVELY DELEGATE RESPONSIBILITY?					X	
3 TRANSMIT ORDERS, INSTRUCTIONS AND PLANS?					X	
4 ORGANIZE HIS WORK AND THAT OF THOSE UNDER HIS COMMAND OR SUPERVISION?					X	
5 MAINTAIN DISCIPLINE AMONG THOSE UNDER HIS COMMAND OR DIRECTION?					X	
1 ABILITY TO WORK WITH OTHERS?					X	
2 ABILITY TO ADAPT TO CHANGING NEEDS AND CONDITIONS?					X	
3 MILITARY CONDUCT—BEARING, DRESS, COURTESY, ETC.?					X	

None

I CONSIDER THIS REPORT TO BE [X] SATISFACTORY [ ] UNSATISFACTORY

Personal and military character excellent. Has been performing his duties in exceptional manner under extremely difficult conditions. Fit for promotion. This officer has not seen this report.

90-A

(Last)	(First)	(Middle)	RANK AND CLASSIFICATION	FILE NO.
THOMSEN	Niels	Peter	Lieut. Comdr., USCG	30 611

STATION
DCGO 17:D

| | | | | DATE FROM 4-1-45 | DATE TO 9-30-45 |

☐ DETACHMENT OF   ☐ DETACHMENT OF   ☒ REGULAR   ☐ QUARTERLY   ☐ SPECIAL
   OFFICER REPORTED ON   REPORTING SENIOR   SEMI ANNUAL

			MO	DA	MO	YR
t Guard League Committee, ODCGO 17:D			9	45	9	45
s nel Officer, ODCGO 17:D			8	45	9	45

BEA   KIND OF DUTY SHAWNEE   LOCATION Eureka, California
SHORE   KIND OF DUTY Marine Inspection Service   LOCATION As assigned

NAME OF REPORTING OFFICER   RANK   OFFICIAL STATUS RELATIVE TO OFFICER REPORTED ON
E. H. FRITZSCHE   Captain, USCG   ADCGO 17:D

OFFICER QUALIFIED TO PER...   ☒ YES   ☐ NO

Administrative   AFLOAT C.O.

RATING FACTORS	Not Observed	Within Bottom 10%	Within Next 20%	Within Middle 40%	Within Next Top 20%	Within Top 10%
STANDING DECK WATCHES UNDERWAY	X					
ABILITY TO COMMAND	X					
PERFORMANCE IN PRESENT DUTIES AS DESCRIBED IN SECTION 7 ABOVE						X
REACTIONS DURING EMERGENCIES	X					
PERFORMANCE AT BATTLE STATION OR IN BATTLE DUTIES	X					
ASSUME RESPONSIBILITY WHEN SPECIFIC INSTRUCTIONS ARE LACKING						X
GIVE FRANK OPINIONS WHEN ASKED OR VOLUNTEER THEM WHEN NECESSARY TO AVOID MISTAKES						X
FOLLOW THROUGH IN SPITE OBSTACLES IN CARRYING OUT RESPONSIBILITIES ASSIGNED OR ASSUMED						X
GRASP INSTRUCTIONS AND PLANS GIVEN TO HIM						X
USE IDEAS AND SUGGESTIONS OF OTHERS						X
RATE IN TECHNICAL COMPETENCE IN HIS SPECIALTY IF ANY Name Specialty	X					
INSPIRE SUBORDINATES TO WORK TO THE MAXIMUM OF THEIR CAPACITY						X
EFFECTIVELY DELEGATE RESPONSIBILITY						X
TRANSMIT ORDERS INSTRUCTIONS AND PLANS						X
ORGANIZE HIS WORK AND THAT OF THOSE UNDER HIS COMMAND OR SUPERVISION						X
MAINTAIN DISCIPLINE AMONG THOSE UNDER HIS COMMAND OR DIRECTION						X
ABILITY TO WORK WITH OTHERS						X
ABILITY TO ADAPT TO CHANGING NEEDS AND CONDITIONS						X
MILITARY CONDUCT—BEARING DRESS COURTESY, ETC						X

UR ATTITUDE TOWARD OFFICER UNDER YOUR (Check one)
☐ DEFINITELY NOT WANT HIM (UNSATISFACTORY)   ☐ PREFER NOT TO HAVE HIM (UNSATISFACTORY)   ☐ BE SATISFIED TO HAVE HIM   ☒ BE PLEASED TO HAVE HIM   ☐ PARTICULARLY DESIRE HIM

ADVERSE COMMENTS TO MAKE REGARDING THIS OFFICER'S "PERFORMANCE?"   ☐ YES ☒ NO   If yes, explain in Section 12.
PHYSICAL OR MORAL WEAKNESS WHICH ADVERSELY AFFECTS   ☐ YES ☒ NO

Check one of these boxes—I CONSIDER THIS REPORT TO BE ☒ SATISFACTORY   ☐ UNSATISFACTORY

Thomsen has grasped the details of the current personnel demobilization
program with extraordinary ability and under arduous circumstances. Discharges
functions, duties, and responsibilities of his office in a highly
commendable manner. Is fit for promotion. This officer has not seen this report.

SIGNATURE OF REPORTING OFFICER
E H Fritzsche

HAVE YOU READ THE ATTACHED INSTRUCTION SHEET? Yes

PLEASE TYPE THIS FORM

If no typewriter is available use ink but be sure all copies are legible

DATE _____

1. NAME	(last)	(first)	(middle)	RANK AND CLASSIFICATION	FILE NO.

SHIP OR STATION

PERIOD OF REPORT (mo., day, year)

DATE FROM _____ DATE TO _____

DATE OF REPORTING TO PRESENT SHIP OR STATION

OCCASION FOR REPORT

☒ DETACHMENT OF OFFICER REPORTED ON ☐ DETACHMENT OF REPORTING SENIOR ☐ REGULAR SEMI-ANNUAL ☐ QUARTERLY ☐ SPECIAL

2. DESCRIPTION OF DUTIES SINCE LAST FITNESS REPORT (List most recent first and describe accurately. Include periods of leave, transit, etc., also include employment of ship.)

	FROM		TO	
	MO	YR	MO	YR

Personnel Officer

Has present duty changed since last fitness report was submitted? ☐ Yes ☒ No

3. IF COURSES OF INSTRUCTION WERE COMPLETED DURING PERIOD OF THIS REPORT, LIST TITLE OF COURSE, LOCATION OF SCHOOL, LENGTH OF COURSE AND DATE COMPLETED.

Are you physically qualified for Sea Duty? ☒ Yes ☐ No ☐ Don't Know

4. If Aviator, Indicate No. of Flight Hours Last Two Years for Each Type Aircraft (List Most Recent Type First) — TYPE OF AIRCRAFT / NO. OF HOURS — TOTAL

5. MY PREFERENCE FOR NEXT DUTY IS: SEA — KIND OF DUTY / LOCATION
SHORE — KIND OF DUTY / LOCATION

6. SECTIONS 6 THROUGH 12 TO BE FILLED IN BY REPORTING OFFICER

NAME OF REPORTING OFFICER / RANK / FILE NO. / OFFICIAL STATUS RELATIVE TO OFFICER REPORTED ON — Commanding Officer

IS THIS OFFICER QUALIFIED TO PERFORM ALL HIS PRESENT DUTIES? ☒ YES ☐ NO

INDICATE MORE RESPONSIBLE DUTIES FOR WHICH HE IS IN TRAINING. (If none, so state)

DATE OF EXPECTED QUALIFICATION

Comment on special or outstanding qualifications as well as any physical defects, which should be considered in determining the kinds of duty to which he should be detailed. Only comments on qualifications significant in detailing should be entered here. ANY COMMENTS REGARDING FITNESS FOR PROMOTION SHOULD BE ENTERED IN SECTION 12 ONLY OF PAGE 1.

None

FOR WHAT DUTIES IS HE RECOMMENDED?

ASHORE — None   AFLOAT —

7. FOR EACH FACTOR OBSERVED CHECK THE APPROPRIATE BOX TO INDICATE HOW THE OFFICER COMPARES WITH ALL OTHERS OF THE SAME RANK, CLASSIFICATION AND CORPS WHOSE PROFESSIONAL ABILITIES ARE KNOWN TO YOU PERSONALLY. DO NOT LIMIT THIS COMPARISON ONLY TO THE OTHERS NOW UNDER YOUR COMMAND. DO NOT HESITATE TO MARK "NOT OBSERVED" ON ANY QUALITY WHEN APPROPRIATE. NO ENTRY WHICH IS MADE IN THIS SECTION WILL BE CONSIDERED AN UNSATISFACTORY REPORT WHICH MUST BE REFERRED TO THE OFFICER FOR STATEMENT. ONLY ENTRIES DESIGNATED IN SECTIONS 8, 9, 11 AND 12 WILL BE SO CONSIDERED.

RATING FACTORS	Not Observed	Within Bottom 10%	Within Next 20%	Within Middle 40%	Within Next Top 20%	Within Top 10%
A. SEA OR ADVANCE BASE DUTY 1. STANDING DECK WATCHES UNDERWAY*						
2. ABILITY TO COMMAND*						
3. PERFORMANCE IN PRESENT DUTY AS DESCRIBED IN SECTION 2, ABOVE*						
4. REACTIONS DURING EMERGENCIES*						
5. PERFORMANCE AT BATTLE STATION OR IN BATTLE DUTIES*						
B. INITIATIVE AND RESPONSIBILITY 1. ASSUME RESPONSIBILITY WHEN SPECIFIC INSTRUCTIONS ARE LACKING*					X	
2. GIVE FRANK OPINIONS WHEN ASKED OR VOLUNTEER THEM WHEN NECESSARY TO AVOID MISTAKES*						
3. FOLLOW THROUGH DESPITE OBSTACLES*						

C. UNDERSTANDING

D. LEADERSHIP

This officer is highly intelligent, and has a good knowledge of administrative procedure. He is also a good seaman, with plenty of experience in all phases of seamanship, and navigation. He made a good record as District Personnel Officer due to his good knowledge of regulations. He is understanding of the problems of enlisted men, and has a sympathetic attitude towards them. He is inclined to be tempermental and argumentative, but there is no question of his ability, intellectually as well as in practical matters. Recommended for promotion.

Niels Haugen, Captain
U.S. Coast Guard
Chief of staff

ADMIRAL LESLIE

Chapter 24

NINTH COAST GUARD DISTRICT

TOLEDO, OHIO

1947-1950

The TUPELO was a steel 180-foot ice breaker and Aids to Navigation Cutter-tender, whose mission was the servicing of floating navigation buoys and shore lights on Lake Erie, and be available to perform marine rescue work. The TUPELO with her sharp, armored bow, and her powerful engines was also a formidable icebreaker. One of her numerous duty assignments was to assist ice-breaking vessels in Lake Michigan and Lake Superior whenever the need arose. Another function was representing the Coast Guard in maintaining a close public relationship with the Lake Erie Coast Guard Auxiliary and yachting fraternity, and patrolling the annual yacht races at Put-in-Bay Island in Lake Erie. All new and interesting tasks.

When my 30-day leave expired, and my family located, I reported to the TUPELO to replace the Commanding Officer, Lieutenant (jg) Frank Hilditch, USCG, also a former Lighthouse shipmaster. During my initial inspection and change of command ceremony, and while inspecting the enlisted crew's quarters, I could not help but notice that all of the eight black crew members were packed tightly together in the narrow bow of the vessel. Over two years had elapsed since giving up command of the USS MENKAR (AK-123) in Honolulu.

That evening after retiring to my cabin on the TUPELO, my mind went back to the MENKAR at Morotai, New Guinea, and the gentle, brown-eyed, dark-faced Mexican boy, George Ybarra, who gave his life for his country and was buried on a remote island in the South Pacific and of the two all black after gun crews who stood steadfast at their stations and gunned down the Japanese Kamikaze as it dove towards them on the MENKAR at Okinawa, and I came to a decision.

In the morning my first official act as Commanding Officer, was to instruct the Chief Yeoman to prepare a list giving the date each man reported to the ship for duty. My second order of the day was to the Executive Officer to have all enlisted men on the foredeck with their seabags at one o'clock. At one p.m. the crew mustered on deck with their belongings, and as the Yeoman read off the names of the men in the order of their reporting on board, they went below and chose their berth. The Chief Boatswain's Mate in charge of the crew quarters was from the State of Georgia named Robert E. Lee. He was in a state of shock, as were the ship's officers. The incident was never again referred to. Robert E. Lee was still a member of the crew when I departed three years later.[1]

---

[1] Robert E. Lee retired from the Coast Guard fifteen years later, and for ten years was employed by me as Officer-in-Charge on several of my fishing vessels in the Bering Sea and the Aleutian Islands. He now lives in Duluth, Michigan. We phone one another at least once a month to discuss my arthritis and his rheumatism.

5. MY PREFERENCE FOR NEXT DUTY IS:

	KIND OF DUTY	"YOCONA" (WAT) or WAGL	LOCATION	Pacific Coast
SEA				
SHORE	KIND OF DUTY	Aids to Navigation –Base	LOCATION	Pacific Coast or Outside

6. SECTIONS 5 THROUGH 12 TO BE FILLED IN BY REPORTING OFFICER

NAME OF REPORTING OFFICER — RANK — OFFICIAL STATUS RELATIVE TO OFFICER REPO

James A. Hirshfield, Commodore, Commander 9th Coast Guard Dist

IS THIS OFFICER QUALIFIED TO PERFORM ALL HIS PRESENT DUTIES? [X] YES [ ] NO

INDICATE MORE RESPONSIBLE DUTIES FOR WHICH HE IS IN TRAINING. (If none, so state)

Aids to Navigation Duties Ashore

DATE OF QUALIFI... Now

Comment on special or outstanding qualifications as well as any physical defects, which should be considered in determining the kinds of duty to which he should be detailed. Only qualifications significant in detailing should be entered here. ANY COMMENTS REGARDING FITNESS FOR PROMOTION SHOULD BE ENTERED IN SECTION 12, ONLY.

Especially well qualified in Aids to Navigation duties. There is no doubt that he wou

perform other duties in an efficient manner.

FOR WHAT DUTIES IS HE RECOMMENDED?

ASHORE Aids to Navigation   AFLOAT Aids to Navigation

7. FOR EACH FACTOR OBSERVED CHECK THE APPROPRIATE BOX TO INDICATE HOW THE OFFICER COMPARES WITH ALL OTHERS OF THE SAME RANK WHOSE SIONAL ABILITIES ARE KNOWN TO YOU PERSONALLY. DO NOT LIMIT THIS COMPARISON ONLY TO THE OTHERS NOW UNDER YOUR COMMAND. DO NOT TO MARK "NOT OBSERVED" ON ANY QUALITY WHEN APPROPRIATE. NO ENTRY WHICH IS MADE IN THIS SECTION WILL BE CONSIDERED AN UNSATI REPORT WHICH MUST BE REFERRED TO THE OFFICER FOR STATEMENT. ONLY ENTRIES DESIGNATED IN SECTIONS 8, 9, 11 AND 12 WILL BE SO CONSID

RATING FACTORS	Not Observed	Within Bottom 10%	Within Next 20%	Within Middle 40%	Within Next Top 20%
A. SEA OR ADVANCE BASE DUTY How does this officer compare in: 1. STANDING DECK WATCHES UNDERWAY?					X
2. ABILITY TO COMMAND?					X
NOTE: ITEM (A) TO BE MARKED ONLY FOR OFFICERS ON SEA OR ADVANCE BASE DUTY DURING THE PERIOD OF THIS REPORT 3. PERFORMANCE IN PRESENT DUTIES AS DESCRIBED IN SECTION 2, ABOVE?					X
4. REACTIONS DURING EMERGENCIES?					X
5. PERFORMANCE AT BATTLE STATION OR IN BATTLE DUTIES?	X				
B. INITIATIVE AND RESPONSIBILITY How well does this officer: 1. ASSUME RESPONSIBILITY WHEN SPECIFIC INSTRUCTIONS ARE LACKING?					X
2. GIVE FRANK OPINIONS WHEN ASKED OR VOLUNTEER THEM WHEN NECESSARY TO AVOID MISTAKES?					X
3. FOLLOW THROUGH DESPITE OBSTACLES IN CARRYING OUT RESPONSIBILITIES ASSIGNED OR ASSUMED?					X
C. UNDERSTANDING AND SKILL How well does this officer: 1. GRASP INSTRUCTIONS AND PLANS GIVEN TO HIM?					X
2. USE IDEAS AND SUGGESTIONS OF OTHERS?					X
3. RATE IN TECHNICAL COMPETENCE IN HIS SPECIALTY, IF ANY? (Name Specialty)					X
D. LEADERSHIP How well does this officer: 1. INSPIRE SUBORDINATES TO WORK TO THE MAXIMUM OF THEIR CAPACITY?					
2. EFFECTIVELY DELEGATE RESPONSIBILITY?					X
3. TRANSMIT ORDERS, INSTRUCTIONS, AND PLANS?					X
4. ORGANIZE HIS WORK AND THAT OF THOSE UNDER HIS COMMAND OR SUPERVISION?					X
5. MAINTAIN DISCIPLINE AMONG THOSE UNDER HIS COMMAND OR DIRECTION?					
E. CONDUCT AND WORK HABITS How does this officer compare in: 1. ABILITY TO WORK WITH OTHERS?					
2. ABILITY TO ADAPT TO CHANGING NEEDS AND CONDITIONS?					X
3. MILITARY CONDUCT—BEARING, DRESS, COURTESY, ETC.?					X

8. INDICATE YOUR ATTITUDE TOWARD HAVING THIS OFFICER UNDER YOUR COMMAND, WOULD YOU: (Check one)
[ ] DEFINITELY NOT WANT HIM? (UNSATISFACTORY)   [ ] PREFER NOT TO HAVE HIM? (UNSATISFACTORY)   [ ] BE SATISFIED TO HAVE HIM?   [X] BE PLEASED TO HAVE HIM?   [ ] PARTICULA... DESIRE HI...

9a. CONSIDERING ALL OFFICERS OF THE SAME RANK WHOSE PROFESSIONAL ABILITIES ARE KNOWN TO YOU PERSONALLY, WOULD YOU PROMOTE HIM: (Check one)
[ ] UNDER NO CIRCUMSTANCES? (Unsatisfactory)   [ ] IF 90% WERE TO BE PROMOTED?   [ ] IF 70% WERE TO BE PROMOTED?   [X] IF 30% WERE PROMOTED?   [ ] IF ONLY 10% WERE TO BE PROMOTED?

9b. How many Officers are inc... group used for the compar... [ ] 10 OR LESS [X] 10 TO 50

10. COMMENT IN SECTION 12 AND GIVE REFERENCE HERE TO ANY COMMENDABLE OR ADVERSE REPORTS THAT HAVE BEEN MADE ON THE OFFICER DURING THI...

See attached letter

11. HAVE YOU ANY ADVERSE COMMENTS TO MAKE REGARDING THIS OFFICER'S QUALITIES OR PERFORMANCE? [ ] YES [X] NO
HAS HE ANY MENTAL OR MORAL WEAKNESS WHICH ADVERSELY AFFECTS HIS EFFICIENCY? [ ] YES [X] NO
If yes, explain in Section 12.
UNSATISFACTORY. Yes in either ... constitutes an unsatisfactory report and must to the officer for statement.

12. Give in this space a clear, concise appraisal of the officer reported on and his performance of duty, including any worthy of special mention. Include recommendations as to promotion. Statements of unsatisfactory performance, ability, character, or conduct must be referred to the officer for statement. Statements of a constructive nature which refer to minor imperfections qualifications do not constitute an unsatisfactory report. For example: "This officer was a little slow in getting started but is now making good progress" or "This officer is well qua... present duties but has had no experience at sea" would not be unsatisfactory in nature.

Check one of these boxes — I CONSIDER THIS REPORT TO BE [X] SATISFACTORY [ ] UNSATIS...

This officer is very interested in Aids to Navigation duties and devoted much of his ti...
to pertinent details resulting in a marked improvement in the functioning of Aids to
Navigation for which he is responsible. His relations with the public are noteworthy.
He is recommended for promotion whenever others in his classification are so considered

J. P. GERMAN
CDR, USCG

(If additional space is needed attach extra sheet)

SIGNATURE OF OFFICER REPORTED ON (Applies only to Sections 1 through 5)   SIGNATURE OF REPORTING OFFICER   HAVE YOU RE... THE ATTACHE... INSTRUCTION SHEET?

J. A. HIRSHFIELD, Commodore, USCG

When completed remove carbon paper, forward Pages 1 and 2, not detached, to BuPers. Retain Page 3 for "Officer's Qualification Record

PAGE 1

	TYPE OF AIRCRAFT		

(In Aviator, Indicate No. of Type Hours Last Two Years; For Each Type Aircraft List Most Recent Type First, No. of Hours)

ANY PREFERENCE FOR NEXT DUTY	SEA	KIND OF DUTY	No preference	LOCATION	Pacific Coast
	SHORE	KIND OF DUTY	Shore duty not desired	LOCATION	

Sections 6 Through 12 to be Filled in by Reporting Officer

NAME OF REPORTING OFFICER	RANK	FILE NO.	OFFICIAL STATUS RELATIVE TO OFFICER RE
James A. Hirshfield Commodore			Commander, 9th CG Distr

IS THIS OFFICER QUALIFIED TO PERFORM ALL HIS PRESENT DUTIES?	☒ YES ☐ NO	INDICATE MORE RESPONSIBLE DUTIES FOR WHICH HE IS IN TRAINING. (If none, so state) None	DATE QUALIFIED

Comments on special or outstanding qualifications as well as any physical defects which should be considered in determining the kinds of duty to which he should be detailed. Only that which is significant in detailing should be entered here. ANY COMMENTS REGARDING FITNESS FOR PROMOTION SHOULD BE ENTERED IN SECTION 12 ONLY

None

FOR WHAT DUTIES IS HE RECOMMENDED?

ASHORE General   AFLOAT General

7. FOR EACH FACTOR OBSERVED CHECK THE APPROPRIATE BOX TO INDICATE HOW THE OFFICER COMPARES WITH ALL OTHERS OF THE SAME RANK, CLASSIFICATION, CORPS WHOSE PROFESSIONAL ABILITIES ARE KNOWN TO YOU PERSONALLY. DO NOT LIMIT THIS COMPARISON ONLY TO THE OTHERS NOW UNDER YOUR COMMAND. DO NOT HESITATE TO MARK "NOT OBSERVED" ON ANY QUALITY WHEN APPROPRIATE. NO ENTRY WHICH IS MADE IN THIS SECTION WILL BE CONSIDERED AN UNSATISFACTORY REPORT WHICH MUST BE REFERRED TO THE OFFICER FOR STATEMENT. ONLY ENTRIES DESIGNATED IN SECTIONS 8, 9, 11 AND 12 WILL BE SO

	RATING FACTORS	Not Observed	Within Bottom 20%	Within Next 20%	Within Middle 40%	Within Next 20%
A. SEA OR ADVANCE BASE DUTY How does this officer compare in: NOTE: *Item (A) 5 To Be Marked For ALL Officers.*	1. STANDING DECK WATCHES UNDERWAY?	X				
	2. ABILITY TO COMMAND?					X
	3. PERFORMANCE IN PRESENT DUTIES AS DESCRIBED IN SECTION 2, ABOVE?					X
	4. REACTIONS DURING EMERGENCIES?	X				
	5. PERFORMANCE AT BATTLE STATION OR IN BATTLE DUTIES?	X				
B. INITIATIVE AND RESPONSIBILITY How well does this officer:	1. ASSUME RESPONSIBILITY WHEN SPECIFIC INSTRUCTIONS ARE LACKING					X
	2. GIVE FRANK OPINIONS WHEN ASKED OR VOLUNTEER THEM WHEN NECESSARY TO AVOID MISTAKES?					X
	3. FOLLOW THROUGH DESPITE OBSTACLES IN CARRYING OUT RESPONSIBILITIES ASSIGNED OR ASSUMED?					X
C. UNDERSTANDING AND SKILL How well does this officer:	1. UNDERSTAND INSTRUCTIONS GIVEN, AND USE SUGGESTIONS OFFERED?					X
	2. EXERCISE JUDGMENT?				X	
	3. RATE IN TECHNICAL COMPETENCE IN HIS SPECIALTY, IF ANY (Name Specialty) Aids to Navigation Duties				X	
D. LEADERSHIP How well does this officer:	1. INSPIRE SUBORDINATES TO WORK TO THE MAXIMUM OF THEIR CAPACITY					X
	2. EFFECTIVELY DELEGATE TASKS AND AUTHORITY?					X
	3. TRANSMIT ORDERS, INSTRUCTIONS, AND PLANS?					X
	4. ORGANIZE HIS WORK AND THAT OF THOSE UNDER HIS COMMAND OR SUPERVISION?					X
	5. MAINTAIN DISCIPLINE AMONG THOSE UNDER HIS COMMAND OR DIRECTION?					X
E. CONDUCT AND WORK HABITS How does this officer compare in:	1. ABILITY TO WORK WITH OTHERS?					X
	2. ABILITY TO ADAPT TO CHANGING NEEDS AND CONDITIONS?					X
	3. MILITARY CONDUCT- BEARING, DRESS, COURTESY ETC?					X

8. INDICATE YOUR ATTITUDE TOWARD HAVING THIS OFFICER UNDER YOUR COMMAND. WOULD YOU: *(Check one)*

☐ DEFINITELY NOT WANT HIM (UNSATISFACTORY)   ☐ PREFER NOT TO HAVE HIM? (UNSATISFACTORY)   ☐ BE SATISFIED TO HAVE HIM?   ☒ BE PLEASED TO HAVE HIM?   ☐ PARTICULARLY DESIRE HIM

9a. Considering all Officers of the same rank, classification and corps, whose professional abilities are known to you personally, would you promote him? *(Check one)*   ☐ UNDER NO CIRCUMSTANCES (UNSATISFACTORY)   ☐ IF 50% WERE TO BE PROMOTED?   ☐ IF 70% WERE TO BE PROMOTED?   ☒ IF 90% WERE TO BE PROMOTED?   ☐ WILL BE PROMOTED

9b. How many Officers in group used for the comparison?   ☐ LESS   ☒

10. COMMENT IN SECTION 12 AND MAKE REFERENCE HERE TO ANY COMMENDABLE OR ADVERSE REPORTS THAT HAVE BEEN MADE ON THE OFFICER DURING THIS P

None

11. HAVE YOU ANY ADVERSE COMMENTS TO MAKE REGARDING THIS OFFICER'S QUALITIES OR PERFORMANCE?   ☐ YES ☒ NO   If yes, explain in Section 12.

HAS HE ANY MENTAL OR MORAL WEAKNESS WHICH ADVERSELY AFFECTS HIS EFFICIENCY?   ☐ YES ☒ NO

UNSATISFACTORY. Yes in either box constitutes an unsatisfactory report and referred to the officer for statement.

12. *Give in this space a clear, concise appraisal of the officer reported on and his performance of duty, including any words of special mention. Include recommendations. Any statements of unsatisfactory qualities in ability, character, or conduct must be referred to the officer for statement. Statements of a constructive nature which refer to lions or lack of qualifications do not constitute an unsatisfactory report. For example: "This officer was a little slow in getting started but is now making good progress" or "is well qualified in his present duties but has had no experience at sea" would not be unsatisfactory in nature.*

Check one of these boxes — I CONSIDER THIS REPORT TO BE ☒ SATISFACTORY   ☐ UNFAVORABLE   ☐ UNSAT

This officer assumed the responsibility of his duties with a minimum amount of instruc from the District Office. He is cooperative and his ability to work with others is outstanding.

J. P. GERMAN
Commander, U. S. Coast Guard
Chief, Aids to Navigation Section

SIGNATURE OF OFFICER REPORTED ON (Applies only to Sections 1 through 5)	SIGNATURE OF REPORTING OFFICER	(If additional space is needed attach extra sheet)

NAVY DAY MEMORIAL SERVICE

At approximately eight o'clock the evening before a scheduled Navy Day memorial ceremony to be held at Bayview Park Auditorium, Toledo, Ohio, I received a telephone call to my home from Washington, D.C. The caller was the Coast Guard Aide to the Coast Guard Commandant. He informed me that the Commandant was scheduled to appear on the speakers' rostrum the following morning together with Admiral Robert Carney, USN, Chief of Naval Operations. He further stated that due to a sore throat, the Commandant would be unable to attend, and instructed me to represent the Coast Guard in his stead, and that the addresses were to be recorded and forwarded to Headquarters.

I had no experience in speaking to a large audience, and I felt especially lacking in my capacity to adequately voice my feelings on such a solemn and sensitive subject. It was only two years since the tragic events of World War Two, and I was filled with strong pacifist leanings. To me it was not an occasion for rejoicing. What could I say to mothers, widows, fathers and children who were without their loved ones. Like many others who had managed to survive, I nursed a feeling of guilt because I was alive and able to speak to them.

I sat up all night as when writing poetry and found words that satisfied me. When it was finished and memorized, I crawled into bed to sleep for an hour until daylight.

On the speakers' rostrum, seated in the following order were the local Congressman, Admiral Robert Carney, USN, Chief of Naval Operations, a Marine Corps General, the Mayor of Toledo, myself and Commander Flucky, USN, the Commander of the submarine that had entered Tokyo Bay during the height of hostilities with Japan.

In 1947 the news media was filled with rhetoric proclaiming the warlike intentions of the Soviet Union, and the necessity for the United States to prepare itself for eventual conflict and the importance of the United States to remain strong militarily.

The Admiral came out in a fighting stance, blasting the Soviet Union, to all intents ready to take on the enemy single-handed. I was temporarily struck dumb, thinking about my pacifist, peaceful, memorized message to the two thousand people present. When I stumbled to my feet and began to speak, I was certain that at any moment someone would grab me by my coat tails and tell me to sit down. I was even more certain that my brilliant Coast Guard career had come to an end. On completion of the ceremony, Admiral Carney singled me out and congratulated me, leaving me with a feeling that we were not too far apart in our private beliefs, and I was intensely relieved.

Transcript of a Recording of an Address

NAVY DAY MEMORIAL SERVICE

At Bayview Park - Toledo, Ohio 1947

CONGRESSMAN THOMAS

Thank you, Admiral Carney, for those very appropriate words. That other great arm of the United States Navy, the Coast Guard, will be represented by Commander Niels P. Thomsen, who will pay tribute to the Members of the United States Coast Guard who made the Supreme Sacrifice.

COMMANDER NIELS P. THOMSEN, UNITED STATES COAST GUARD

On this Navy Memorial Day I am humbly proud to represent on this platform the Coast Guard's honored dead. We are gathered here today amidst the memories of those we once knew, of those who are not here today - to live, and to love, to work and to worship with us. If only they could stand in my place today - for their vision of a better world was never blurred by the tragic, mortal shortcomings of those they left behind. For they died with lofty dreams in the belief that by their sacrifice they were helping to create a better and more beautiful world for those they loved - and if they could but speak to us today, they might say, "that when drums roll and feet march in places far away, that we not too easily forget how, why, and wherefore they died," and they might also remind us - that on the field of battle there is no true glory - there is only food for tears.

For those amongst you who have found no comfort, it might help for you to remember - that to have felt an inconsolable sorrow, is in itself, a rare and signal privilege - for it is only if we have these feelings that we can ever hope to attain, for our children and our children's children - the kind of a world for which they died - those whom we honor here today. Thank you all, and may God keep you always.

Freighter Watt Rescued From Massive Ice Pack

Vessel Forced Aground Off Monroe Cut Loose By Coast Guard Cutter Tupelo

The 405-foot freighter James Watt was back on her regular coal run between Toledo and Detroit today after a weekend during which the vessel went aground in shoal waters off Monroe, Mich., and the 35 crew members stood

It Might Have Been Her Last Voyage

FREIGHTER JAMES WATT IN CRUSHING GRIP OF LAKE ERIE ICE
Driving winds forced the ship aground and piled tons of ice on her deck

by ready to abandon ship.

Forced shoreward by a massive, floating ice pack, driven by a 40-mile-an-hour east wind, the Watt radioed for aid Friday afternoon shortly after she left Toledo. The tug Atomic, out of Detroit, and the U.S. Coast Guard cutter Tupelo, based at Toledo, proceeded to her aid through heavy rain and sleet squalls, bucking a strong westerly ice movement.

Ice Piled On Deck

During the 36-hour operation in which 200 tons of ice piled to heights of 20 feet on the deck of the Watt, the Tupelo skippered by Lieut. Comdr. Neils P. Thomsen, was maneuvered to the Watt's port side.

The hulls of both vessels were under heavy ice pressure. Port holes on the Watt were broken, ice was entering the holds and the vessel, which has a 19-foot draft light, was being forced aground. Orders were issued from the coast guard vessel to Capt. W. J. Edgar of the Watt to "fill all tanks" to raise her draft to 22 feet.

After both vessels grounded, crew members on the Watt stood by to abandon ship. Standing by in Cheboygan, Mich., to aid the vessels was the coast guard icebreaker Mackinaw. But her services were not needed.

Ice Pressure Decreases

At dawn Saturday ice was piled high on each side of the Watt, and fore and aft of the Tupelo. But ice pressure which through the night had made those aboard the vessels feel as if they "were in the midst of an earthquake" had decreased.

Captain Edgar, who described the ice conditions as the worst in 10 years, ordered ballast pumped from the Watt to put her draft back to 19 feet. By Saturday afternoon the tug Atomic had moved in closer and with the Tupelo was cutting the Watt from the ice.

A 45-mile-an-hour southwesterly wind which dropped the water level 3 feet, held the Watt aground in 19 feet of water until 1:30 a.m. Sunday. After the vessel was floated, she was escorted to Detroit Harbor Light by the Tupelo and the Atomic. Though her rudder was damaged, she was partially maneuverable and able to proceed at 5 miles an hour, coast guardmen said.

Watt Leaves For Detroit

The Watt, after repairs in Detroit, arrived back in Toledo at 9:30 last night, took on a cargo at the C. & O. docks, and cleared at 2:30 a.m. today for Detroit.

The vessel is owned by the Nicholson Transit Co., Detroit.

The Watt, which with the freighter Pope carries coal throughout the winter to the Ford Motor Co., was aided three other times this winter by the Tupelo. The coast guard described the rescue as a "routine operation."

The massive, floating ice pack today was in eastern Lake Erie. Moving with shifting winds, the pack is windrowed to heights of 20 and 30 feet and is about 10 feet in depth, according to lake sailors.

92-F

92-G

UNITED STATES COAST GUARD

CLEVELAND 15, OHIO

15 September, 1948
File: dca 650, 625

From: Patrol Commander, Gold and Silver Cup Races
To: Lieutenant Commander N. V. Thomsen, USCG, Commanding TUPELO
Via: Commander, Ninth Coast Guard District

Subj: Commendation for assistance in patrol activities.

1.   During the Gold and Silver Cup Races in Detroit, Michigan,
28 and 29 August, and 4, 5, and 6 September, 1948, CGC TUPELO operated
under the orders of the undersigned.

2.   Personnel and boats from TUPELO assisted in surveying and laying
the buoys marking the race courses, and in actual patrol of the races.
You and your officers gave help and co-operation to the patrol Commander
and his staff in excess of reasonable requirements, and made yourselves
available at all times for any duty. The officers and men attached to
your command gave evidence of good training and discipline, and upheld
the highest traditions of the Coast Guard during this period.

3.   You are hereby highly commended for your initiative, leadership,
and co-operation while operating under the orders of the Patrol Commander.
A copy of this letter will be forwarded to Headquarters for insertion in
your official record.

J. C. WENGLAND
J. C. WENGLAND

Ind-1   14 January, 1949
Comdr., 9th CG District   File: d 650 625

From: Commander, Ninth Coast Guard District
To: Lieutenant Commander N. V. Thomsen, USCG, Commanding TUPELO

Forwarded with pleasure.

J. A. HIRSHFIELD

Chapter 28

COAST GUARD BASE
KETCHIKAN, ALASKA

 In 1951, I was transferred back to Alaska as Commander of the Coast Guard Base in Ketchikan. One afternoon in 1952 I had severe abdominal pain while at the office. Feeling weak, I went home and lay down in the bedroom. Suddenly, my throat filled with blood that gushed all over the bedspread. All along, since Guadalcanal, it had been stomach ulcers, not gall bladder. A major vein in my stomach had ruptured. After nine blood transfusions in six days and several weeks in the hospital, I survived, but my Coast Guard career was at an end.

I was only 44 years old.

14 February, 1951
P17-2/00

From: Lieutenant Commander Niels P. Thomsen (1697)
To: Commandant (PO)
Via: 1. Commanding Officer, CG Base, Ketchikan
       2. Commander, 17th CG District (p)

Subj: Duty classification; promotion; status of

1.   A recent promotion list to Commander, for temporary service, passed over in entirety a group of ten Lieutenant Commanders of Chief Warrant and Warrant Officer origin. These officers were the remainder of twenty-eight Chief Warrant and Warrant Officers selected for commissions as Lieutenant (junior grade) in early 1941. All have served continuously in the grade of Lieutenant Commander since 1 June, 1943.

2.   It appears unlikely that Personnel Circular No. 24-49 could have been applied to prevent the promotion of these former Chief Warrant and Warrant Officers, whose versatile duty assignments and qualifications for all types of duty, including Marine Inspection, are a matter of record over a ten year period as Commissioned Officers, especially in view of the promotion to Commander of approximately ninety-five officers of Marine Inspection and Reserve origin, all of whom are junior to these officers.

3.   A request to be classified for general duty was submitted by this officer in May, 1949, on receipt of Personnel Circular 24-49.

4.   The present status of this officer, with respect to duty classification and future opportunity for promotion, is requested.

                                        Niels P. Thomsen

Ind-1   14 February, 1951
                                        P17-2/00

From: Commanding Officer, BASE, Ketchikan
To: Commandant (PO)
Via: Commander, 17th CG District (p)

Forwarded.

                                        N. P. THOMSEN
                                        Acting

UNITED STATES COAST GUARD

PO
. 12 March, 1951
FILE: P17-2/0 0

RECEIVED

MAR 14 1951

U. S. COAST GUARD
Office CDR 17th CG District

.From: Commandant'
To: LCDR Niels P. Thomsen (1697), USCG - Base
Via: Commander, 17th CG District (p)

Subj: Appointment for temporary service.

Ref: (a) Treasury Department letter dated   8 March, 1951.

1.   Pursuant to the authority provided by an Act of Congress approved 24 July, 1941 (34 U. S. Code 350), as amended, and as stated in reference (a), the President of the United States on 8 March, 1951, appointed you to the grade of   commander for temporary service in the U. S. Coast Guard, effective 8 March, 1951, to rank from 26 January, 1951.

2.   The procedures prescribed in Personnel Circular No. 5-49 will be carried out in effecting this appointment. If this letter is not delivered within thirty (30) days after receipt at the unit to which the addressee is attached, the responsible officer concerned is directed to return it to the Commandant (PO) with suitable explanation and await further instructions. If you are physically qualified and if you accept the appointment, the office vests in you and pay and allowances accrue from 8 March, 1951.

3.   In the case of enlisted personnel promoted for temporary service, the provisions of Personnel Circular No. 52-50 also apply and acceptance must be made on the form letter enclosed.

HERBERT F. WALSH
By direction

Ind-1

p
14 March, 1951
P17-2/00

From: Commander, 17th Coast Guard District
To: LCDR Niels P. Thomsen (1697), USCG - Base, Ketchikan

Forwarded.

V. F. TYDLACKA
By direction

93-B   TREASURY-CGHQ-WASH.,D.C.

Address reply to:
Commandant
U.S. Coast Guard
Headquarters
Washington 25, D.C.

6 September, 1949
File: PMM 670

From: Commandant
To: Lieutenant Commander Niels P. Thomsen, USCG
Via: 1. Commander, 9th Coast Guard District
       2. Commanding Officer, CGC TUPELO (WAGL 303)
Subj: Retirement benefits; eligibility for

Ref: (a) Memorandum from the Acting Secretary of the Navy,
            dated 21 July, 1948.

       (b) The Act of June 6, 1942 (56 Stat. 328, ch. 383;
            14 U.S.C. 174 a).

1.   The Navy Department Board of Decorations and Medals, by letter dated
1 June, 1949, file QB4/ AFB/emb, Serial 0787, has informed the Commandant
that, in accordance with the instructions contained in reference (a), the
Navy Department Board of Decorations and Medals has carefully considered the
cases of all lieutenant commanders in the United States Coast Guard as to
their eligibility for retirement benefits in accordance with the provisions
of reference (b).

2.   The Board was of the opinion that you have been specially commended
for your performance of duty in actual combat by the Head of the Executive
Department under whose jurisdiction such duties were performed, and, therefore, recommended that you be accorded the benefits accruing by law to those
officers who have been so commended.

3.   This recommendation of the Board, dated 25 May, 1949, file QB4/WAPM/rd,
Serial 0749, was approved by the Acting Secretary of the Navy on 31 May,
1949.

                                        R. M. WEST
                                        By direction

B 2297

TREASURY DEPARTMENT
Washington

Office of
The Secretary

COAST GUARD GENERAL COURT-MARTIAL ORDER NO. 788 (G.C.M. 9678)

On 14 November, 1950, Charles Marion Scott, chief boatswain's mate, U. S. Coast Guard, was tried by general court-martial, convened by order of the Commander, Seventeenth Coast Guard District, on charges and specifications and with resulting findings and sentence as follows:

CHARGE I:

PRESENTING FOR PAYMENT A CLAIM AGAINST THE UNITED STATES KNOWN TO BE FALSE (one specification).

CHARGE II:

FALSEHOOD (one specification).

FINDINGS:

The court found the specification of Charge I not proved and the accused of the charge not guilty. The specification of Charge II was found proved and the accused of the charge guilty.

SENTENCE:

The court sentenced the accused to lose sixty dollars ($60) per month of his pay for a period of six (6) months, total loss of pay amounting to three hundred sixty dollars ($360), and to deprivation of liberty on shore for a period of one (1) month.

The Government's case was ably presented and the trial record carefully prepared by Lieutenant Commander Niels P. Thomsen, U. S. Coast Guard, the Judge Advocate. The accused was conscientiously defended and with equal capability by Lieutenant Robert E. Emerson, U. S. Coast Guard. The record of this difficult case reflects credit on the administration of justice by courts-martial in the Coast Guard.

The proceedings, findings and sentence of the court in the foregoing case are approved, but the loss of pay is reduced to twenty-nine dollars and forty cents ($29.40) per month for a period of six (6) months, total loss of pay amounting to one hundred seventy-six dollars and forty cents ($176.40). The Commander, Seventeenth Coast Guard District, is to execute the sentence as mitigated.

(Signed) E. H. Foley
Acting Secretary of the Treasury
Dated: Jan. 9, 1951

93-D

CLEVELAND 15, OHIO

ADDRESS REPLY TO
DISTRICT COAST GUARD OFFICER
NINTH NAVAL DISTRICT
REFER TO FILE:

26 June 1950

LCDR, Neils P. Thomson, USCG,
CGC TUPELO,
Coast Guard Base,
Toledo, Ohio.

Dear Neils:

You will be pleased to know that Captain Hirshfield has advised me of his choice for CO of the TUPELO – none other than your present Exec.

Frank Hilditch is going south to St. Petersburg, at his own request.

There have been few officers in my experience who have brough to their duties the enthusiasm, ability, and cooperation that you have shown on the TUPELO. Civilian and military personnel alike are unanimous in their praise and appreciation. Your departure from the Toledo area and the Ninth District leaves me with a feeling of personal loss and regret, and I send you my sincere thanks for the many fine things you have done for me, the Coast Guard, The League, and the Auxiliary.

With best regards,

R. R. WAESCHE, JR.,
Commander, U.S.C.G.

USS MENKAR (AK-123)

ADDENDUM

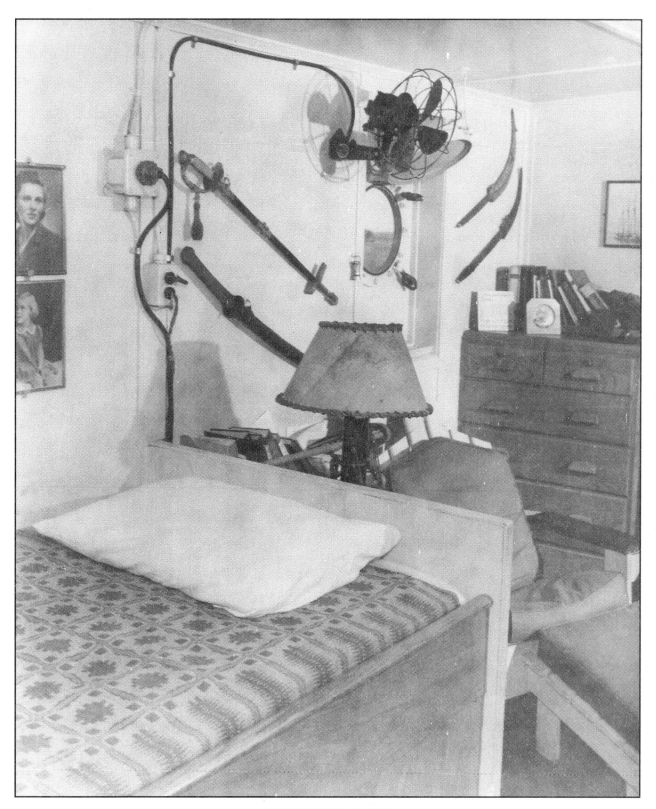

CAPTAIN'S CABIN

My Two Lives

BY DAY
IN
THE HURRIED
STREAM OF LIFE
I CAN
CLOSE
MY MIND
TO
EMPTY HOPES
AND
SHATTERED
DREAMS.

BY NIGHT
I AM SHORN
OF THE MANTLE
THAT
I HAVE WOVEN
ABOUT MY HEART
TO
GIVE ME WARMTH
AND
COMFORT ME
IN MY
SEARCH FOR PEACE.

WHY
DO THEY COME
THESE CREATURES
OF THE NIGHT
THESE FIGURES
FROM THE PAST
TO BECKON
AND
TO LURE ME ON
TO GREATER FOLLY
BECAUSE
OF MY
IMPATIENT HEART.

I WISH
TO KNOW
WHICH LIFE
IS REAL
AND WHICH
IS FALSE
THE LIFE
I LEAD BY DAY
OR
THAT
I DREAD BY NIGHT.

IF BUT
THIS WHIRLING
EARTH
WOULD SPEED
ITS PACE
TO GREET THE SUN
SO I COULD
BANISH
ALL THESE
POINTING GHOSTS
AND EASE
MY ACHING SOUL.

—NIELS THOMSEN

Daddy to Carol Ann

LIEUTENANT SKILLIN

LIEUTENANT DOSSETT

DR. O.B. DOYLE

LIEUTENANT BROWN

SAND ISLANDS, HONOLULU

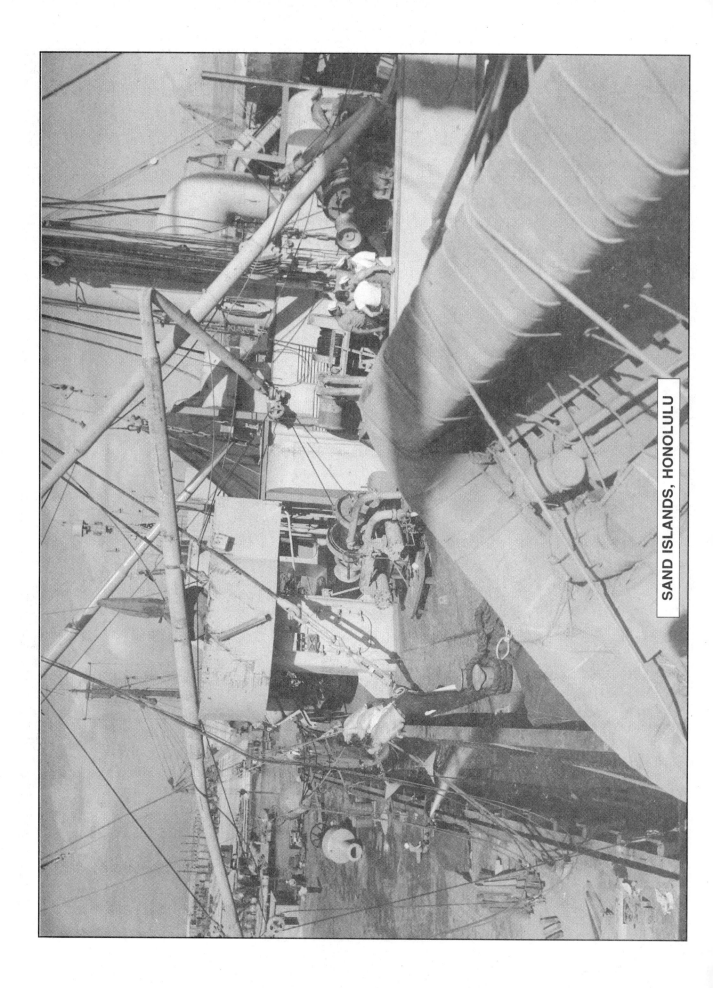

SAND ISLANDS, HONOLULU

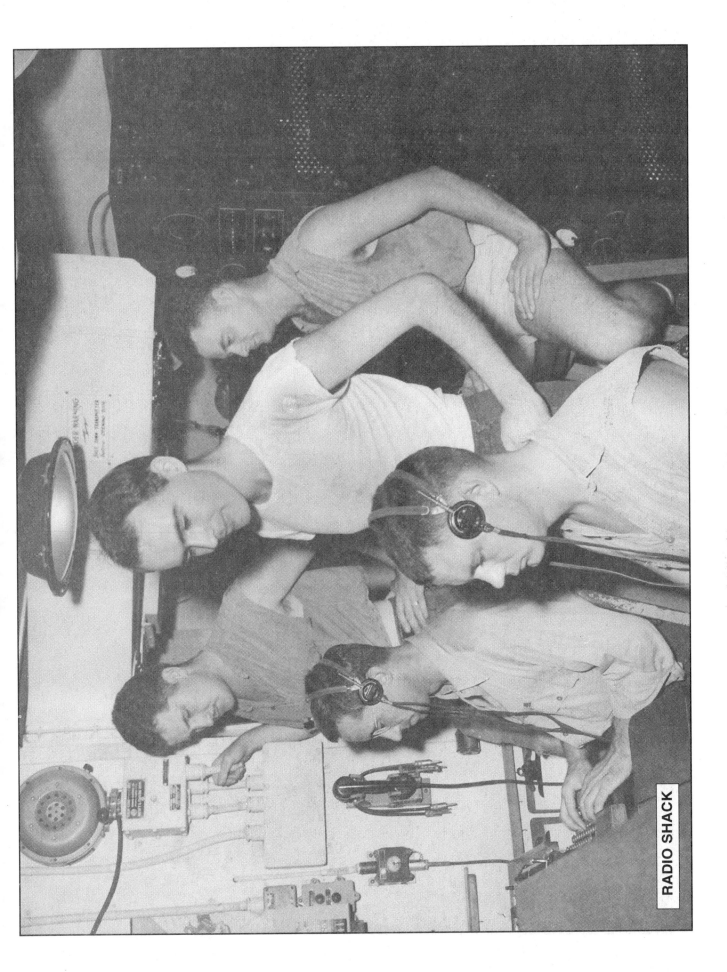

RADIO SHACK

GUARD DOGS AND TRAINERS

TRAINING

TRAINING

POSTSCRIPTS

From Rear Admiral F.A. Zeusler, U.S. Coast Guard, 12th Coast Guard
District Commander, June 8, 1945. My former Commander in Ketchikan,
Alaska. My much admired mentor and benefactor who believed in me and to
whom I owe so much.

My Dear Commander:

Your most interesting letter with picture arrived today. It
is always a pleasure to receive a letter from you, because
you seem to speak my language and we see eye to eye on the
events of today and those of tomorrow. Mrs Zeusler likes
your style and the delightful presentation of the events
that you see and encounter. I get terribly homesick for the
sea and for action as I read of your experiences. With the
many transports and Coast Guard vessels coming in here for
repairs, I see many of our personnel, and I am able to keep
track of some of our doings. I have a nice organization, and
my gang is working fine. Our naval and military contacts
are the finest, and our cooperation the best that can be
expected, but we are at war, and I sort of feel that my 26
years at sea, my war college course, my basic C.G. course,
are all going to waste as far as I am concerned by remaining
on the beach, but Headquarters says "no soap, you are too
old for your rank".You are good for administrative work and
that is all. I guess I have therefore joined the ranks of
the old Fuddle Duddies, and so must remain content.

We are very busy. Our ammunition loadings are up 120 % and
last month our patrols were more active. Our C.O.T.P. are
very busy. our bases are beehives of activity all because
the duties have been directly vested in me, and I have so
been designated by the Commander of the 13th Naval Distrct,
but that does not appeal to me. I am gradually getting most
of my Staff from Alaska, so that I will be right at home
when it comes to talking about Alaska, the Country that I
am very fond of.
I begrudge your experience in the Southwest Pacific with the
varied work you can see in the development of the War.
Congratulations on your successful attack on the Jap planes.
Here is hoping that you get all the others that take a crack
at you. I gather from the hard work that your gang is doing,
and their enthusiasm, that they must be a fine bunch of
boys. I think that your idea of patting them on the
back,is responsible for the efficiency that exists onboard.
I have been on the road, inspecting equipment, personnel and
units, so that I have been away on and off. This week I go
to San Francisco, and I will see what we have there. I have
heard all kinds of reports about that place.

So you will have another kiddie in a week or so. I tell you
there is nothing like it. I am so pleased with my girls.
They are real pals and their husbands fine fellows. I keep
young because of them. Give our kindest regards to Mother
and Babes when you write. Thanks again for your pictures and
letter.

Sincerely,

F.A. Zeusler

U.S. Coast Guard Headquarters
Washington, D.C..   Thursday, 14 June, 1945

Dear Captaian Thomsen:

When I received your letter of 6 June I realized that had not
written you in a long time. I don't have any excuse however and I
hope you will forgive.

I am sorry to hear of your illness. Your work is, as we all
realize, very nerve-wracking. It is hard to say now if the next
trip will be the last one or not, but the way things look now there
is a good chance that it won't be as we have orders to fill up Sand
Island as soon as you move the material now there. I would however
try to make the next trip without major overhauls, as the gear is
needed out there.

Your reports have been most interesting and informative, and have
enjoyed wide circulation in Headquarters. You really have had some
close calls, and good luck must be with you. I see from the
interesting photos you sent with your last letter that you have
grown a mustache.

I am pleased that That Lieutenant Commander Donnell is able to help
you and that your relations are of the best. There is no reason why
they should not be. You really have a bulky load when you have both
Station Fox and Mike aboard. That is really hard cargo to handle.
We follow all your moves with interest, and never a day goes by
when we don't talk about where the MENKAR is.

I wish that I could say that I will see you at Sand point, but the
way things look here I will never get out. I did get a trip to
San Juan, Trinidad, and the Canal Zone in April, and may get to the
West Coast this summer, but any further looks impossible. I am sure
that your work, as well as that of the Constructon Detachments, is
really appreciated by the Aviators who get home only because of the
aid they receive from Loran. It is hard to know just how much good
it does, but we do receive some praises.

I hope that you will be able to get home to see your new child
soon.

Best of luck to you and your crew.

                                        P.W.N. Gustafson

Letter received from Lt(jg) P.W. N. Gustafson, USCGR, assistant
to Captain Tinkham, USCG, Chief of Loran Section, Engineering
Department, Coast Guard Headquarters, Washington, D.C.

2 August, 1945

Dear Mr Thomsen:
Your letter of July 25th was received. The photos enclosed were
very interesting. Your being relieved on arrival in Honolulu was
a surprize to us. When I received your last letter in which you
told me of your poor health, I went to Captain Tinkham with a note
in which I called his attention to your health and that you had
been skipper for nearly ten months, most of which was on the go in
the forward areas, and probably you had been under strain long
enough, and inasmuch as the program indicates many more months, you
might be relieved if you wished. Captain Tinkham and I then talked
to Admiral Park and he requested me to write you a personal
letter asking if you wanted to be relieved, but before I could get
a letter off, a copy of your orders, or rather Lieutenant Commander
Krestensen was received. From what I can learn, the whole thing was
handled from Alameda by Commander Evans with, no doubt, Captain
Stiles verbal permission. If anyone had expected that the MENKAR
would return to the West Coast, they would no doubt have changed
command then. She is bound for Puget Sound Naval Yard.

I imagine that you are now home and happy to be with your wife and
children, especially to see the new arrival. There is one thing you
might not realize that we in Headquarters do, and that is that the
higher ups in the Coast Guard do not seem to realize the importance
of the Loran program. We who have been closely connected with it
feel that of all the things that the Coast Guard is doing, the
Loran program is one of the few Coast Guard things that are
directly connected with the war effort. The Navy says do a job, and
we do it. All other things such as ship manning are under the direct
supervision of the Navy, such as your assignment to command the MENKAR.
The Coast Guard is merely a personnel agency. You should be very
proud to have been a part of the Loran program, and realize by your
interest and efforts the stations were able to get on the air
sooner, which saved many planes. We feel that the first stations
built with the aid of the MENKAR has made many things possible,
which without it, would not have been possible. As skipper of the
MENKAR you have done your part.

Lieutenant Commander Donnell ~~Donnell~~ has gone back to Guam. We feel
that he is doing an excellent job. He has been recommended for
Commander, but it is almost impossible to get a spot promotion for
an engineering officer. He certainly needs the additional rank.
I hope you get your wish, and get assigned to Alaska.

In closing please realize that I have written the above as I have
been able to see it, and in no way is it official.

Best of luck, and do write.

P.W.N. Gustafson

Coast Guard Headquarters
Washington, D.C.

POSTSCRIPT

Forty-seven years have elapsed since the voyage of the MENKAR, and I never met or heard from anyone who served on her until the day after I finished this book, when I came across a photograph taken by the MENKAR's combat photographer, COOK. Attached to the photograph was the name of the Navigator, Lieutenant James T. Challenger, Jr., USCGR of Wilmington, Delaware.

I called the long distance operator in Wilmington, saying, "Forty-seven years ago I knew a man by the name of James T. Challenger, Jr. Would you by any chance have the telephone number of a man by that name?" The operator immediately gave me his telephone number.

I dialed the number and James Challenger was at the other end of the line. I said, "This is Captain Thomsen."

Jim said, "Oh, My God!" He then told me that he had been in a nursing home for the past nine years.
I said that I had just completed writing a book on the voyage of the MENKAR, and would he like me to send him a copy of the book.

Jim said, "Yes, but I must tell you that although I am blind, I am having a great time, and I can have someone in the home to read it to me."

I sent Jim the first copy, and on the cover page inscribed the following:
"To Lieutenant James T. Challenger, Jr. the Navigator of the USS MENKAR (AK-123) and one of the best."

A week later I received a telephone call from Jim Challenger. His first words were, "I am so thrilled over receiving the Men of the MENKAR. Now <u>ALL</u> the people in the nursing home who never believed me, know that I was a Lieutenant and a Navigator on a Coast Guard combat ship in World War Two, and that it was not just a figment of my imagination."

This was for me a heart-warming experience which made my research and literary efforts completing this work worthwhile. We corresponded for two years until Jim Challenger passed away at the age of ninety-one.

2,623,255

THE UNITED STATES OF AMERICA

TO ALL TO WHOM THESE PRESENTS SHALL COME:

Whereas   Niels P. Thomsen,

of

Toledo,   Ohio,

PRESENTED TO THE **Commissioner of Patents** A PETITION PRAYING FOR
THE GRANT OF LETTERS PATENT FOR AN ALLEGED NEW AND USEFUL IMPROVEMENT IN

RELEASABLE CHAIN STOPPER,

A DESCRIPTION OF WHICH INVENTION IS CONTAINED IN THE SPECIFICATION OF WHICH
A COPY IS HEREUNTO ANNEXED AND MADE A PART HEREOF, AND COMPLIED WITH THE
VARIOUS REQUIREMENTS OF LAW IN SUCH CASES MADE AND PROVIDED, AND

Whereas UPON DUE EXAMINATION MADE THE SAID CLAIMANT   is
ADJUDGED TO BE JUSTLY ENTITLED TO A PATENT UNDER THE LAW.

NOW THEREFORE THESE **Letters Patent** ARE TO GRANT UNTO THE SAID

Niels P. Thomsen, his heirs   OR ASSIGNS

FOR THE TERM OF SEVENTEEN YEARS FROM THE DATE OF THIS GRANT

EXCLUSIVE RIGHT TO MAKE, USE AND VEND THE SAID INVENTION THROUGHOUT THE
ND STATES AND THE TERRITORIES THEREOF. Provided, however, that
said invention may be manufactured and used by or for the
nment for governmental purposes without the payment of
yalty thereon. In testimony whereof, I have hereunto set my
hand and caused the seal of the Patent Office
to be affixed at the City of Washington
this thirtieth day of December,
in the year of our Lord one thousand nine
hundred and fifty-two, and of the
Independence of the United States of America
the one hundred and seventy-seventh.

Attest:

John A. Marzall

Attesting Officer.   Commissioner of Patents

UNITED STATES COAST GUARD

ADDRESS REPLY TO:
COMMANDANT
U. S. COAST GUARD
HEADQUARTERS
WASHINGTON 25, D. C.

C

P15

From: Commandant
To: CDR Niels P. Thomsen (1697) USCG

Subj: Letter of Commendation

1.   The Commandant notes with pride your services in developing a device known as the mechanical chain stopper, which constitutes a material advance in buoy handling equipment, and which is now being installed on the majority of Coast Guard buoy tenders. The device, essentially a lockable hinge with a slot to hold anchor chain, makes it possible to service buoys more rapidly, by fewer men, with greater safety. With working models and motion pictures produced at your own expense, demonstrations were held which resulted in a decision to service test the device to determine its general applicability. These tests have now resulted in a program of installation on all tenders where the device is usable.

2.   You are commended for your inventive ability and initiative, and your great interest in the Service is appreciated.

3.   A copy of this letter will be made a part of your record at Headquarters.

Cutter Tupelo Experiments With

New Method of Handling Buoys

ABOUT EIGHTEEN months ago there began aboard the *Tupelo* at Toledo, Ohio, the design and development of a mechanical chain stopper and safety lead to replace the present methods of handling chain on the buoy deck by the use of manila lines, chain stoppes, grab hooks, and pelican hooks. After more than a year of building and experimenting with various scale-size models, a full-size working model weighing approximately 500 pounds was constructed. This full-size model was installed on the edge of the dock at the Toledo Depot for testing and further improvemnt. After a considerable number of alterations the device was considered workable and its installation on the *Tupelo* buoy deck was authorized for further experimentation. Since July, 1949, the *Tupelo* has worked a considerable number of buoys of all types and handled a great amount of buoy chain under varied conditions, using the device exclusively.

A series of structural tests were performed aboard the *Tupelo* with an 8,500 pound sinker. The sinker with 90 feet of 1¼ inch chain attached was towed at 12 MPH in 30 feet of water while made fast in the chain stopper. The same sinker with 60 feet of 1½ inch chain attached was hoisted on board through the device. At no time during these tests did the chain drop back through the port more than eight inches before being caught by the chain stopper, and no visible signs of undue strain to the device have been noted since its installation.

In practical tests aboard the *Tupelo* the Mechanical Chain Stopper and Safety Lead rendered the handling of buoy chain through the buoy port comparatively safe under all conditions for the deck can be completely cleared of all personnel until the chain is automatically and safely secured at the outside edge of the buoy port. The device simplifies the dropping of sinkers and takes the place of "teeterboards," slip lines and pelican hooks.

When relieving buoys it is un-necessary to take the sinkers actually aboard if they are to be re-used for the next buoy. The sinker is left hanging over the side and ready to release. Once the buoy is hooked by the boom hoist, control passes from the buoy deck to the bridge until the chain is automatically secured in the chain stopper. This permits instructions, if required, to the boom handler by word of mouth from the Commanding Officer instead of signals from the deck 50 feet away. From the standpoint of observing danger, the Commanding Officer with an overall view of the buoy deck and knowledge of the movements being made by the ship, is in a more logical position to issue instructions. This factor also minimizes the importance of the role played by the Petty Officer in charge of the buoy deck.

The use of this device on the *Tupelo* has eliminated certain operations and speeds up overall buoy handling from 30 to 50 percent and permits buoy handling in unfavorable current and weather conditions.

THE CHAIN IS BEING RELEASED from the stopper, allowing the buoy sinker to fall into position. Demonstrating this procedure is Lieutenant Commander N. P. Thomson, Commanding Officer of the Tupelo.

NEW MECHANICAL chain stopper and safety lead aboard the CGC Tupelo is shown holding a buoy sinker prior to its release. The sinker can be carried in this position while the buoy marker is removed or adjusted on the ship's buoy deck.

CLOSE-UP VIEW FROM THE SHIP'S DECK showing chain being held in mechanical chain stopper. Since its installation the chain has never slipped more than eight inches before being caught securely in the jaws of the chain stopper.

"MECHANICAL BUOY CHAIN STOPPER AND SAFETY LEAD"

Ninth Coast Guard District (pi) color film demonstration on board the Cutter TUPELO. Introductory comment by Lieutenant. Commander Niels P. Thomsen, U. S. Coast Guard.

You are about to witness one of the Coast Guard 180 foot combination Tender-Cutters and Ice-breakers demonstrate a new and safer method of handling heavy weights and buoy chain through the buoy port. A device, known as a "Mechanical Buoy Chain Stopper and Safety Lead", has been developed and installed on the Cutter TUPELO in the interests of reducing the mental strain and tremendous physical hazards associated with this particular type of duty.

The Commandant recently, in Safety Circular 7-49, subject, "ACCIDENT PREVENTION", stated that the primary humanitarian loss to the service appeared to result from accidents occuring on board buoy tenders and elsewhere incident to the handling of buoys.

Safety Circular No. 7-49 also sets forth three outstanding causes for these buoy handling accidents.

By a coincidence, the device which you will see demonstrated, specifically tends to partially, if not wholly, eliminate these three major hazards outlined by the Commandant. A fourth reason for these accidents is believed to be the lack of standardization of work methods and buoy handling equipment.

The safe and efficient handling of heavy buoys and chain through the buoy port with the nineteenth century methods presently in use throughout the service, requires a team of experienced seamen who through years of experience with nautical gear have acquired a physical and mental alertness to danger that can come only with maturity. We are primarily a military service performing a specialized and exacting duty with respect to Aids to Navigation functions, and because a military service necessitates constant transfer of personnel, and because of the extreme youthfulness and inexperience of the personnel available, the buoy deck today is far more dangerous to life and limb, than in former years when trained and matured seamen were recruited from the Merchant Marine.

This same situation exists with regard to Officers and Petty Officers assigned to Tender duties.

The hazards of duty incident to the handling of buoys has always been recognized, and under the old Lighthouse Service such personnel were classed as field duty personnel, and were entitled to special retirement and physical disability benefits.

With the objective of reducing the possibilities of casualties to personnel and equipment on the buoy deck, the TUPELO approximately twenty months ago, began the design and development of a Mechanical Chain Stopper and Safety Lead, that would replace the present established and dangerous methods of handling chain on the buoy deck by the use of manila lines, chain stoppers, snatch blocks, grab hooks and various types of pelican hooks. All of this equipment is dangerous in the hands of other than experienced seamen. The optimum in equipment is that which can be most easily operated and understood by inexperienced personnel.

More than a year was spent in building and experimenting with various scale size models, ranging from a 1/32 scale of the forward part of the ship, including the hoisting gear, to a 1/8 scale model of the buoy port containing the device. A full size working model was finally constructed on the TUPELO from scrap steel. It was patterned after the principle of the "Wildcat" on the anchor windlass, weighs approximately 500 pounds, and is capable of handling chain from 5/8" to 2" in diameter.

In May of 1949 this full size working model was installed on the edge of the dock at the TOLEDO DEPOT for further testing and development. After a number of alterations, the device was considered workable, and tests were viewed by the District Engineering and Aids to Navigation Officers. Their findings resulted in Headquarters authorization to install the device on the TUPELO for further study. Installation on board ship was completed on 8 July, 1949. Since its installation a number of improvements have been made, among them a curved steel lip welded below the jaws and extending under the shaft on the outboard side to prevent a reversed shackle from catching under the device. Also, a spring steel shock absorber, requiring 2500 lbs. to compress, has been attached to the tripping chain. Since the filming of these operations, the spring has been so adjusted that the device automatically reseats itself on deck after being tripped.

The following structual tests have been made on the device installed on the TUPELO.

(a) An 8,500 lb. sinker with 90 feet of 1-1/4 inch chain attached, was towed at ten miles per hour in thirty feet of water while secured in the stopper.

(b) An 8,500 lb. sinker with 60 feet of 1-1/2 inch chain attached, was hoisted on board through the device, and the carrying away of the chain at the boom block was simulated by cutting a manila sling at the block and letting the chain go with a run. This test was made with the boom in eight different positions. At no time did the chain drop back through the buoy port more than eight inches before being caught and securely held by the chain stopper. No visible signs of casualty or undue strain to the device has been noted since its installation.

Practical tests on board the CGC TUPELO under various operating conditions, both favorable and unfavorable, have demonstrated that this **MECHANICAL CHAIN STOPPER AND SAFETY LEAD** renders the handling of buoys and buoy chain through the buoy port, a comparatively safe operation. This is evidenced by the following:

(1) The buoy deck can be completely cleared of all personnel until the chain is automatically and safely secured at the outside edge of the buoy port.

(2) It eliminates entirely the use of manila lines, snatch blocks, chain stoppers and pelican hooks from the buoy deck, insofar as the securing of chain is concerned.

(3) In the event of casualty to hoisting gear the device prohibits the chain from going over the side.

(4) It particularly simplifies the dropping of sinkers, taking the place of "Teeterboards", slip lines and pelican hooks such as recommended on pages #1825 to #1828 of Maintenance of Aids to Navigation Manual, Cutters of the Tender Class. In the relieving of a buoy with appendages, it is not necessary to bring the sinker on board if it is to be reused. The sinker is left hanging over the side until the chafe has been renewed and a new buoy attached.

(5) It removes for the greater part, the strain and tension on personnel directly handling or supervising buoy handling operations, by eliminating the probability of sudden and serious injury through circumstances beyond their control.

(6) **By eliminating certain operations, and by releasing personnel from fear of injury, speeds up overall buoy handling from 50 to 100 per cent, and permits buoy handling in unfavorable current and weather conditions without unduly endangering personnel.**

(7) **It substantially reduces the personnel requirements on the average buoy deck. In the TUPELO class tender the vang lines are eliminated and the vessel rigged with two motor-operated guys by utilizing the relief and whip as triple purchase guys to port and starboard. It is actually possible to take a buoy and chain on board with but one man on the buoy deck. The maximum number used on the TUPELO buoy deck are four, including the petty officer in charge.**

(8) Once the buoy is hooked on for hoisting aboard the immediate control of the operation passes from the buoy deck to the bridge until such time as the chain is automatically secured in the MECHANICAL CHAIN STOPPER. This permits the Commanding Officer on the bridge to have complete control of the operation by issuing orders direct to the boom operator either by word of mouth or other communication device. The conning officer on the bridge who has an over all view of the buoy deck and has complete knowledge and control of the movements of the ship is in a far better position than any officer stationed on the buoy deck, as is the present custom, to directly control the complete operation. It is believed that this elimination of chain of command and centralization of control is one of the most important features of the device. The responsibility at that critical period, before the chain is secured, then rests directly on the responsible officer who is in the best possible position to safely conduct the operation.

(9) Lastly, and perhaps one of the most important items where safety is concerned is that this device will standardize to a great extent the work methods employed in buoy handling. This cannot be over-emphasize in a military organization performing a specialized duty with everchanging and inexperienced personnel.

In the past five months the TUPELO has worked a great many buoys of all types peculiar to the Ninth Coast Guard District, and has handled a large amount of chain through the buoy port under varied conditions and in all types of weather, using the device exclusively. During this period no manila lines, pelican hooks, snatch blocks or chain stoppers have been used on the buoy deck. The overall performance of the device has been excellent, and beyond the original expectations, with new uses constantly being discovered.

For the purpose of this buoy handling demonstration the TUPELO operated off the Toledo Entrance Channel buoys on Lake Erie. The depth of the water is approximately 25 feet. The wind is force 30 mile per hour with a small to moderate sea running.

Buoy problems are shown in the following order:

(1) Close up demonstration of the device alongside the Toledo Depot.

(2) A 35 foot wooden spar with sinker attached directly to the bail will be taken on board and then replaced in the water.

(3) A 35 foot wooden spar with fifteen feet of 5/8 inch chain attached between spar and sinker will be dropped in the water and recovered on board.

(4) A third class nun buoy with 60 feet of inch chain attached will be taken on board and then replaced in the water.

(5) A 7-18(BLII) Acetylene gas buoy with 75 feet of 1-1/4 inch chain attached will be taken on board for the purpose of recharging and replacing in the water.

(6) A 7-18 Acetylene gas buoy will be taken on board.

In closing, your attention is again invited to Commandant's Safety Circular 7-49 which states that the three outstanding causes of buoy handling accidents are:

(a) The failure of hooks, blocks, straps, hoisting lines and vang lines.

(b) The imposing of live loads on booms by hoisting against short scope moorings.

(c) The hazard of falling objects.

Note in preceeding films the almost total elimination of these three possible casualties.

PATENT OFFICE MODEL

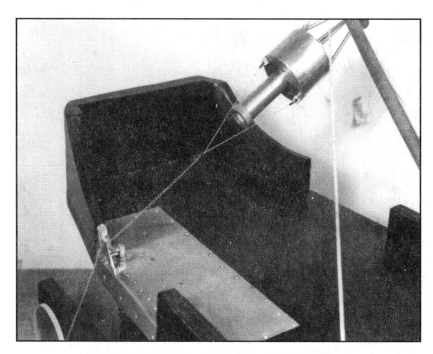

MECHANICAL CHAIN STOPPER

MODEL EXPERIMENTS

THE AUTHOR

UNITED STATES COAST GUARD

ADDRESS REPLY TO

THE COMMANDANT   (PMM)

REFER TO FILE: CG-71

WASHINGTON

28 December, 1943

To: Commanding Officer, U.S.S. HUNTER LIGGETT

Subj: Lieutenant Neils P. Thomsen; award of Legion of Merit

1.   The inclosed citation is forwarded for presentation
to Lieutenant Thomsen along with the Legion of Merit that has
been shipped under separate cover by registered mail. The
presentation should be made with appropriate ceremony. It is
requested that in so doing, you convey to Lieutenant Thomsen
my congratulations for this well-deserved recognition of his
exceptionally meritorious conduct.

2.   Please note that the citation has not been censored
for publication. If such is anticipated, it will be necessary
to clear through the Public Relations Officer of the Navy.

3.   It is requested that Lieutenant Thomsen acknowledge
receipt of the Legion of Merit by a letter to Headquarters.

                        R. R. WAESCHE
                        Commandant

Incl
Citation

   Ind-1
   DCGO 12th Naval District
   12 February, 1944

   To: Lieutenant Neils P. Thomsen

   Delivered with pleasure.

                        R. S. PATCH

The President of the United States takes pleasure in presenting the LEGION OF MERIT to

LIEUTENANT NEILS P. THOMSEN
UNITED STATES COAST GUARD

for service as set forth in the following

CITATION:

"For exceptionally meritorious conduct in the performance of outstanding services to the Government of the United States as Commanding Officer of the YP-251 during action against a hostile submarine in North Pacific Waters, July 9, 1942. After a prolonged and determined search for a submarine reported to be in the area, Lieutenant Thomsen made contact with the enemy undersea craft and, quickly maneuvering into attack position, repeatedly dropped depth charges set for detonation at varying depths. Although an air driven torpedo passed 28 yards astern of the YP-251 during the engagement, Lieutenant Thomsen relentlessly pursued his target until spreading oil slicks and continuous air bubbles gave evidence of the probable destruction of the enemy vessel."

For the President,

Frank Knox
Secretary of the Navy.

THE AUTHOR

Born in Ribe, Denmark   1907
Immigrated to the United States   1912
Attended Jackson Grade School in Fresno, CA until   1922

– BOOK ONE –

VOYAGE OF THE FOREST DREAM AND OTHER SEA ADVENTURES

1922-1925   Seaman on Coastwise vessels and steamers.

1925   One of the survivors of a crew of twelve on the voyage of the five-masted Barkentine FOREST DREAM on a 200 day voyage at sea enroute from Victoria, B.C. Canada to Port Louis, Mauritius in the Indian Ocean.

1927-1928   Seaman & First Mate on the fur-trading, four-masted sailing schooner C.S. HOLMES out of Seattle, WA as far north as east of Point Barrow, Arctic Ocean.

1928   Unlimited License as Second Mate of ocean vessels. Unlimited Master and Pilot licenses.

– BOOK TWO –

JOURNEY OF AN IMPATIENT HEART
MERCHANT MARINE

1929-1930   Deck Officer, American Merchant Marine.

1930   Six months in Hollywood, CA, pursuing a Motion picture career. Protegé of Evangelist Amy Semple McPherson while studying singing, dancing, acting and voice. Extra & stand-in Warner Brothers Studio.

1913-1938   Deck Officer & Master in American Merchant Marine.

1934   Commissioned as Ensign in U.S. Naval Reserve.

1939   U.S. Lighthouse Service as Master U.S.L.H.S. COLUMBINE, San Francisco Bay. Naval reserve training on U.S.S. NEVADA

UNITED STATES COAST GUARD

U.S. Lighthouse Service absorbed by U.S. Coast Guard. Appointed Warrant Deck Officer, and on request assigned to Coast Guard Cutter ARIADNE at San Francisco.

WAR YEARS

1941

U.S. Coast Guard taken over by the U.S. Navy, comissioned as Lieutenant (JG) and assigned to Alaska as Executive Officer Coast Guard Cutter CYANE. Later appointed Director U.S. Coast Guard Reserve and Navigational Instructor to Alaska Air Force Surface Rescue Division.

1942

As Commanding Officer U.S. Naval Vessel Y.P. 251 (85 foot patrol vessel), as Senior Officer Present, and in conjunction with Cutter McLANE, rammed and sank the Japanese submarine RO-32 off Alaska Coast on July 12, 1942 sinking later confirmed. Subsequently decorated with Legion of Merit with Combat Insignia.

1942

Assigned to Combat Transport HUNTER LIGGETT at Guadalcanal in Solomon Islands as Ship's Navigator. Appointed Staff Navigator and Chief Pilot to Admiral Laurence F. Reifsnider, USN, Commander Third Amphibious Group consisting of twelve Troop Transports throughout the Solomon and Bougainville Island invasions. Letter of Commendation from the Commander, Third Amphibious Group.

1944

Assigned to Morro Bay, California as Commander Local Naval Defense, and Commander Coast Guard Patrol Stations Monterey to Santa Barbara.

– BOOK THREE –

MEN OF THE MENKAR

1944

On request for assignment to Forward Combat Area was given command of USS MENKAR (AK-123) and on this top secret independent assignment carried out installation of Loran stations in forward areas from Halmahera, New Guinea to Iwo Jima, which permitted high altitude precision bombing of the Japanese home islands. While at anchor in Buckner Bay, Okinawa, the MENKAR shot down one Japanese suicide aircraft as it dived on the vessel.

1945

In July assigned to Alaska as district Personnel Officer. In August was appointed additional duties of Chief demobilization Officer of Reserve Officers and Enlisted Personnel in Alaska.

1947

Commanding Officer Coast Guard Cutter TUPELO, and Commander Coast Guard Base, Toledo, Ohio. Invented, developed and Patented the Mechanical Chain Stopper and Safety Lead, now in use by all buoy handling vessels worldwide. Commendation from U.S. Coast Guard Commandant.

1950

Commander, U.S. Coast Guard Base, Ketchikan, Alaska.

1952

Combat Service Connected Disability retirement from the United States Coast Guard with the rank of Commander, and promoted to Captain on the retired list due to wartime Decoration of the LEGION OF MERIT with Combat Insignia.

1952

Founded Ketchikan Merchants Charter Association, a small refrigerated shipping service between Seattle, Washington and Southeastern Alaskan ports. President and General Manager.

1952	Founded Alaska Marine Transport Company servicing Alaskan ports.
1954	Awarded U.S. Mail contract for Aleutian Islands, Alaska. This contract held until 1964 when boat service was discontinued by the Postal Department. President and General Manager.
1954-1964	Founded and operated the following business enterprises in Seattle and Alaska:

Alaska:

Ketchikan Merchants Charter Association'
Southeast Alaska Marine Transport Company
Rainbird Equipment Company
Tiare-Tahiti Sailing Cruises
Thomsen Art Gallery and Appraisers
Salmon Royal Restaurant and Delicatessen
Aleutian Seafoods, Ltd. Salmon Curers
Coral Sea Boat Company
Pelican Boat Company
Fairbanks Boat Company
Aleutian Newspaper "MAILBOAT MONITOR," Editor
Aleutian Representative of Bank of Kodiak

1964	Successful Primary Democratic candidate as State Representative for the Aleutian Islands with a view to unseating the ineffectual Demoncratic Incumbent. Stepped aside to ensure election of qualified Indpendent Alaskan Native. Involved in advancing Alaska land claims movement which ultimately resulted in compensation to Native peoples. Politically active in furthering stricter conservation measures of Alaska king crab resources.
1964	Formed Aleutian King Crab, Inc. at Unalaska, Dutch Harbor, Alaska. Major stockholder, President and manager. Mayor of Unalaska.
1969	Sold Aleutian King Crab, Inc. to Brown and Williamson Tobacco Company in Louisville, Kentucky for four million dollars. Established Tax exempt charitable foundation "Community Cooperative of Seattle" in form of "Halfway House" to enable distribution of monies to needed projects, principally in the educational field in the West Indies, this project brought me to the Island of Bequia in the St. Vincent Grenadines, West Indies.
1970	Purchased and developed FRIENDSHIP BAY HOTEL, a luxury resort hotel on the Island of Bequia, representing a private investment of in excess of one million dollars.
1970-1981	Operated FRIENDSHIP BAY HOTEL and spent time sailing the waters of the West Indies in his 56 foot sailing yawl ZORBA, and 100 foot Schooner Yacht LILLI in the Spanish Mediterranean.
1980	Married Airdrie Anne Amtmann, Artist Illustrator, age 30.
1984	Moved to Seattle, Washington.

1985	Civil Service appointment as Pilot on U.S. Army Corps of Engineer dredge YAQUINA, sea-going hopper dredge operating on the Oregon and Washington coasts.
1987	Compulsory age retirement from Army Corps of Engineers.
1990-1996	Author, *The Voyage of the Forest Dream and Other Sea Adventures, U.S. Coast Guard World War II Naval Exploits, The Men of the Menkar.*
1993-1996	Counsel to Kuyédi Thlingit Tribe of Kuiu Island, Alaska. Financial and Economic Advisor.

Book One

VOYAGE OF THE FOREST DREAM AND OTHER SEA ADVENTURES

This first book of memoirs begins with the Author's abduction from his parents at the age of four in Denmark and the first twenty years of his life.

~ Reviews of the Forest Dream and Other Sea Adventures ~

I enjoyed the book thoroughly and recommend it to anyone interested in sailing ships. It is not only a good read, but it is safe to say that it may be the last book of it's kind.
Andrew J. Nesdall,
Massachusetts National Maritime Museum Society Sea History Magazine

This is an unusual, and one of the best stories I have read in a long time. It is an account of the author's coming of age on one of the last sailing ship ventures in this country. You will encounter the full gamut of emotions, from hatred for the afterguard, frustration, pathos. To the crew members who held an unspoken love, as brothers, for one another, and more. Love for their ship, which I doubt any of them ever forgot. You will love the story.
Gordon Jones,
Reviewer Maritime Museum of San Diego, California

Please send me four more copies of the Voyage of the Forest Dream to give to four of my friends. It will mark their day, month and year. Thank you so much. Your book is something I will always keep.
David Smith,
Campbell, California

Truly believe your book is a remarkable, and important contribution of maritime and historical literature. Few have written so eloquently about their lives and the historical context of their sea-faring experiences. You have blessed us with a very special gift.
Dan Lanier,
Rehoboth, Massachusetts

What a beautiful book. I have not been able to put it down. I am already halfway through it. What a wonderful life in spite of adversities.
Neil McCormack, Member of the Society of Naval Architects
and a Companion of the Royal Institute, Adelaide, Australia

I bought the Voyage of the Forest Dream and Other Sea Adventures for my husband. I had no idea how I would enjoy it myself. I laughed when you laughed, cried when you cried, even though Frank's death was due to the negligence of the Captain. Perhaps dying doing something you love may be all we can hope for. Thanks again.
Cathy Beeman,
Creswell, Oregon

Volume One
Voyage of the Forest Dream and Other Sea Adventures
$25.00 Postpaid

Volume Two
Men of the Menkar and Other WW Two Coast Guard Naval Exploits
$30.00 Postpaid

Both Volumes – $50.00 Postpaid

19222 Olympic View Drive, Edmonds, WA 98020
Fax: 425-712-1880   Phone: 425-771-7137   Email: grenadines@earthlink.net
Web site: http://www.geocities.com/soho/studios/3409